SOCIETY FOR NEW TESTAMENT STUDIES
MONOGRAPH SERIES

GENERAL EDITOR
MATTHEW BLACK, D.D., F.B.A.

16

'AND THE TWO
SHALL BECOME ONE FLESH'

'AND THE TWO SHALL BECOME ONE FLESH'

A STUDY OF TRADITIONS IN EPHESIANS 5: 21–33

J. PAUL SAMPLEY

*Associate Professor of New Testament and
Christian Origins, Indiana University*

CAMBRIDGE

AT THE UNIVERSITY PRESS

1971

Published by the Syndics of the Cambridge University Press
Bentley House, 200 Euston Road, London N.W.1
American Branch: 32 East 57th Street, New York, N.Y.10022

Library of Congress Catalogue Card Number: 77–152644

ISBN: 0 521 08131 9

Printed in Great Britain
at the University Printing House, Cambridge
(Brooke Crutchley, University Printer)

CONTENTS

To Sally

ὀστοῦν ἐκ τῶν ὀστέων μου καὶ σὰρξ ἐκ τῆς σαρκός μου

PREFACE

Outside my window the seventeen-year cicadas have appeared. The male cicadas boast while their impregnated females lace the branches of trees with their eggs, thus beginning the cycle that will finally visit its offspring upon Indiana once again in 1987.

The study here offered for discussion is the result of a rather lengthy process that had its inception in a study of the NT Haustafeln, begun under my father in the faith, Prof. Fred D. Gealy, at Perkins School of Theology in 1959. Unlike the cicadas, however, the fertilization of the minuscule egg did not take place until I came under the tutelage of Prof. Nils A. Dahl in a graduate seminar on Colossians and Ephesians offered at Yale University in 1961–2. The seminar elicited my first efforts to unite my interest in the Haustafel with Prof. Dahl's sensitivity both to Ephesians and to the wealth of traditions circulating within the early church. My dissertation, 'The Form and Function of Ephesians 5: 21–33', grew out of the paper submitted from Prof. Dahl's seminar.

With the completion of a metamorphosis in which considerable parts were changed, many features sloughed and extensive additions made, the current work is offered in the hope of contributing to both the illumination of the traditions of the early church and a relatively new phase in the study of Ephesians.

J. P. S.

May 1970
Indiana University
Bloomington, Indiana

vii

ACKNOWLEDGMENTS

Any endeavor such as this monograph places one in the debt of others with whom pertinent matters have been discussed and from whom suggestions and critiques have been received. In this regard, Professors Paul Schubert, Paul Minear and Nils A. Dahl were of greatest aid. To them I am especially indebted.

Without question, however, Prof. Dahl's encouragement and insightful suggestions at each stage of the study have been of paramount importance. His comments and critiques draw upon his phenomenal resourcefulness and have the special virtue of encouraging the recipient to stake out his own position in considerable independence. Whatever of merit is found in this investigation, therefore, may be understood as my saying 'thanks' to a dear teacher and friend. It stands to reason that any deficiencies in this study devolve on me and should in no fashion be associated with anyone else.

Thanks are also due to many other persons who in various ways have contributed to my work. Among them I make particular mention of Bob and Jean Carros, to whom I express my special gratitude for their support at some critical junctures in the investigation of this topic.

A special word of thanks is directed to Prof. Matthew Black and his co-editor of the SNTS Monograph Series, Prof. R. McL. Wilson. Their cooperation and suggestions have been most helpful.

Finally, I turn to my wife, Sally. Those who have been through the joys and tortures that are involved in writing and preparing a monograph will know both the sympathies due to a wife in these circumstances and the deepest satisfactions of sharing the joys and tumults with one who is truly 'flesh of your flesh'. Sally's patience, encouragement and love surely signal the full humanity to which any of us might well aspire.

CHAPTER I

INTRODUCTION OF PROBLEM
AND PERSPECTIVE

In recent years, studies in Ephesians have begun to enter into a new phase. Previous investigations of the epistle were dominated by questions of authenticity, relation to Colossians and the homologoumena and by dogmatic inquiries into themes that by historical accident occur in Ephesians. The newer approach to the study of Ephesians is dominated primarily by the hypothesis that the document is a unique, syncretistic collection of a variety of traditions extant in the early church. Ernst Käsemann has clearly posited this viewpoint in his insistence that Ephesians be understood as a mosaic of early Christian traditions and conventions that reach far beyond a compilation of fragments from the Pauline homologoumena.[1] As Käsemann puts it: 'The entire letter appears to be a mosaic composed of extensive as well as tiny elements of tradition, and the author's skill lies chiefly in the selection and ordering of the material available to him.'[2] While recognizing that the Ephesian mosaic is complex and composed from sources more diverse than the homologoumena, more recent contributions to the study of Ephesians have attempted to assess not only the origin and extent of the traditions incorporated in Ephesians but also the new messages and purpose conveyed through this association of diverse materials. Studies of a dogmatic or thematic nature, however, properly continue, although, in and of themselves, they contribute little to the advancement of the study of Ephesians.

[1] Käsemann's approach is of broader scope and purpose than earlier attempts such as those represented by Edgar J. Goodspeed, *The Meaning of Ephesians* (Chicago: University of Chicago Press, 1933) and C. Leslie Mitton, *The Epistle to the Ephesians: Its Authorship, Origin and Purpose* (Oxford: The Clarendon Press, 1951). Käsemann himself explicitly distinguishes his work from that of Mitton: cf. 'Ephesians and Acts', *Studies in Luke–Acts*, ed. L. E. Keck and J. L. Martyn (Nashville: The Abingdon Press, 1966), p. 297, n. 1.

[2] *Ibid.* p. 288.

At this stage in the study of Ephesians, further detailed and critical investigation is required on the following matters: (1) the full range of traditions incorporated in any given passage of Ephesians must be more carefully and critically identified and, insofar as possible, traced to their sources. In this procedure a more critical methodology and more judicious application of it ought to dominate the quest for the identification of the sources of the traditions incorporated in Ephesians. (2) When the traditions in a given passage have been identified as fully as possible, the attention of the investigator should be turned to an examination of the train or movement of thought achieved by the author in his assimilation of these diverse traditions. It is in a context provided by such rigorous investigation that (3) the passage may be examined in its function in the entire epistle. The understanding of the entire letter, its purpose and occasion, may thereby be improved. The results of such an investigation offer not only an increased understanding of Ephesians, but also promise further insight into the life and worship of the early church as it found its place *vis-à-vis* the world.

To be sure, such a critical investigation of Ephesians must be the shared task of many exegetes and will occupy the attention of scholarship for some time to come. Eph. 5: 21–33 has been chosen for this investigation for several reasons. First, it is a passage that has vexed exegetes. Second, it is heavily laden with conventional formulations such as the Haustafel and the hieros gamos of Christ and the church, each of which has been the subject of independent studies. Third, it represents the opening section that deals with the family as the microcosmic unit that reflects the cosmic purposes of God.

Eph. 5: 21–33 is also ideally suited for such detailed investigation since it is an identifiable and isolable literary unit whose themes and concerns are integral to the remainder of Ephesians and thereby provides a small vantage point for surveying the purposes and concerns of the author in the entire epistle.

The investigation that follows will be guided by an identification and assessment of the material incorporated into 5: 21–33 and will assess the author's creative association of diverse formulations into a flow of thought.[1] Since the concerns of 5: 21–33

---

[1] This study of 5: 21–33 and its traditional materials represents an effort to examine the traditions that may be traceable to the richness of pre-

relate to matters dealt with in the remainder of the epistle certain ramifications for the study of Ephesians will result.

Since Ephesians stands out so clearly as a mosaic of traditions current in the early church, the detailed study of such a passage will offer as a by-product further insight into the complex of traditions circulating in the early church as well as increased understanding of the hymnic, liturgical and catechetical traditions of the early Christians.

During the course of the following investigation three statements by Ernst Käsemann will be kept in view. The first, that Ephesians is a mosaic of traditional materials,[1] is a working hypothesis of this study. The scrutiny and analysis of that part of the mosaic contained in 5: 21–33 is a task basic to this investigation. The other two statements by Käsemann, however, are retained for examination in the light of possible results of this study. Käsemann asserts that the recipients of the epistle to the Ephesians, being themselves Gentiles, are in danger of divorcing themselves from their Jewish heritage as preserved in Jewish Christianity. 'Eine heidenchristliche Gemeinde...die Bindung an das Judenchristentum zu vorlieren droht.'[2] Rom. 11 is cited by Käsemann as a similar case where Gentile Christians are warned against taking any pleasure whatsoever from the possible exclusion of the Jews and the inclusion of Gentile Christians in their place. Whereas in Romans Paul argues against such haughtiness by reference to various OT passages, Käsemann asserts in his third statement that the author of Ephesians is scarcely interested in the OT as a context for understanding the present life of the church. In comparing Luke and Ephesians, Käsemann declares that 'Luke relates this [the history of Christianity] backward to the history of Jesus and to the Old Testament – matters in which Ephesians, despite several Old Testament reminiscences, is scarcely interested'.[3] Whereas there can be no quarrel with Käsemann that the author of Ephesians lacks interest in the history of

Ephesian Christian conventions and adopted Jewish traditions contemporary and prior to Ephesians. By this focus I intend no judgment about the light that may be cast upon 5: 21–33 from the gnostic and more purely Hellenistic traditions.

[1] *Ibid.*

[2] 'Epheserbrief', *Die Religion in Geschichte und Gegenwart* (*RGG*), 3rd ed., II, 518.   [3] 'Ephesians and Acts', p. 293.

Jesus, the study that follows indicates that serious questions can be raised against this third assertion of Käsemann.

It is understandable that 5: 21–33 has vexed interpreters. It is structurally akin to the remainder of Ephesians in that its style is complex and its sentences long. Its laconic reference to traditional materials undoubtedly summoned to the early reader's mind a complex of traditions available to the researcher only by arduous investigation. This stylistic convolution and laconic reference to traditional formulations extant in the early church, however, need not cause the interpreter to despair of understanding, but impose more rigorous requirements on him. Too often, in complex constructions such as 5: 21–33, the interpreter is tempted to express his frustration at the difficulty of understanding by crediting the author of the passage with ineptitude, carelessness or obtuseness. The style, content and scope of Ephesians do little to ease this temptation. As Markus Barth has observed: 'There are extremely long sentences into which apparently is pressed in rather obscure, helpless, un-aesthetical, or disorderly fashion, almost every topic between heaven and earth.'[1] About the passage to be examined in this study, F. C. Synge makes a similar, but more reserved, comment when he states that 'verses 22–33 constitute a strangely elaborated, not to say laboured passage'.[2]

[1] Markus Barth, *The Broken Wall: A Study of the Epistle to the Ephesians* (Chicago: The Judson Press, 1959), p. 15.

[2] F. C. Synge, *St Paul's Epistle to the Ephesians: A Theological Commentary* (London: SPCK, 1941), p. 49. Markus Barth and Synge are noted here only as examples of the frustration expressed by many commentators on Ephesians. Others could equally well have been cited. E. F. Scott, for example, speaks of 5: 27 as a 'digression' (*The Epistles of Paul to the Colossians, to Philemon and to the Ephesians*, New York: Harper and Brothers Publishers, 1930, p. 240) and calls vv. 31 and 32 'a flight of speculation' (*ibid.* p. 244). C. L. Mitton suggests that the marriage imagery of Christ and the church may well have been 'somewhat unnaturally forced into the context from an outside source' (*The Epistle to the Ephesians*, p. 146). F. W. Beare, commenting on the phrase 'as to the Lord' in v. 22, states: 'The writer has allowed himself to be carried a step too far in pressing the analogy between the marriage relationship and the relationship between Christ and the Church' ('The Epistle to the Ephesians', *The Interpreter's Bible*, ed. G. A. Buttrick. Abingdon Press, 1953, x, 719). In so doing, Beare suggests that the author's thought in 5: 21–33 is not entirely disciplined. Still further examples could be cited. The ensuing study will assume that the author's thought is ordered and calculated throughout, unless overwhelming evidence calls for a judgment to the contrary.

After a preliminary analysis of the place of 5: 21–33 in the epistle to the Ephesians, the investigation will proceed from an identification and analysis of the traditional formulations in 5: 21–33 and passages especially related to it, to the movement or train of thought in the passage, and finally to a verse-by-verse analysis. The study will close with the assessment of conclusions and implications for the investigation of Ephesians.

CHAPTER II

OUTLINE OF THE EPISTLE TO THE EPHESIANS AND THE AUTHOR'S KNOWLEDGE OF HIS READERS

In order to understand the place of the Haustafel in the epistle to the Ephesians, and in order to establish a context for the entire investigation, there follows an outline of the epistle.

Ephesians bears many of the formal characteristics of the epistolary style common to the homologoumena.[1] There is the opening greeting (1: 1–2) that credits the letter to Paul. In 6: 23–4 there is the conventional benediction. In place of the customary thanksgiving found in five letters of the homologoumena immediately following the greeting, there is in Ephesians, as in 2 Corinthians (1: 3 ff.), a section that opens with the blessing of God the Father (1: 3 ff.). Within the body of the letter a division is made rather easy by the appearance of a doxology at the close of chapter 3 (3: 20–1). As in the homologoumena there is no absolute distinction between theological and ethical or didactic and hortatory sections. Throughout Ephesians these are interwoven.

The letter opens with the greeting 'to the saints who are also faithful in Christ Jesus' (1: 1–2). There follows the blessing and praise of God for his blessing received in and through Christ, his beloved, in accordance with God's plan and purpose (1: 3–14).

Structurally, 1: 15–2: 10 may be considered a unit because of its special relationship to Ps. 110. In 1: 15 ff., the author, having heard of the readers' faith and love, gives thanks for them and prays that they may know that they are called by God to a hope, an inheritance and a power as a consequence of what God has 'accomplished in Christ when he raised him from the dead and made him sit at the right hand in the heavenly places...' (v. 20). Ps. 110: 1 provides the language for portraying Jesus as

---

[1] In the homologoumena I include Rom., 1 and 2 Cor., Gal., Phil., 1 Thess. and Philem.

sitting at the right hand of God (v. 20). That Eph. 1: 15–23 uses Ps. 110 has long been recognized.[1] Compare Ps. 110 (109): 1 κάθου ἐκ δεξιῶν μου ἕως ἂν θῶ τοὺς ἐχθρούς σου ὑποπόδιον τῶν ποδῶν σου with Eph. 1: 20, 22 ἐγείρας αὐτὸν ἐκ νεκρῶν καὶ καθίσας ἐν δεξιᾷ αὐτοῦ ἐν τοῖς ἐπουρανίοις . . . καὶ πάντα ὑπέταξεν ὑπὸ τοὺς πόδας αὐτοῦ.

The section 1: 15–23 is related to 2: 10 in what is described in 1: 15–23 of God's doing in and to *Christ* is said in 2: 1–10 to include the *believers*. The verbal parallels between 1: 20 and 2: 6 are striking verification that the thought begun in chapter 1 about Christ in terms of Ps. 110 is completed in chapter 2: 'he raised him from the dead and made him sit at his right hand in the heavenly places. . .' (1: 20); 'and raised us up with him, and made us sit with him in the heavenly places in Christ Jesus' (2: 6).[2]

In addition to the language from Ps. 110 which speaks generally of exaltation and of sitting at the right hand of God, there is related the terminology of life and death so that 2: 1 ff. opens with the assertion 'You he made alive'. The present situation of the Christians' being alive is set in contrast to that time when they were dead 'through the trespasses and sins in which you once walked'.[3]

This introduces a theme involving a contrast of the readers' predicament apart from Christ and their new situation resulting

[1] For example, cf. T. J. Abbott, *A Critical and Exegetical Commentary on the Epistles to the Ephesians and to the Colossians* (Edinburgh: T. & T. Clark, 1897), p. 31. Cf. also Barnabas Lindars, *New Testament Apologetic* (London: SCM Press Ltd, 1961), esp. pp. 45–51.

[2] The first finite verb of 2: 1–10 occurs in v. 5 and the material prior to that (2: 1–5) depends upon the verb in 2: 5: συνεζωοποίησεν; he, God, made alive with Christ (τῷ χριστῷ). The addition of the incorporative prefix συν reiterates the connection between what was said of Christ in 1: 15–23 with what is said about the believers in 2: 1–10. Significantly, the other two main verbs that follow immediately in v. 6 also have the same prefixed preposition συν. Those verbs are συνήγειρεν and συνεκάθισεν: 'God. . .made us alive together with Christ. . .and raised us up with him, and made us sit with him in the heavenly places in Christ Jesus' (2: 4–6). Συνεκάθισεν (2: 6) is the same root verb found in Ps. 110 (109): 1 (κάθου) and imported into Eph. 1: 20 (καθίσας). The prepositional phrase ἐν δεξιᾷ αὐτοῦ (Eph. 1: 20, cf. Ps. 110 (109): 1) is not repeated in Eph. 2: 6 since the phrase ἐν τοῖς ἐπουρανίοις associated with it in 1: 20 is sufficient to carry the point in 2: 6.

[3] Cf. 1: 20 ἐγείρας αὐτὸν ἐκ νεκρῶν and 2: 6 συνήγειρεν.

from God's action in Christ. This theme is important in every chapter of Ephesians except chapter 6. The description of the former circumstances of the readers (2: 1–3), that they were children of wrath, captive to the desires of body and mind and the passions of the flesh, points up the significance of God's action in Christ: 'But God, who is rich in mercy, out of the great love with which he loved us, even when we were dead through our trespasses, made us alive together with Christ' (2: 4–5).

The section 2: 11–22 also focuses upon the difference between the former predicament of the readers and the present situation and calls upon them to remember what characterized their earlier life. The contrast is set up in terms of phrases such as 'at one time', 'but now'.[1] The previous circumstances are dwelt upon for the purpose of emphasizing the blessings of the present in which the readers are told that they now stand as 'fellow citizens with the saints and members of the household of God' (2: 19). The conclusion of chapter 2 states that this household of God rests upon the foundation of the apostles and prophets with Christ Jesus as the cornerstone.

The initial verses of chapter 3 claim for Paul an important role as one of the chief conveyors of 'the promise in Christ Jesus through the gospel' (v. 6).[2] Chapter 3, especially vv. 1–13, is set forward as a semipersonal statement, but in fact says more about the mystery of Christ than about Paul himself. The mystery of Christ mentioned in v. 4 is specified in v. 6 as: 'how the Gentiles are fellow heirs, members of the same body and partakers of the promise in Christ Jesus through the gospel'. For Paul, preaching the gospel is equivalent to preaching 'the unsearchable riches of Christ' (v. 8). Disclosed in this gospel is God's plan (οἰκονομία) which involves a particular role for the church. In 3: 10, for the first time, the author specifies the function of the church. It is a mission of profound importance

---

[1] This corresponds to the way that Rudolf Bultmann characterizes one division of his *Theology of the New Testament*, trans. Kendrick Grobel (New York: Charles Scribner's Sons, 1951), I, 190 ff., viz. that dealing with what he takes to be Paul's speaking of 'Man prior to the Revelation of Faith'. Cf. also the corresponding 'Man Under Faith', *ibid.*, pp. 270 ff.

[2] The third chapter opens with an anacoluthon – 'For this reason I, Paul, a prisoner for Christ Jesus on behalf of you Gentiles...' – that is resumed in 3: 14: 'For this reason I bow my knees before the Father....'

and cosmic in scope: 'that through the church the manifold wisdom of God might now be made known to the principalities and powers in the heavenly places. This was according to the eternal purposes [πρόθεσις] which he [God] has realized in Christ Jesus our Lord' (vv. 10–11). Chapter 3 closes with the author's prayer for the readers (vv. 14–19). The benediction in vv. 20–1 concludes not only the third chapter, but the whole first section of the epistle to the Ephesians.[1]

The paraenetic section of the letter begins with 4: 1. All of chapter 4 might be entitled 'Lead a life worthy of the call to which you have been called' (4: 1).[2] This admonition to a life worthy of the calling is expressed in mutually reinforcing ways. The author appeals to the broad use of unity shared by all those who are called (4: 1–6). It is a solidarity founded on 'one hope... one Lord, one faith, one baptism, one God and Father of us all' (vv. 4–6). This unity provides the context for the discussion of a variety of gifts, which variety should work 'for building up the body of Christ' (v. 12). The imagery of the body of Christ and of Christ's headship (v. 15) enables the author to express his concern for unity among believers. In this way he can speak of 'bodily growth' and a resultant upbuilding of the body in love.

The passage 4: 17–32 establishes the background for the injunction to imitation of God in 5: 1 f. The readers must 'put off your old nature' (v. 22) and 'put on the new nature'. Putting off the old nature means that they no longer walk as the Gentiles (vv. 17–19). The injunctions of 4: 25–32 provide

---

[1] The close of chapter 3 has two noteworthy points of contact with Eph. 6. At the end of chapter 3, it is the author's prayer that the readers be 'strengthened with might' through the Spirit. The section in Eph. 6: 10 ff. exhorts the readers: 'Finally, be strong in the Lord and in the strength of his might' (v. 10), and in v. 18 grounds this injunction to 'be strong' in the action of the Spirit: 'Pray at all times in the Spirit, with all prayer and supplication.' Eph. 6: 10–20 is, in effect, the closing statement of the letter and is a development of the theme that concludes the first half of the epistle.

[2] 4: 1 by its reference to 'the calling to which you have been called' possibly harks back to 1: 18: 'that you may know what is the hope to which he has called you'. The association of 'hope' and 'call' in 4: 4 – 'you were called to one hope that belongs to your call' – confirms the possibility of a relation between 4: 1 ff. and 1: 18. The emphasis has, however, shifted to a question of unity and the 'one hope' of 4: 4 is now a basis for concord.

guidelines for their new life. When they put on the new nature, the one 'created after the likeness of God in true righteousness and holiness' (v. 24), it follows that they will no longer lie, sin, steal, etc. (vv. 25 ff.). Instead, they will 'be kind to one another, tenderhearted, forgiving one another, as God in Christ forgave you' (v. 32). In short, putting on the new nature created after the likeness of God (4: 24) signifies that they imitate God (5: 1), or, to put it differently, they walk in love (5: 2).

'Walking in love' is expounded in 5: 3–20 by the use of two antitheses. The readers of the epistle are urged to 'walk as children of light' (v. 8). Conversely, they are warned not to be 'sons of disobedience' (v. 6; cf. 2: 2). This 'walking in love' is further explicated in the exhortation to walk as wise men, not as unwise men (v. 15). The language in this section, 5: 3–20, is heavily laden with materials paralleled in Qumran and in the OT.[1] It closes with the exhortation: 'Be filled (πληροῦσθε) with the Spirit' (v. 18). Dependent upon the verb πληροῦσθε are five participles, the last of which, ὑποτασσόμενοι, stands at the conclusion of this section, 5: 3–20, in v. 21.

5: 21 plays a peculiar role in the train of thought of chapter 5. It functions as a heading for the entire following section, 5: 22–6: 9, but is probably also to be considered structurally dependent upon πληροῦσθε of v. 18. Thus it is a transitional statement.

5: 21 to 6: 9 is the Haustafel, or the table of household duties that exist in the mutual relationships of the family. Addressed in order are wives (5: 22), husbands (5: 25), children (6: 1), fathers (6: 4), slaves (6: 5) and masters (6: 9).

A quantitative assessment of the Haustafel role in Ephesians shows that it contains 1/8 of the total letter and consists of 1/5 of the paraenetic section. Its total function in the letter will be the subject of one of the closing phases of this study.

Following upon the Haustafel is the final substantive statement of the epistle (6: 10–20). It consists of an exhortation that may be summed up in the words of its opening verse: 'Be strong in the Lord, and in the strength of his might' (v. 10). The author urges his readers to stand fast by means of taking upon themselves 'the whole armor of God' (vv. 11, 13). The framework

[1] Cf. K. G. Kuhn, 'Der Epheserbrief im Lichte der Qumrantexte', *NTS*, **7**, 334 ff.

of the language of armament of this section is ultimately dependent upon the traditional formulation that may be traced back to Isaiah (esp. Isa. 11: 4–5 and 59: 16–17) and Wisdom (5: 17–21), where the panoply of God is discussed in detail. The readers are to be strong in the Lord by putting on the whole armor of God through prayer: 'Pray at all times in the Spirit, with all prayer and supplication' (v. 18).

The epistle concludes with the personal commendation and commission of Tychicus (6: 21–2) and the benediction (6: 23–4).

Apart from the standard type of outline for the epistle to the Ephesians, it is possible to make some observations concerning an identifiable pattern that emerges in the movement of thought of the entire letter. Prof. Nils A. Dahl has called attention to such a pattern.[1] The rhythmic movement that he observed is not so rigid as to be found at every point in Ephesians, but it occurs regularly enough to be considered characteristic.

Dahl finds that the author of Ephesians follows a movement of thought that involves an alternation between two stages: (1) a specific reference to his readers and to something that pertains to them as they are or have been. From this, the author turns to (2) a rehearsal of what Christ, or God in Christ, has accomplished for them. The pattern is then completed by a return to (1) an application to the situation of the readers. The stage is then set for a return to (2), and so forth. One could describe this movement of thought as an alternation between references to the readers' problems and to what Christ, or God in Christ, has done for them. Or, one could say that the author begins with a reference to the readers, then turns to some christological or theological development, and finally comes back full circle to the situation of the readers.

For the purpose of illustrating this hypothesis briefly, the examination is somewhat arbitrarily restricted to chapters 2 and 3. Other passages would show a similar pattern. Chapter 1 closes with a christological statement (stage 2 above) strongly

---

[1] Seminar on Colossians and Ephesians, Yale University, 1961–2. His position in this matter is also reflected in his 'Bibelstudie über den Epheserbrief', to be found in *Kurze Auslegung des Epheserbriefes* (Göttingen: Vandenhoeck & Ruprecht, 1965), pp. 7–83, in comments such as this on p. 24: 'Der Apostel wendet sich wieder an seine Leser.'

determined by Ps. 110. Chapter 2 opens (2: 1–3) with a description of the readers' past (stage 1 above), which past the author
also recognizes as his own (2: 3). With v. 4 is begun stage (2) in
which the author turns to a rehearsal of what God has done for
the readers with and in Christ. Beginning with v. 10 there are
signs of transition back to the situation of the readers, which
is treated directly in v. 11. Almost immediately the circumstances of the readers are eclipsed by God's activity in Christ
Jesus (stage 2 again). As chapter 2 closes, the author is again
moving more directly into the situation of the reader, and as
chapter 3 opens, Paul is speaking of his ministry in behalf of
'you Gentiles' (stage 1). The first part of chapter 3 is dominated
by matters of the source and accreditation of that ministry.
Verse 8 begins the move that finally leads the author into a
statement concerning God's purposes and plan (stage 2). With
v. 13 there is the return to particular problems (stage 1) facing
the author and the resulting prayer for his readers. This prayer
leads to the benediction and the close of the chapter.

It is to be noted that this pattern is not a bifurcation of
'practical' and 'theological' or of 'hortatory' and 'dogmatic'
considerations. Instead it is evidence of the interrelatedness of
these concerns since the author moves so freely and so often
from the one to the other and back again.

On the surface, the epistle to the Ephesians does not tell much
about the readers, but it does yield a few clues. The author
refers to the readers as 'you Gentiles' at two different points
(2: 11 and 3: 1). In 4: 17, however, the readers are urged: 'no
longer walk as the Gentiles do'. Here the Gentiles seem to be
persons other than the readers, unless 'Gentiles' is here used to
refer to a way of life which the author wishes to reject.

The author has something less than full knowledge of his
readers. He states in 1: 15: 'I have heard of your faith in the
Lord Jesus, and your love toward all the saints.' Such a quotation is not conclusive but, in fact, suggests a lack of detailed
first-hand information.[1] Further evidence may be seen in
Eph. 3: 2–4. The chapter moves from a portrayal of Paul

---

[1] Cf. Philem. 5 where Paul apparently does know the recipient of the
letter entitled Philemon: 'I hear of your love and of the faith which you
have toward the Lord Jesus and all the saints.'

speaking as a prisoner on behalf of the Gentiles to another assertion: 'assuming that you have heard of the stewardship of God's grace that was made known to me by revelation, as I have written briefly. When you read this, you can perceive my insight into the mystery of Christ' (3: 2–4). The phrase 'assuming that you have heard' rests on the Greek construction εἴ γε that is translated 'assuming'. The idiomatic association of the particle εἴ with the emphatic or intensive particle γε in contexts such as this may be translated 'at least'.[1] According to Blass–Debrunner–Funk the combined use of these particles 'implies a...definite assumption'.[2] Thus, the author is at least certain of his readers' knowledge of his commission from God for them. Now from their reading of this epistle the readers are expected to gain further knowledge about Paul: they now have opportunity to 'perceive my insight into the mystery of Christ' (3: 4).

The same observations hold true for a similar occurrence in 4: 20 f.: 'you did not so learn Christ! – assuming that you have heard about him and were taught in him, as the truth is in Jesus'. Εἴ γε is best understood here as it was in 3: 2 – viz., as implying a definite assumption.

Apart from such explicit evidence, the epistle to the Ephesians sheds little light on the relation of the author to his readers. There are no references to the content of his preaching delivered to the readers in the past, as may be seen in most of the homologoumena (e.g., 1 Cor. 11: 23 ff., 15: 3 ff.). Further, there are no personal greetings extended to acquaintances. The lack of most indications of the situation into which the letter is directed may be explained by the assumption widespread in scholarship: Ephesians is a general epistle intended for several congregations.[3]

[1] Friedrich Blass, Albert Debrunner and Robert Funk, *A Greek Grammar of the New Testament and Other Early Christian Literature*, trans. Robert Funk (Chicago: The University of Chicago Press, 1961), par. 439 (2).

[2] *Ibid.*, par. 454 (2).

[3] The chief evidence for considering Ephesians as a catholic epistle is found in the greeting, where P 46, B and ℵ, among others, show a blank at the point where one would rightfully expect to find the name of the community to which the letter was addressed. For a full statement and examination of the evidence pertinent to this question, see Nils Dahl's article, 'Addresse und Prooemium des Epheserbrief', *ThLZ*, **7**, 24 ff.

The author's limited personal acquaintance with his readers does not, of course, necessarily preclude his having knowledge of some specific problems to which he may address himself. Since the author lacks extensive, detailed information about his readers and since the readers have not been tutored personally by him, the author must draw heavily upon materials and ideas that he has reason to assume will be known to his readers in other ways.

It is precisely in this perspective that the author's comment in 4: 21 must be understood: 'assuming that you have heard about him [Christ] and were taught in him'. He has been exhorting the readers to lay aside their former way of life (walking as the Gentiles do) when he departs from a description of that former life to comment about what they have learned as Christians. Though the author does not know his readers personally, he can confidently assume that they have been taught or know certain things. In writing to them he can draw upon those traditions.

What the author of Ephesians makes explicit in 4: 21 is, in fact, characteristic of the whole letter. Ernst Käsemann has observed that 'die kompositionelle Einheit wie bei einem Mosaik aus unzähligen Überlieferungssplittern zusammengefügt wird'.[1] When this characteristic of Ephesians is taken seriously, the methodology of research into any passage must be governed by the primary task of identifying and tracing the different traditional elements that have been combined to constitute the mosaic. Only then can the various elements be fully appreciated in their interplay with one another.

Ephesians' extensive traditional materials may be traced to the OT and Judaism, to the early church and to the world that

---

[1] Ernst Käsemann, 'Das Interpretationsproblem des Epheserbriefes', *Exegetische Versuche und Besinnungen* (Göttingen: Vandenhoech & Ruprecht, 1964), II, 255. The position thus suggested is not to be confused with that set forth by Edgar J. Goodspeed, *The Meaning of Ephesians* and followed by C. Leslie Mitton, *The Epistle to the Ephesians: Its Authorship, Origin and Purpose*, viz., that Ephesians is composed of a mosaic of the homologoumena. One may indeed refer to Ephesians as a mosaic, but the materials came from far more diverse sources; it is a creative mosaic built out of traditions that the author has reason to assume his readers know. The focus of Goodspeed and Mitton does not do justice to the complexity of the composition and milieu of Ephesians.

provided its context. Scholarship on Ephesians has in part recognized the presence of these traditional materials. In Eph. 5: 21–33, notice must be taken of Dibelius' investigation of the Haustafel form,[1] and Weidinger's pursuit of Dibelius' discovery.[2] It was Dibelius' and Weidinger's conclusion that the author of Ephesians took over the Haustafel form from his contemporaries.[3]

Traditional materials of a liturgical and hymnic nature have been widely recognized in earlier studies of Ephesians. One of the clearest examples of such a construction is to be found in Eph. 1: 3–14. Other studies that have no special relevance to this investigation in terms of content, but that are germane in their clarification of Ephesians' penchant for and extensive use of traditional materials are, among others: G. Schille's *Frühchristliche Hymnen*,[4] W. Nauck's article: 'Eph. 2: 19–22 ein Tauflied?',[5] and J. C. Kirby's, *Ephesians: Baptism and Pentecost*.[6]

Studies of a broader scope also manifest the incorporation of materials from the early church and its context: Nils A. Dahl, in his article entitled 'Dopet i Efesierbrevet',[7] has cast light upon some of the impact of early Christian baptismal practices and liturgy on the terminology now reflected in Ephesians. In this connection, another suggestive article is that of K. G. Kuhn, 'Der Epheserbrief im Lichte der Qumrantexte'.[8]

Most of the above studies are fairly recent and portray a renewed interest in the identification and assessment of traditional formulations in Ephesians. The scope and various foci of the above articles make clear that traditional materials are not restricted to one passage in Ephesians, but really pervade the various parts of the letter.

[1] Martin Dibelius, *An die Kolosser Epheser an Philemon* (3. Auflage, Tübingen: J. C. B. Mohr (Paul Siebeck), 1953), pp. 48–50.

[2] Karl Weidinger, *Das Problem der urchristlichen Haustafeln* (Leipzig, 1928), and *Die Haustafeln: ein Stück urchristlicher Paränese* (Leipzig, 1928).

[3] Dibelius, *An die Kolosser Epheser an Philemon*; Weidinger, *Die Haustafeln*.

[4] Berlin: Evangelische Verlagsanstalt, 1965.

[5] *EvTH*, **13**, 362 ff.

[6] Montreal: McGill University Press, 1968. With Kirby I share the conviction of the pervasiveness of Jewish traditions incorporated into Ephesians. His concern with 5: 21–33 and its traditional roots is limited. Cf. pp. 148 f.

[7] *SvTeolKv*, **21**, 85–103.

[8] *NTS*, **7**, 334 ff.

IDENTIFICATION AND STUDY OF TRADITIONAL MATERIALS IN 5:21–33

In previous studies of Eph. 5: 21–33, the identification of and concern with traditional materials have focused primarily on two matters: (1) the extent and importance of the Haustafel form, and, more often, (2) the assessment of that part of 5: 21–33 often spoken of as the hieros gamos or 'Bride of Christ'.

Studies of the imagery having to do with the hieros gamos usually converge on 5: 25–7, with occasional brief mention of other pertinent verses in 5: 21–33. Books and monographs that treat of this subject are numerous. Illustrative of one such approach to the examination of Eph. 5: 21–33 are the relevant sections of Claude Chavasse's book, *The Bride of Christ*,[1] and Paul S. Minear's work, *Images of the Church in the New Testament*.[2] Such studies have their own function as dogmatic considerations of a problem that appears in some of the NT writings. They do, however, leave open the question of the importance of contextual considerations and the larger problem of the function of such imagery in the epistle as a whole.

Other studies treat the hieros gamos from a *religionsgeschichtliche* perspective. Of greatest significance from this standpoint is the section in Heinrich Schlier's commentary, *Der Brief an die Epheser*, in which he devotes several pages to a study of the hieros gamos in Ephesians as seen against his reconstruction of its background.[3]

In their predominant concerns with the Haustafel and the hieros gamos, past discussions of traditional material in 5: 21–33 have failed to note the extent of the incorporation of other traditions and have not given adequate consideration to the

[1] *The Bride of Christ: An Enquiry into the Nuptial Element in Early Christianity* (London: The Religious Book Club, 1939), esp. pp. 72–82.

[2] *Images of the Church in the New Testament* (Philadelphia: The Westminster Press, 1960), pp. 54–6. On pp. 218 f., Minear does relate other images to that of the bride of Christ found in 5: 21–33.

[3] Pp. 264–76.

interrelationship of these materials into an integrated, sequential whole.

The first concern, therefore, is to identify every traditional formulation in 5: 21–33 and, insofar as possible, to trace them to their sources. When this has been accomplished, the interrelationship of these various traditions to one another in Eph. 5: 21–33 can be assessed.

The materials that the author has appropriated for his own purposes center about six major poles. They are as follows:

A. the Haustafel form;

B. the use of Lev. 19: 18*b*: 'You shall love your neighbor as yourself';

C. the hieros gamos;

D. the citation of Gen. 2: 24: 'For this reason a man shall leave his father and mother and be joined to his wife, and the two shall become one flesh';

E. the terminology of head, body and member;

F. the traditions of purity.

This list has the advantage of being comprehensive of the various lines of tradition that feed into 5: 21–33 and is not of a predetermined focus due to concentration on some dogmatic theme. Being intertwined as they are, these six considerations can be differentiated from one another only for the ultimate purpose of understanding the nature of their interrelation.

A. THE HAUSTAFEL FORM

The evidence for a pre-Christian Haustafel form has been set forth by several students of the problem.[1] The assessment of the matter has varied from the affirmation that such a form had an independent existence prior to the NT[2] to a statement from Edgar J. Goodspeed, that 'As for the haustafeln [*sic*] idea, we at Chicago were never able to find any such "haustafeln" as it is claimed anciently existed'.[3]

---

[1] Dibelius, *An die Kolosser Epheser an Philemon*, pp. 48–50; Weidinger, *Das Problem der urchristlichen Haustafeln*, and *Die Haustafeln: ein Stück urchristlicher Paränese.*

[2] Dibelius, *op. cit.* Weidinger, *Die Haustafeln.*

[3] Excerpt from personal letter quoted in F. W. Beare, *The First Epistle of Peter* (Oxford: Basil Blackwell, 1958, 2nd ed. rev.), p. 195.

Martin Dibelius made the first detailed study of the NT Haustafeln and their possible non-canonical antecedents. He treated the question in an excursus in his commentary, *An die Kolosser Epheser an Philemon*.[1] His student, Karl Weidinger, pursued his suggestions concerning the Haustafel in a dissertation, *Die Haustafeln*,[2] and its companion, *Das Problem der urchristlichen Haustafeln*,[3] became the standard treatment of the problem and these were hardly ever questioned until the last decade when interest in the Haustafeln was renewed.[4]

With the ultimate goal of establishing the form, content and extent of the Haustafel in Eph. 5: 21–33, the investigation will proceed by the following steps: (1) an analysis of the form as it appears in the NT, with a view to determining both its characteristics and the general ways in which it is used in the various writings; (2) a comparison of the forms as they appear in Colossians and Ephesians; (3) general observations concerning the Ephesian Haustafel as seen against the NT occurrences of the form; (4) justification for focusing on one section of the Ephesian Haustafel (5: 21–33) and for considering it to be a literary unit; and (5) the final delineation of the formal extent of the Haustafel addresses to wives and husbands in 5: 21–33.[5]

1. *An investigation of the Haustafeln in the NT*

Apart from any argument concerning the existence of an Haustafel form prior to the writings of the NT, there is sufficient evidence within these writings so that a formal analysis of the NT Haustafeln may be undertaken with some profit. It is

[1] Dibelius, *An die Kolosser Epheser an Philemon*, pp. 91–2.

[2] Weidinger, *Die Haustafeln*.

[3] Weidinger, *Das Problem der urchristlichen Haustafeln*.

[4] Hein Dietrich Wendland, 'Zur sozialethischen Bedeutung der neutestamentlichen Haustafeln', *Die Leibhaftigkeit des Wortes* (Theologische und seelsorgerliche Studien und Beiträge als Festgabe für Adolf Koberle zum 60. Geburtstag, Hrsg. Otto Michel und Ulrich Mann) (Hamburg, 1958), pp. 34–46. David Schroeder, 'Die Haustafeln des Neuen Testaments: Ihre Herkunft und ihr theologischer Sinn' (unpublished dissertation, Hamburg, 1959). Eduard Lohse, *Die Briefe an die Kolosser und an Philemon* (Göttingen: Vandenhoeck and Ruprecht, 1968). See esp. pp. 220–4.

[5] Wherever possible research such as that done by Dibelius, Weidinger and Wendland will be presupposed in this section so that the study may center on considerations more germane to 5: 21–33.

generally agreed that the following passages constitute the NT Haustafeln: Eph. 5: 21–6: 9, Col. 3: 18–4: 1, 1 Pet. 2: 17–3: 9, 1 Tim. 2: 8–15, 6: 1–10, Titus 2: 1–10.[1]

The investigation of the characteristics of the NT Haustafeln begins with an examination of those in Ephesians, Colossians and 1 Peter, since they are the most complete forms. A study of these forms produces certain observations that can then be checked against the remaining NT evidence.

The Haustafeln in Ephesians, Colossians and 1 Peter are unsurpassed in the total classes of individuals addressed.[2] In Ephesians, three sets of classes are involved: wives and husbands (5: 21–33), children and fathers (6: 1–4), and slaves and masters (6: 5–9). The identical sets in the same order are found in Col. 3: 18–4: 1. In 1 Peter the situation is somewhat different: (1) not all the above classes of individuals are addressed; (2) not all of the above sets are complete; and (3) a new feature – a final address to 'all of you' – is to be observed. The Haustafel in 1 Peter is introduced by an additional injunction calling for submission 'to every human institution' (2: 13 ff.) and succeeded by commands addressed to servants[3] (2: 18–25), wives (3: 1–6), husbands (3: 7) and 'all of you' (3: 8 f.). It is apparent that (1) the Haustafel form was adaptable with regard to the total number of classes addressed and with regard to the order of their presentation, but that (2) it did offer a list of classes, some of which served the purposes of one author, while others, with some overlapping, best suited the needs of another author.

The Haustafeln in Ephesians, Colossians and 1 Peter also show that (3) the classes are addressed collectively and directly:

[1] According to Dibelius, Rom. 13: 1–7 and Titus 3: 1 f. should be listed here as well: *An die Kolosser Epheser an Philemon*, p. 48. They are not considered here since they might more properly be called Gemeindetafeln or Staatstafeln. One could also mention in this connection 1 Pet. 2: 13–17. It is clear that, by the time of 1 Peter and Titus, there is no necessary separation between Gemeindetafel or Staatstafel and Haustafel.

[2] Hereafter, for clarity two terms will be used: 'class' designates any particular group of individuals addressed in part of the Haustafel; 'set' designates any two related classes such as wives *and* husbands or slaves *and* masters.

[3] In contrast to Ephesians and Colossians, 1 Pet. 2: 18 uses οἰκέται instead of δοῦλοι.

αἱ γυναῖκες, οἱ ἄνδρες, τὰ τέκνα, etc. Further, (4) the different classes are generally joined with related classes to form sets of relationships: wives and husbands, children and fathers, slaves and masters. Ephesians and Colossians do not deviate from this pattern; 1 Peter conforms to this arrangement in the case of wives and husbands (3: 1–8), but breaks it when the admonitions to the servants (2: 18–25) are not followed by corresponding exhortations to the masters.

Also (5) the authors exercise considerable freedom within the framework provided by the form. For example, the admonitions to one class may be expanded without necessitating a similar development in the injunction to the corresponding class.[1]

Furthermore, expansions within the addresses to particular classes have certain identifiable characteristics. First, there is sometimes an explication of the admonition along pragmatic lines on the basis of commonplace expressions. In Col. 3: 22, for example, the slaves are enjoined to 'obey in everything those who are your earthly masters'. In the remainder of v. 22 and in vv. 23 and 25 there follow pragmatic delineations of the meaning of that obedience. On the surface, some of these explanations are commonplace remarks such as 'whatever your task, work heartily' (3: 23) and 'the wrongdoer will be paid back for the wrong he has done' (3: 25).[2]

The Colossian address to the slaves yields an example of a second line of expansion that may be found within the Haustafeln. Very often the class addressed is reminded of its obligations by a specific christological reference or by an application of some aspect of Jesus' ministry to the problem at hand. The author of Colossians urges slaves to work 'as serving the Lord

---

[1] A good example of this may be seen in Colossians where the Nestle text shows the admonition to slaves (3: 22–5) with 57 words while the corresponding injunction to masters (4: 1) shows only 18 words. Such a phenomenon is not restricted to Colossians: in 1 Peter the admonition to the wives (3: 1–6) contains 98 words while the corresponding address to the husbands (3: 7) contains only 25 words. Furthermore, one of the classes or sets can be expanded while all the others are retained in very brief form, as may best be seen again in Colossians. As indicated, the injunction to slaves contains 57 words according to the Nestle text; in contrast the words addressed to *all* the other classes in that Haustafel total 61, only four more words than the exhortation to the slaves alone.

[2] Further, cf. 3: 19*b* and 3: 21.

and not men, knowing that from the Lord you will receive the inheritance as your reward; you are serving the Lord Christ' (3: 24).[1]

Third, the expansion of the admonitions within the Hausta-feln may be founded upon a reference to an OT verse as in Eph. 5: 31 or an OT character as in 1 Pet. 3: 5 f. In 1 Peter, for example, Sarah's obedience to Abraham in calling him Lord (LXX Gen. 18: 12) is set forth as the pattern that women are urged to emulate by submission to their own husbands.[2]

Finally, there stands the question of the reason for the presence of any expansions within the Haustafel form. Of course, it must be considered a possibility that the Haustafeln have been mediated in expanded form to a given author. Certainly no blanket answer may be assumed; each decision must be made on the basis of the evidence at hand. In at least one case, however, an interpreter posits that the expansion of one Haustafel admonition provides a major clue to the purpose or occasion of the letter containing it. John Knox, in his *Philemon Among the Letters of Paul*, takes the expansion of the injunction to slaves in Colossians as one further indication that the purposes and occasions of Philemon and Colossians are interrelated.[3]

Such may be the situation in Colossians and in the other letters that contain Haustafeln. Only further detailed study of the matter can make judgment possible.

This brief survey of some major characteristics of the three most complete Haustafeln in the NT provides guidelines for a few comments about the other NT occurrences of the form, all of which are to be found in the pastoral epistles. First, the pastoral Haustafeln are not as complete in classes addressed as

[1] Or, note the christological development in 1 Pet. 2: 21 ff., patterned on Isa. 53. That statement is found in the framework provided by the Haustafel injunction to the servants (2: 18 ff.). It can only be observed that christo-logical expansions within the Haustafel framework are quite prevalent and would provide the basis for a much broader study than is possible here. It is one such christological expansion that in part will demand attention in Eph. 5: 21–33.

[2] A similar case is found in 1 Tim. 2: 13 f., where submission of the wife to the husband is grounded in stories about Adam and Eve.

[3] John Knox, *Philemon Among the Letters of Paul* (2nd ed. rev., New York: Abingdon Press, 1959), pp. 36–45.

are those in Ephesians, Colossians and 1 Peter. At no point in the pastorals is there an address to masters. Children are not admonished either.

Second, sets – corresponding classes – are not as frequent in the pastoral epistles as in Ephesians, Colossians and 1 Peter. Twice (1 Tim. 6: 1 ff. and Titus 2: 9–10) slaves are to be admonished, without any accompanying directions for the masters. But even more important, where there are complete sets the admonition to one class within the set seldom directs the attention of that class towards its corresponding member.[1] This is a significant difference from the Haustafeln of Ephesians, Colossians and 1 Peter, and probably is to be understood as a shift designed to encourage exemplary behavior as a witness to those outside the church. Such witness is the basis for behavior not only in the pastoral Haustafeln, but throughout the pastoral epistles.[2]

Third, the pastorals evidence no concern to maintain the integrity of the Haustafeln, but in fact manifest them in smaller fragments. This is in marked contrast to Ephesians, Colossians and 1 Peter where the Haustafeln appear as units.

Fourth, there is at one point a specification within the sets that would not be expected on the basis of the Haustafeln in Ephesians, Colossians and 1 Peter. In Titus 2: 2–6 there is a division within groups of men and women on the basis of age. As a result, the classes encountered are: πρεσβύτας (2: 2), πρεσβύτιδας (2: 3), νέας (2: 4) and νεωτέρους (2: 6). In no other NT Haustafel is there such a division within a set.

Finally, the direct address that was so common to the Haustafeln of Ephesians, Colossians and 1 Peter is entirely lacking from the Haustafeln found in the pastoral epistles. In place of direct address of the classes one finds instructions to an individual – a Timothy or a Titus – that prescribed requirements be placed upon the Christians that are his congregation. This change from direct address is probably governed by the

---

[1] For example, the directive in 1 Tim. (2: 8) concerning the duties of men makes no mention of any responsibility to their wives. Similarly, the orders in Titus (2: 2 ff.) to older men and women are entirely separate and involve no mutual obligations of either class to the other. The same is true in 2: 6 where the 'younger men' are urged 'to control themselves'.

[2] Cf., for example, C. K. Barrett, *The Pastoral Epistles* (Oxford: Clarendon Press, 1963), pp. 19–32.

pretense under which 1 and 2 Timothy and Titus were written as pastoral letters addressed to individuals.[1]

Thus, even though there is a recognizable minimal conformity between all of the NT Haustafeln, there is at the same time considerable freedom in the use of the form. It is not a rigid tradition that must be taken over in a fixed fashion, but may be adapted for the particular purposes of the author. For this reason, modifications or additions are frequently indicative of the author's special concerns.

2. *A comparison of the Haustafeln in Colossians and Ephesians*

Since there exists some special literary relationship[2] between Ephesians and Colossians, some comments are in order concerning the Haustafeln in these two writings. As noted, the classes of individuals and the sets of relationships that they compose are identical in order of occurrence and in number. Six classes forming three sets are found in both Ephesians and Colossians: wives and husbands, children and fathers, slaves and masters.[3] On the basis of the Nestle text the entire Ephesian Haustafel has 324 words while Colossians has 117; when allowance has been made for similar root words, etc., Ephesians and Colossians have 70 words in common in the Haustafeln. Too much could easily be asserted for these figures, but it should be clear that, though there is some basic verbal similarity, there is also a considerable latitude of independent development. To be sure, the Colossian Haustafel is briefer than that of Ephesians by a considerable number of words;

---

[1] Cf. Ehrhard Kamlah, *Die Form der katalogischen Paränese im Neuen Testament* (Tübingen: J. C. B. Mohr (Paul Siebeck), 1964), p. 199, n. 3. There Kamlah declares: 'Der Kern des 1 Tim ist ein "Paraklese", deren Gerippe einen Haustafel ist.' He is inclined to view 1 Timothy as an overgrown Haustafel and says accordingly that 'das Haus spielt deswegen eine so grosse Rolle, weil die Gemeinde in Analogie dazu gesehen wird'.

[2] The precise nature of this literary relationship need not be argued at this point.

[3] Parallel column presentations of the relationship between the Haustafeln of the two letters are available in Goodspeed and Mitton: Goodspeed, *The Meaning of Ephesians*, pp. 146–50, see also his *The Key to Ephesians* (Chicago: University of Chicago Press, 1956), pp. 58–62; Mitton, *The Epistle to the Ephesians*, pp. 307–9. In these tables one can readily observe the extent of the verbal similarities.

in fact, Colossians is the briefest full Haustafel form in the NT.

Because of its brevity the Colossians form has often been assumed to be the most pristine Haustafel in the NT. For those who advocate this position, simplicity and conciseness of form point to an early stage in an assumed development towards complexity.[1] For this view the ἐν κυρίῳ of 3:18 and 20, for example, is to be regarded as the 'christianizing' of the form.[2] While it must be acknowledged that Colossians presents the briefest Haustafel, the judgment that it is therefore the most primitive form must be suspended in view of other considerations that may in fact argue in a different direction.

Of all the Haustafeln discussed above, only Colossians – and with it Ephesians – has such a symmetrical pattern in which every class of individuals has its corresponding class immediately after it. Thus admonitions to husbands follow those to wives, those to parents follow those to children, and masters are addressed after slaves. Here are three full sets of classes. Also, without exception, the class upon which obedience or submission is incumbent is admonished prior to the corresponding class that exercises some authority over it. Though the Haustafel in Colossians is concise, it is highly stylized and systematically arranged. Brevity of form is not unambiguous as a canon for early dating of a tradition; formalization sometimes serves a limiting and refining function. Such observations caution against a too facile declaration that Colossians contains the most primitive NT Haustafel.

While Colossians presents the briefest full Haustafel form in

---

[1] Philip Carrington, *The Primitive Christian Catechism* (Cambridge: Cambridge University Press, 1940), pp. 92–3. There Carrington reconstructs 'a basic Colossian catechism' including the entire Haustafel and states: 'it may well be that Colossians provides a primitive version of the teaching.' Cf. H. J. Holtzmann, *Kritik der Epheser- und Kolosserbriefe* (Leipzig: Wilhelm Engelmann, 1872). Though his overall theory accounting for the relationship of Ephesians and Colossians is unduly complex, Holtzmann points to many of the difficulties that make impossible a facile reconstruction of that relationship. However, concerning the point at issue here, Holtzmann reconstructs the original letter to the Colossians (pp. 325–30) and finds the Haustafel of canonical Colossians to be the original form.

[2] Werner Ochel, *Die Annahme einer Bearbeitung des Kolosser-Briefes im Epheser-Brief* (Marburg: Konrad Triltsch, Würzburg, 1934), p. 65. 'In Kol 3, 20 gibt nämlich allein das ἐν κυρίῳ den Zusammenhang christliche Farbe.'

the NT, Ephesians contains the most expanded such form. The enlargement comes not in the number of classes addressed, but within the framework provided by those very classes. At every point – even where Colossians' Haustafel is expanded concerning slaves (3: 22–5) – Ephesians' Haustafel is more extended than that of Colossians.[1] The expansion within the form in Ephesians raises the question of the role this aggrandized form plays in Ephesians.

3. General observations: Ephesians' Haustafel in light of NT Haustafeln

The typical NT expansions within the Haustafel form are also in evidence in Ephesians. First, commonplace expressions are present within the framework of the form: 'no man ever hates his own flesh' (5: 29), and 'Masters...forbear threatening' (6: 9). Secondly, christological references and reminders of some aspect of Jesus' ministry are to be found rather often (e.g., 5: 29, 6: 6). Finally, the use of the OT – implicitly and explicitly – is greater in Eph. 5: 21–6: 9 than in any other Haustafel in the NT. For example, within the section dealing with the obligations of wives and husbands there is the quotation of Gen. 2: 24 'A man shall leave his father and mother and cleave to his wife, and they shall become one [flesh]' (5: 31).[2]

---

[1] Sheer numerical tabulation of words does not in itself establish a full picture of the relationship of Colossians to Ephesians, but it may provide some clarification. Within the Haustafeln of Colossians and Ephesians the least difference, of course, may be seen in the set dealing with slaves and masters: Ephesians has 88 words compared to 75 for Colossians. When one allows for similarities of root words, Ephesians and Colossians share 42 of these words in this set. In the set dealing with children and fathers, Ephesians uses 49 words to Colossians' 23, of which 16 are used in common by both writings. The greatest difference may be seen in the first set, that dealing with wives and husbands. Whereas Colossians devotes 19 words to this set, Ephesians uses 187, with only 12 held in common.

[2] Concerning 5: 31, Masson (*L'Épître de Saint Paul aux Éphésiens*, p. 215) states that 'Paul ne cite pas ici l'Écriture'. In a footnote to this statement, Masson gives the reason for his judgment: 'Cela ressort de l'absence de toute formule de citation, dont l'auteur sait user (4. 8; 5. 14).' On the contrary, in Ephesians indebtedness to the OT is not generally acknowledged by introductory phrases, but is part of the language that the author weaves directly into the flow of his thought. Some examples may be seen (1) in the way Ps. 110 is used in 1: 20–2, (2) in the use of Isa. 57: 19 in 2: 17, (3) in the

Some MSS even show part of Gen. 2: 23 inserted just prior to this quotation.[1] Also, the section of the Haustafel addressed to children (6: 1 ff.) contains the decalog commandment to honor father and mother, and even includes the accompanying OT promise that such honor results in long life for those who bestow it (6: 2–3; cf. Exod. 20: 12).

Of all three sets that constitute the Ephesian Haustafel, one set – that of wives and husbands (5: 21–33) – is expanded disproportionately. Judged merely from the standpoint of quantity, over one-half or nearly 60 per cent of the bulk of Ephesians' total Haustafel is contained in the set of admonitions to wives and husbands – just one-third of the form. The question of the purpose of this unparalleled expansion may find its answer in a whole series of answers to other questions.

Focusing this investigation upon 5: 21–33 makes possible an intensive study of the form and function of this passage in Ephesians. This work should lay the foundation for an even broader assessment of the form and function of the total Haustafel in Ephesians.

Eph. 5: 21–33 may legitimately be studied as a unit for several reasons. First, it contains a set of addresses to corresponding classes. Wives are addressed (5: 22 ff.) just prior to husbands (5: 25 ff.). The admonition to the wives speaks of their behavior to their husbands; similarly, the injunction to the husbands concerns itself with their obligations towards their wives. This set (5: 21–33) is followed by two other distinguishable sets (6: 1–4 and 6: 5–9). Second, Eph. 5: 33 must be considered as strong evidence for the necessity of treating the

configuration of OT verses woven into 4: 25 ff. and (4) the incorporation of armament imagery into the admonitions of 6: 14 ff. Only two certain exceptions – and possibly a third – may be noted where traditional material is introduced with a formula: (1) in 4: 8 διὸ λέγει introduces very explicitly the quotation of Ps. 68: 19 and (2) in 5: 14 διὸ λέγει marks the insertion of the bit of traditional material whose source is unidentifiable. The third case might also be considered a slight exception because of the insertion of 6: 2b that identifies 6: 2a as the first commandment with a promise; the promise is then stated in 6: 3, but the commandment stands with no such introductory formula as the first two cases have. Thus Masson takes what in fact are numerically the exceptions (4: 8 and 5: 14) and mistakenly considers them the rule by which to judge 5: 31.

[1] The MS evidence for the insertion of ἐκ τῆς σαρκὸς αυτου και ἐκ των οστεων αωτου is the Koine text, D Gpl latt sy and Ir.

admonitions to wives and to husbands as one unit. It stands as the last verse in the section and reads: 'however, let each one of you [husbands] love his wife as himself, and let the wife see that she respects her husband.' If someone were inclined to argue that the injunctions to the husbands (vv. 25 ff.) are only tangentially related to the preceding admonitions to the wives (vv. 22 ff.), then he would have to ignore v. 33 since it ties together the admonitions to both classes of individuals in summary fashion. Eph. 5: 33 rules out any bifurcation of 5: 21–33.

Third, the materials employed to expand the passage beyond the minimal Haustafel admonitions are permeated throughout with references to Christ and the church and their relationship. The concentration on the Christ–church theme permeates all of 5: 21–33, but is not prevalent in the remainder of the Haustafel.

Fourth, regardless of what one must finally say about the relation of 5: 21 to the material immediately prior to it, 5: 22–33 is syntactically tied to 5: 21 because of the assumption in v. 22a of the verb ὑποτασσόμενοι already stated in 5: 21.[1] The rather general nature of 5: 21 – 'Be subject to one another out of reverence for Christ' – argues for its being superscription or introduction and specific injunction. Any treatment of 5: 22 ff., therefore, must also treat 5: 21 as a part of the passage.

From these observations it can be posited that any analysis of 5: 21–33 that does not consider it as a unit must be judged as inadequate. The formal analysis of the Haustafel in 5: 21–33 may now be undertaken.

---

[1] The MS evidence for v. 22 yields two derivative efforts to supply a verb for the Haustafel admonition to the wives. One set of MSS supports ὑποτασσέσθωσαν (the Hesychian family, the Vulgate, Egyptian translations and part of Clement of Alexandria). The other reading ὑποτασσέσθε is supported by the Koine group of MSS as well as the Syriac and Marcion. Both ὑποτασσέσθωσαν and ὑποτασσέσθε are in fact secondary attempts to resolve the problem created in v. 21 by the presence of the participle ὑποτασσόμενοι so far removed from a finite verb. The substitution of either variant would provide a closer finite verb, but neither is necessary. Supporting the reading chosen by Nestle – αἱ γυναῖκες τοῖς ἰδίοις ἀνδράσιν – are the Chester Beatty papyrus, Vaticanus – these two provide formidable evidence – and parts of Clement and Origen.

4. *Formal extent of the Haustafel in 5: 21–33*

The Haustafel form as it relates to wives and husbands in 5: 21–33 is best seen when all such NT admonitions are set forth in tabular fashion:

Eph. 5: 22 αἱ γυναῖκες (ὑποτάσσομαι) τοῖς ἰδίοις ἀνδράσιν
Col. 3: 18 αἱ γυναῖκες ὑποτάσσεσθε τοῖς ἀνδράσιν
1 Pet. 3: 1 γυναῖκες ὑποτασσόμενοι τοῖς ἰδίοις ἀνδράσιν
1 Tim. 2: 11 γυνὴ ἐν ἡσυχίᾳ μανθανέτω ἐν πάσῃ ὑποταγῇ
Titus 2: 4 f. ἵνα σωφρονίζωσιν τὰς νέας φιλάνδρους εἶναι . . .
ὑποτασσομένας τοῖς ἰδίοις ἀνδράσιν
Eph. 5: 25 οἱ ἄνδρες, ἀγαπᾶτε τὰς γυναῖκας
Col. 3: 19 οἱ ἄνδρες, ἀγαπᾶτε τὰς γυναῖκας
1 Pet. 3: 7 οἱ ἄνδρες ὁμοίως συνοικοῦντες κατὰ γνῶσιν ὡς
ἀσθενεστέρῳ σκεύει τῷ γυναικείῳ
Titus 2: 6 τοὺς νεωτέρους ὡσαύτως παρακάλει σωφρονεῖν

From these occurrences it can be deduced that the Haustafel form of the admonitions to wives and husbands contains at a minimum the following elements:

(1) a mention of the class of individuals in question – usually but not necessarily in direct address;

(2) one main verb that specifies the action or posture that the class of individuals should undertake or assume;[1]

(3) a direct object that mentions the other class of individuals constituting the set: e.g., the address to the wives will mention in its object the husbands, and vice versa.

About the verb it is possible to be even more specific. Within the NT Haustafeln the wives are consistently urged to be submissive to their husbands. The regularity of the idea of submission in these contexts indicates that the basic form of the Haustafel injunction to wives contained some form of ὑπο-τάσσομαι. Where the verbal form is missing the substantive ὑποταγή may be found (1 Tim. 2:11).[2] The same certainty concerning the identification of the particular verb used in the

[1] The verb can be an imperative or a participle functioning as an imperative and may be associated with an infinitive.

[2] Even in Titus, where the Haustafel has been modified to address two different age groups of men and women, the admonition reserved for younger women retains among other things the standard form of the injunction: ὑποτασσομένας τοῖς ἰδίοις ἀνδράσιν (2: 5).

Haustafel address to the husbands is not attainable. It can at least be noted that the form of ὑποτάσσομαι is used in the NT Haustafeln as a specification of the way husbands should relate to their wives. Beyond this, no pattern emerges.

Thus, the Haustafel form reduced to its barest details would include: Wives, be submissive to (possibly 'your own') husbands; Husbands, (some verb) wives.

There is confirmation of this formal judgment within Eph. 5: 21-33 itself. As will be examined in more detail, the author of Ephesians enlarges upon the Haustafel form with various materials and then returns to a statement that may be called a recapitulation of the basic Haustafel construction with which he began. For example, the section addressed directly to the wives (5: 22-4) opens with the Haustafel formulation: αἱ γυναῖκες (ὑποτάσσομαι assumed from v. 21) τοῖς ἰδίοις ἀνδράσιν. After this construction there is the comparative phrase ὡς τῷ κυρίῳ and a development of the thought that man is κεφαλή of the woman as Christ is of the church. Verse 24 continues the discussion about Christ and the church and lays the foundation for the concluding statement to the wives: 'As the church is subject (ὑποτάσσεται) to Christ' οὕτως καὶ αἱ γυναῖκες τοῖς ἀνδράσιν ἐν παντί. The parallelism between v. 22 a and v. 24 b, though clear, has been overlooked in the past. Verse 24 b leaves out ἰδίοις – a debatable part of the basic Haustafel form as seen from the other NT evidence – and adds the phrase ἐν παντί, probably signifying the extent of the demand for submission.

The judgment that the Haustafel form of address to the husbands contained the mention of the class, some verb, and the naming of the wives is further substantiated in 5: 33 a: 'however, let each one of you love his wife as himself'. Since this is the conclusion of the passage addressed to the husbands, the 'each one of you' is a specification and individualization of the general address given to the Haustafel form in v. 25 a. After the verb in v. 33 a comes the same object that was specified in the Haustafel construction in v. 25 a. The identical pattern that was noted in the verses directed to the wives (5: 22-4) is repeated in the section devoted to husbands (5: 25-33 a). The Haustafel injunction is given, developed and extended, and then repeated or recapitulated. Thus, within the author's own embellishment of the Haustafel form, there is heretofore unrecognized evidence to test and confirm this analysis of the minimal elements of the Haustafel form. The author's faithfulness to his inherited Haustafel form and his sense of literary balance provide a double occurrence of the fundamental Haustafel construction within the same passage.

B. THE USE OF LEV. 19: 18

Although it has never been recognized, Eph. 5: 33a – πλὴν καὶ ὑμεῖς οἱ καθ' ἕνα ἕκαστος τὴν ἑαυτοῦ γυναῖκα οὕτως ἀγαπάτω ὡς ἑαυτόν – bears a close relationship to Lev. 19: 18b. The LXX reflects the following translation of Lev. 19: 18b: ἀγαπήσεις τὸν πλησίον σου ὡς σεαυτόν; translated in the RSV 'You shall love your neighbor as yourself'. In 5: 21-33, v. 33 serves a double function: first, it is the conclusion to the section admonishing the husbands; secondly, it is at the same time a summary admonition both to the husbands and to the wives that terminates this entire section of the Haustafel.

The second occurrence of the Haustafel admonition to the wives (v. 24) is extended by the addition of ἐν παντί. In similar fashion the address to the husbands, seen in v. 25a, οἱ ἄνδρες ἀγαπᾶτε τὰς γυναῖκας, is extended and further specified in v. 33a by the addition of ὡς ἑαυτόν. The conjunction of ὡς ἑαυτόν with the verb ἀγαπάω gives reason to suspect that Lev. 19:18 plays some role as a specification of the Haustafel admonition that husbands love their wives.

There remains one problem in the relationship of 5: 33a and Lev. 19: 18. Even though both verses exhort the reader to love and both share the comparative phrase 'as himself', Ephesians nowhere shows neighbor, πλησίον, as the object of the love, but instead speaks of the wife, γυνή. The evidence of greatest importance in this question is found in Song of Songs, where the LXX on nine different occasions (1: 9, 15; 2: 2, 10, 13; 4: 1, 7; 5: 2; 6: 4) has the lover address his beloved bride with ἡ πλησίον μου. The context of the occurrences of πλησίον in Song of Songs confirms that πλησίον is used as a term of endearment for the bride.[1] This evidence is especially

---

[1] Other Jewish traditions give clear evidence that the wife may be addressed by various titles such as sister; cf. Song of Songs 4: 9, 10, 12 and

noteworthy since the hieros gamos of Ephesians will be seen below to have significant relationship to that of Song of Songs.[1]

Furthermore, as will be seen, tannaitic materials give ample witness to the function of Lev. 19: 18 in treating problems of marriage. Such an application necessitates an identification of wife and neighbor so that in certain contexts the word רֵעַ (or רִיעַ) may be used and understood as wife. Also, other OT verses that refer to neighbor, as does Prov. 3: 29 for example, are similarly used as basis for halakah concerning marriage: 'A man must not marry a woman if it is his intention to divorce her, for it is written "devise not evil against thy neighbour, seeing he dwelleth securely by thee".'[2]

These and other tannaitic passages bear witness that in Judaism the identification of רֵעַ (or רִיעַ) and 'wife' was widespread. Without such an equation the author of Ephesians would not have been able to use Lev. 19: 18.

The author of Ephesians, given the Haustafel form that speaks of the husband's obligations to love his wife, has no need to identify her as πλησίον, neighbor. Once the conventional interchangeability of γυνή and πλησίον is seen, it is clear that the exhortation to love the wife as oneself in 5: 33 a is patterned after Lev. 19: 18: 'Love your neighbor as yourself.' Were this the extent of Ephesians' use of Lev. 19: 18 in 5: 21–33 it would certainly be worth noting; however, Lev. 19: 18 has a far greater role in these few verses.

A portion of 5: 21–33 that has long caused difficulty to interpreters consists of v. 28 and the first part of v. 29. In vv. 25 b–7, the author has completed a rather lengthy statement concerning what Christ has done for the church. He then returns to his exposition of the obligations of the husband to his wife. This section is composed of three terse, somewhat repetitious and loosely connected statements: 'Even so, husbands should love their wives as their own bodies. He who loves his

5: 1 but also Jub. 27: 14–17, Tobit 5: 21 (B text), 7: 15, 8: 4–7; cf. also Gen. 26: 7 which perhaps should be mentioned here as well. Other names for wife, such as 'daughter' and 'mother', need not be discussed for the purpose of this investigation.

[1] Below, pp. 45–9.

[2] BT Yebamoth 37b. Talmudic quotations, unless otherwise specified, come from *The Babylonian Talmud*, trans. under the direction of I. Epstein, London: The Soncino Press, 1935–48.

wife loves himself. For no man ever hates his own flesh, but nourishes and cherishes it.' In one way or another, each of these assertions points up the need for the husband to love the wife. Under close examination all three statements bear a special relationship to Lev. 19: 18: 'Love your neighbor as yourself.' The first – 'Husbands should love their wives as their own bodies', v. 28a – is a pluralized restatement of the imperative in an indicative form, with the simple substitution of 'as his body' for 'as himself'. The next statement, curiously in the singular in contrast to the former pluralized one, is: 'He who loves his wife loves himself', v. 28b.[1] Once again, the imperative form of Lev. 19: 18 is altered to the indicative.[2] Of the three statements in vv. 28–9a, this one is most obviously and directly related in form and content to Lev. 19: 18. The substitution of γυνή for πλησίον continues to be governed by the context provided by the Haustafel. The third statement – 'For no man ever hates his own flesh', v. 29a – is a reflection of the theme of the two preceding declarations.[3] It is cast in the indicative and in the negative. Changed into a positive statement, it would read: 'Everyone loves [nourishes and cherishes, v. 29b] his own flesh.' Or, stated a bit differently, the primary thrust of v. 29a is that everybody loves himself. On the basis that everyone loves himself, the understanding implicit in ὡς ἑαυτόν, it is possible for the author to admonish men to love their neighbors (wives) as themselves. Thus, it seems that the third statement – 'For no man ever hates his own flesh' – is not finally a paraphrase, or restatement of Lev. 19: 18 as such. It is

---

[1] The critical apparatus records a conjectured deletion of v. 28b. Such a conjecture without supporting textual evidence is tantamount to the interpreter's admission that he does not understand what is written. The role of Lev. 19: 18 in vv. 28–9 accounts for the presence of v. 28b.

[2] Though both the imperative form ἀγαπήσεις, and the ὡς σεαυτόν of Lev. 19: 18 are missing in vv. 28–9a, both are found explicitly in v. 33a, the concluding statement in the address to the husband within the Haustafel form. The presence of the indicative instead of the imperative in vv. 28–9a can hardly stand as an argument against the influence and importance of Lev. 19: 18 in these verses.

[3] Cf. Sirach 7: 26: γυνή σοί ἐστιν κατὰ ψυχήν; μὴ ἐκβάλης αὐτήν. Translating from the Hebrew MS A, Box and Oesterley print an even more germane line: 'Hast thou a wife, abhor her not. . . .' R. H. Charles, *The Apocrypha and Pseudepigrapha of the Old Testament* (Oxford: The Clarendon Press, 1913), I, 341.

rather the affirmation or assumption upon which rests the injunction to love neighbor as self. It is, in short, an expansion of the understanding reflected in the ὡς σεαυτόν of Lev. 19: 18.

However, it may be asked if there is any precedent or parallel to the equation of wife to body as is seen in v. 28 – 'Even so, husbands should love their wives as their own bodies' – and therefore, any evidence for the relationship between ὡς ἑαυτόν and wife as body. The clearest extracanonical case of an identification of wife and body is to be found in BT Berakoth 24a. It takes place in the context of a discussion concerning the conditions under which one might recite the Shema.

R. Joseph the son of R. Nehunia inquired of Rab Judah: If two persons are sleeping in one bed, how would it be for one to turn his face away…and recite? – He replied: Thus said Samuel: (It is permitted) even if his wife is with him. R. Joseph demurred to this. (You imply, he said) 'His wife', and needless to say anyone else. On the contrary, (we should argue): His wife is like himself [גופו, literally like his body],[1] another is not like himself.

Another tannaitic tradition reflects a formulation very nearly like 5: 33a – 'Let each one of you love his wife as himself'. In BT Yebamoth 62b, concerning a man's relation to his wife, it is said: 'Our Rabbis taught: Concerning a man who loves his wife as himself, who honors her more than himself, who guides his sons and daughters in the right path…Scripture says, and thou shall know thy tent is in peace.'[2]

In conclusion, the Ephesian Haustafel injunction to the husbands – 'love your wives' (v. 25a) – is in part expounded by the author in light of Lev. 19: 18, 'Love your neighbor as yourself'. The author's use of Lev. 19: 18 is entirely consonant with his quotation of Gen. 2: 24b (5: 31b), which identifies man and wife as one flesh.

By his use of Lev. 19: 18, the author has therefore been able to relate the quotation from Gen. 2: 24 to the Haustafel admonition of the husbands and to develop that thought in some detail in vv. 28 f. Therefore, when in v. 33 he comes to the conclusion of the treatment of husbands and wives, he can draw

[1] Marcus Jastrow, *A Dictionary of the Targumim, the Talmud Babli and Yerushalmi, and the Midrashic Literature* (New York: Pardes Publishing House, Inc., 1950), I, 225.
[2] Cf. a close parallel in BT Sanhedrin 76b.

together most of his admonitions to the husbands with the concluding clause, 'let each one of you love his wife as himself'. This injunction, on the basis of its use of Lev. 19: 18, gives occasion for the confluence of the following elements of 5: 21 ff.: (1) the Haustafel admonition to the husbands (v. 25a); (2) the protracted statement concerning the love due one's wife as one's body or flesh (vv. 28 f.); and (3) the quotation of Gen. 2: 24 that provides a further basis for understanding one's wife as oneself (v. 31).[1]

C. THE HIEROS GAMOS

As noted previously, the part of Eph. 5: 21–33 that has most often been examined with a view to determining the traditional material contained within it has been 5: 25b–7, the section generally taken as treating the hieros gamos. It follows immediately upon the Haustafel address to the husbands (v. 25a) and reads:

Husbands, love your wives, as Christ loved the church and gave himself up for her, that he might sanctify her, having cleansed her by the washing of water with the word, that the church might be presented before him in splendor, without spot or wrinkle or any such thing, that she might be holy and without blemish.

The search for the possible backgrounds for the traditional material in 5: 25b–7 should be guided by the most important components in the marriage image as they present themselves in these verses, rather than by preconceived or imported notions concerning what elements should be present or should be considered. The soundest methodological approach to the understanding of these verses and the identification of the traditions within them involves establishment of their constitutive elements. Then follows the search for the closest verbal parallels that can be found in contexts similar to the one presented in

---

[1] It may also be that Lev. 19: 18 had still one further traditional association with another part of Eph. 5: 21–33. Fear of the Lord (cf. v. 21) is related in the Testament of the Twelve Patriarchs to Lev. 19: 18 'Fear ye the Lord, and love your neighbor...For he that feareth God and loveth his neighbor cannot be smitten by the spirit of Beliar, being shielded by the fear of God', T. Benj. 3: 3–4. Whether or not the Testament of Benjamin is in fact pre-Christian, these two verses provide a direct association of two phrases that are similarly related in Eph. 5: 21–33.

Ephesians. Texts that exhibit parallels to more than one of the features of 5: 25b–7 increase the credibility of some directly mediated relationship.

The basic elements that form these verses, and, therefore, the points for which traditional formulations might be identified are: (1) the love that Christ had for the church – a love of great extent as indicated in Ephesians by Christ's giving himself up for the church; (2) what he did for the church – sanctify or make her holy by the washing of water; and (2) the goal to be attained by his action – that she be presented ἔνδοξος, that is, without spot, wrinkle, blemish, or any such thing.

Eph. 5: 25b – 'as Christ loved the church and gave himself up for her' – correlates Christ's love for the church and his death for her. This half verse may have roots that, in fact, reach beyond the early Christian communities, but it is paralleled in Eph. 5: 2b and traces of it can be identified in the homologoumena.

Of prime importance for understanding 5: 25b is the parallel in 5: 2b. Eph. 5: 25b reads καθὼς καὶ ὁ χριστὸς ἠγάπησεν τὴν ἐκκλησίαν καὶ ἑαυτὸν παρέδωκεν ὑπὲρ αὐτῆς and 5: 2b states καθὼς καὶ ὁ χριστὸς ἠγάπησεν ὑμᾶς καὶ παρέδωκεν ἑαυτὸν ὑπὲρ ἡμῶν.[1] The object of Christ's love and giving of himself is, in Eph. 5: 25b, the church; likewise, the object of his love as depicted in 5: 2b is clearly the church as represented in the believers. The phrases that are associated with 5: 2b at the opening of chapter 5 have already been recognized as containing traditional material of their own. Eph. 5: 2c – 'a fragrant offering and sacrifice to God' – is drawn from the sacrificial language of the OT[2] (cf. Exod. 29: 18 and Ezek. 20: 41), and here specifies that Christ's loving and giving himself up (5: 2b) refer to his death.[3] Into the context provided by the

---

[1] There is some division of the MSS concerning the person of the pronouns that are the objects of both verbs in 5: 2b, but that does not affect the issue in question at this point.   [2] So Schlier, *Der Brief*, p. 232.

[3] One might also be able to argue that imitation of God (5: 1a) or of one of his agents functions as a conventional expression in the early church, cf. Matt. 5: 45, John 8: 39, 1 Cor. 4: 16, 11: 1, Gal. 4: 12, Phil. 3: 17, 4: 9, 1 Thess. 1: 6, 2: 14, 2 Thess. 3: 7–9, Heb. 6: 12, 13: 7. Indeed Abraham in Heb. 6 and all of the individuals recounted in Heb. 11 serve in part as persons to be emulated; cf. Abraham as the type of faithful man in Rom. 4 and Gal. 3.

traditional material incorporated in the first few verses of chapter 5, the author of Ephesians inserts the statement that 'Christ loved us and gave himself up for us'.

That Christ 'gave himself up' for the believers is already stated twice in the homologoumena. In Rom. 8: 32 Paul speaks of the action undertaken by God ὅς γε τοῦ ἰδίου υἱοῦ οὐκ ἐφείσατο, ἀλλὰ ὑπὲρ ἡμῶν πάντων παρέδωκεν αὐτόν. In Rom. 8: 32 God is the subject of the verb παρέδωκεν, whereas Christ is the subject in Ephesians. However, this verb still refers to Christ's death,[1] and it is specified in Rom. 8, as it is in Eph. 5: 2b, as a death ὑπὲρ ἡμῶν.

Gal. 2: 20 is indeed very similar: τοῦ ἀγαπήσαντός με καὶ παραδόντος ἑαυτὸν ὑπὲρ ἐμοῦ. Whereas Rom. 8: 32 lacks the association of ἀγαπάω and παραδίδωμι, Gal. 2: 20 exhibits it just as Ephesians does. In Eph. 5: 25 the object of Christ's love and his giving himself up is the church. In Gal. 2: 20, the same basic verbs are used, but the object is 'me'. In contrast to the example from Rom. 8: 32, but in agreement with both occurrences in Ephesians, Christ, or the Son of God, and not God himself, is the one who loves and gives himself up. At any rate, the same phrase or formula occurs in this verse from Galatians.

Consistently, then, the combination of the verb παραδίδωμι and the preposition ὑπέρ with some pronominal object was very early formalized as a way of speaking of the death of Jesus. There is no question that the occurrences in Eph. 5: 2b and 5: 25b likewise refer to Jesus' death by means of this traditional formula.

In both verses in Ephesians and in Gal. 2: 20, the death of Christ is the supreme sign of love; the paratactical relationship of the two verbs 'love' and 'give up' is itself evidence of a close relationship. These terms do not refer to separable realities or events.

The specific occurrence of ἀγαπάω and παραδίδωμι in Eph. 5: 25 differs only in the change of the object of the preposition ὑπέρ from some personal pronoun such as the ὑμᾶς of 5: 2b, or the με of Gal. 2: 20 to τὴν ἐκκλησίαν. The context of the discussion in 5: 25 ff. requires such a substitution, but still permits the author to retain the basic parts of the formula,

[1] C. K. Barrett, *A Commentary on the Epistle to the Romans* (New York: Harper & Row, 1957), p. 172.

viz., 'loved' plus object and 'gave himself up for' plus object. Since there is never a distinction between the object of the verb ἀγαπάω and the object of the preposition ὑπέρ, the object of ὑπέρ in 5: 25b is altered to αὐτῆς in agreement with τὴν ἐκκλησίαν.

It is therefore clear that the first part of the statement about Christ and the church in 5: 25b–7 is a traditional formulation extant in the earliest Christian communities. The author of Ephesians has adapted it for his own purposes to speak specifically of the church. What remains in 5: 26–7a are two ἵνα clauses that may be understood to hang syntactically upon either ἠγάπησεν or παρέδωκεν as their finite verb.[1] However, from what has been determined about the traditional paratactic association of these two verbs the two ἵνα clauses of vv. 26–7a ought to be understood as dependent on both verbs together. Christ's love for the church was shown in the giving up of himself (his death) for it.

Now that this formulation has been traced in its history in the writings preserved by the earliest church, there remains the possibility that the love ascribed to Christ (5: 25b ff.) may allude to formulations prior to the NT.[2]

Whereas 5: 25b – 'Christ loved the church and gave himself up for her' – may on one level be understood apart from marriage imagery and language, 5: 26–7 may not be so understood. These two verses contain a complex of ideas related primarily to marriage, and they exhibit certain features and characteristics that may be traced directly to two specific OT writings, namely Ezekiel and Song of Songs.

It is ultimately possible to see the milieu of the Ephesian hieros gamos in that elusive portrait of YHWH's marriage to Israel. There are, to be sure, reflections of such an understanding already to be found in Hosea, Ezekiel, Jeremiah and

---

[1] The third ἵνα clause (5: 27c) cannot be considered directly with the first two.

[2] C. H. Dodd, *According to the Scriptures: the Sub-structure of New Testament Theology* (London: James Nisbet and Company Ltd, 1952), p. 94; Lindars, *New Testament Apologetic*, p. 80; C. K. Barrett, *Epistle to the Romans*, p. 172. I find their suggestion not compelling in view of the connections between Ephesians and Ezekiel–Song of Songs about to be set forth. C. H. Dodd, Barnabas Lindars and C. K. Barrett trace this formulation back to Isa. 53: 12, the last of the servant songs.

other writings in the OT; the idea is carried on, developed and, one suspects, at times even suppressed in later Jewish tradition.[1] At this point, however, such a broad background may be assumed while the antecedent task of finding more specific parallels is carried out.

The sixteenth chapter of Ezekiel may be considered a highly relevant parallel, since its context is similar to Eph. 5: 21–33 in that both treat of marriage and share some verbal parallels.[2]

It is generally agreed that among extant OT prophetic traditions Hosea was the first to portray the relationship to Israel of YHWH as that of an unfaithful bride to a husband.[3] Hosea's bride was disposed to harlotry from the beginning (1: 2).[4] Jeremiah and Ezekiel employ and expand the tradition of Israel as YHWH's unfaithful bride. Ezekiel's main interest is in the bride Israel as unfaithful also. But this characterization is prepared for by a rather detailed expression of her early desolation, YHWH's almost paternal care, and her later emergence as a beautiful youth ready to be wed.[5] Zimmerli, by the heading of his treatment of Ezek. 16, 'Die untreue Frau', indicates his opinion that the major emphasis of the author is upon the defection of the wife to other lovers.[6] To be sure, the bulk of chapter 16, as well as chapter 23, does treat

[1] Generalizing treatments of the YHWH–Israel, YHWH–Jerusalem background of the Christ–church hieros gamos are available. Cf., for example, Masson, *L'Épître*, p. 213, n. 4; John A. Allan, *The Epistle to the Ephesians* (London: SCM Press Ltd, 1959), p. 128. Such studies remain superficial and consequently oversimplify the richness of the traditions upon which the author is dependent.

[2] In Ezekiel it is the marriage of YHWH and Jerusalem as a surrogate for Israel; in Ephesians it is the relation of Christ and the church in a context of human marriage.

[3] Johannes Lindblom, *Prophecy in Ancient Israel* (Philadelphia: Fortress Press, 1962), p. 328. Cf. Lindblom also on the earlier history of the erotic terminology used here by Hosea for speaking of the relationship of YHWH to Israel, pp. 328–9.

[4] So Abraham J. Heschel, *The Prophets* (New York: Harper & Row, 1962), p. 52 n. Contrast Lindblom, *Prophecy in Ancient Israel*, p. 166.

[5] This picture is to be found in Ezek. 16, a chapter called an 'extended allegory' (Lindblom, p. 263) and an 'extended parable' (Walther Eichrodt, *Theology of the Old Testament* (Philadelphia: The Westminster Press, 1961), I, 68).

[6] Walther Zimmerli, *Ezechiel* (*Biblischer Kommentar Altes Testament*, Herausg. von Martin Noth, 1958), pp. 331 ff.

of Israel's unfaithfulness to YHWH, but the introductory section (16: 1–14) portrays in considerable detail the beauty of the young maiden Israel and YHWH's choosing of her as his bride.

The chapter opens with the command 'Son of man, make known to Jerusalem her abominations' (16: 2). Then vv. 3–5 describe the desolation and estrangement that characterized her lot at the time of her birth. YHWH passed by her on two different occasions. The first is depicted in vv. 6–7; at this point YHWH saw her weltering in the blood of her birth and commanded her to 'Live and grow up like a plant of the field'. The remainder of 16: 7 sets forth the results of the effective word of YHWH: 'And you grew up...and arrived at full maidenhood; your breasts were formed and your hair had grown; yet you were naked and bare.'

The second occurrence of YHWH's passing by her is described in 16: 8–14; these verses contain the most important parallels to the imagery in Eph. 5: 25*b*–7. They are as follows:

When I passed by you again and looked upon you, behold you were at the age for love; and I spread my skirt over you, and covered your nakedness: yea, I plighted my troth to you and entered into a covenant with you, says the Lord God, and you became mine. Then I bathed you with water and washed off your blood from you, and anointed you with oil. I clothed you also with embroidered cloth and shod you with leather. I swathed you in fine linen and covered you with silk. And I decked you with ornaments, and put bracelets on your arms, and a chain on your neck. And I put a ring on your nose, and earrings in your ears, and a beautiful crown upon your head. Thus you were decked with gold and silver; and your raiment was of fine linen, and silk, and embroidered cloth; you ate fine flour and honey and oil. You grew exceedingly beautiful and came to regal estate. And your renown went forth among the nations because of your beauty, for it was perfect through the splendor which I had bestowed upon you, says the Lord God.

Consider alongside this Eph. 5: 25*b*–7, where the author stresses, more than anything else, the spotless purity and splendor of the bride, the church. Positively, this concern is expressed in the desire that the church be pure, and negatively, or in the converse, that she be without impurity. Christ gave himself up for her 'that he might sanctify her, having cleansed her...that the church might be presented...in splendor, without spot or wrinkle or any such thing, that she might be holy and without blemish'.

The verses from the sixteenth chapter of Ezekiel do not explicitly claim that Jerusalem's purity has to do with her being made without blemish. Her glory is described in terms of a contrast of the desolation that characterized the day of her birth and the change that resulted from YHWH's attention and love for her. In 16: 8–14, there is only one reference to a change from impurity to purity and it is effected in a washing: 'Then I bathed you with water and washed off your blood from you' (v. 9).

By far the greatest emphasis in Ezek. 16: 8–14 lies not on the negative conditions of impurity and lack of splendor to be avoided, but on the great detail of what YHWH did to Jerusalem to bestow splendor upon her. The extensive description of the clothing and ornamentation in vv. 10–13 accounts for the greater mass of the material in this section that describes YHWH's care for and betrothal to Jerusalem. Such ornamentation pertains to the preparation of the bride for marriage.

Ezekiel concludes the description of Jerusalem's ornamentation by saying, 'You grew exceedingly beautiful (ἐγένου καλὴ σφόδρα) and came to regal estate' (16: 13). Jerusalem's beauty was her hallmark among the nations (16: 14a). Likewise in Ephesians, the splendor and purity of the church were to be her insignia in the world as a direct result of Christ's giving himself up for her. Further, Ezekiel notes that Jerusalem was not only beautiful, but that her beauty was also perfected in glory (כִּי כָלִיל הוּא בַּהֲדָרִי) and was personally bestowed by YHWH (אֲשֶׁר־שַׂמְתִּי עָלַיִךְ). Actually the LXX shows an even greater emphasis on beauty than does the Hebrew text. In place of the Hebrew בַּהֲדָרִי the LXX has used two prepositional phrases: ἐν εὐπρεπείᾳ and ἐν τῇ ὡραιότητι. The stress on Jerusalem's beauty, unquestionable in the Hebrew, is even more detailed in the LXX. According to Eph. 5: 27, Christ's actions towards the church were expected to result in her being presented before him ἔνδοξος. Ἔνδοξος is a relatively rare word in the NT, occurring only four times.[1] Though there is no verbal identity

---

[1] Gerhard Kittel, '"Ενδοξος', TDNT, II, 254–5.

between Ezekiel and Ephesians on this point, the ἔνδοξος of Ephesians and the double prepositional phrases used to translate בַּהֲדָרִי in the LXX, namely ἐν εὐπρεπείᾳ and ἐν τῇ ὡραιότητι, share in the same general meaning of splendor or beauty.[1] In both documents a male figure bestows the splendor. In Ezekiel it is explicitly stated, 'the splendor which I have bestowed upon you' (v. 14). In Ephesians, the splendor of the church results from the death of Christ and the love shown in that death.

Thus, the first clear parallel between Ezek. 16 and Eph. 5: 25b–7 has to do with the detailed and overriding concern to set forth the beauty and purity of the bride. Ezekiel's presentation has the function of setting the stage for the impact of v. 15, in which it is stated that Jerusalem 'trusted in your beauty and played the harlot'. Her beauty, as expressed in the description of garments and ornaments, has been misused to advance her harlotries.

A second close affinity may be seen between Ezek. 16: 9 – 'then I bathed you with water and washed off your blood from you' – and Eph. 5: 26 – 'that he might sanctify her, having cleansed her by the washing of water with the word'. Eph. 5: 26 contains the first ἵνα clause that is dependent upon verse 25b – 'Christ loved the church and gave himself up for her'. Within the ἵνα clause is the participial phrase: καθαρίσας τῷ λουτρῷ τοῦ ὕδατος ἐν ῥήματι, 'having cleansed her by the washing of water with the word'. Leaving apart for the present the question of the function of ἐν ῥήματι, Ezekiel provides a certain parallel to this participial phrase. In 16: 8 ff. Ezekiel portrays YHWH as passing by youthful Jerusalem a second time, finding her 'at the age for love' (עֵת דֹּדִים or ἰδοὺ καιρός σου).[2] He plighted his troth to her and made a covenant with her (16: 8). Zimmerli states that there can be no doubt that the Hebrew וָאָבוֹא בִּבְרִית אֹתָךְ indicates that a betrothal is intended.[3] In conjunction with this betrothal and the covenant that signifies it, Jerusalem becomes YHWH's. Ezek. 16: 9, in this connection, reads: 'Then I bathed you with water' (וָאֶרְחָצֵךְ בַּמַּיִם or καὶ ἔλουσά σε ἐν

---

[1] Bauer–Arndt–Gingrich, *A Greek–English Lexicon*, pp. 324, 905 and 262.

[2] דֹּד or דּוֹד may mean friend, lover, or beloved, and is used of YHWH in Song of Songs 1: 4.

[3] Zimmerli, *Ezechiel*, p. 351.

ὕδατι). In Ezekiel, as in Ephesians, the washing with water is directly related to the act of the husband's purifying his bride.

Further reinforcing the lines that may be drawn between Ezekiel and Ephesians on this particular issue is the currency of the association of Jerusalem with the church, as discussed by Paul Minear in his *Images of the Church in the New Testament*.[1] The interplay of conceptions of Jerusalem and of the church in Galatians, Hebrews and Revelation points up the prevalence of these understandings in the early Christian communities, and probably indicates that the author of Ephesians has here taken over earlier church or Christian traditions and informed them with further details from Ezek. 16.

Also in this connection, the identification is even further confirmed if K. G. Kuhn's judgment be correct, that, in rabbinic literature, קָדַשׁ often means 'to espouse a wife'.[2] Kuhn, in his treatment of holiness in rabbinic Judaism, points to what he describes as a 'secular use' of קָדַשׁ with the prefixed preposition לְ that must be translated 'to espouse a wife', literally, 'to select or separate to oneself, as wife'.[3]

In rabbinic literature, קָדַשׁ takes over the function of the biblical word קָנָה to express the action of betrothal. This use of קָדַשׁ pervades the tractate BT Kiddushin. In the marital context, then, קָדַשׁ means that the husband renders his wife as הֶקְדֵּשׁ, a consecrated object, to all other men.[4] BT Kiddushin 41a is illustrative and incorporates many features that are related also in Eph. 5: 21–33: (1) its use of קָדַשׁ for betrothal is the same as Ephesians' use of ἁγιάζω (5: 26a); (2) Kiddushin's 'lest he see something repulsive in her' relates closely to Ephesians' insistence that the church be without spot, blemish, etc.; and (3) both use Lev. 19: 18. In the context of a discussion of betrothal through an agent, the argument continues: 'Rab Judah said in the name of Rab: A man may not betroth a woman before he sees her, lest he see something repulsive in her, and she become loathsome to him, whereas the All-Merciful said, "but thou shalt love thy neighbour as thyself".'

[1] Pp. 92–6.
[2] K. G. Kuhn, 'The Concept of Holiness in Rabbinic Judaism', *TDNT*, I, 98.   [3] *Ibid.*
[4] BT Kiddushin 2a; cf. Jastrow, *A Dictionary*, II, 1319–20.

Corresponding to this use of קָדַשׁ in some sections of rabbinic literature, the ἁγιάζω of Eph. 5: 26a means not only 'set apart', but also 'set apart for wife'. It follows that the 'washing with water' of Eph. 5: 26 must also be interpreted in precisely the same context of betrothal and marriage that, according to Zimmerli, is accomplished by the 'I bathed you with water' of Ezek. 16: 8-9.[1] According to this view, therefore, the ἁγιάζω of Eph. 5: 26a parallels the וָאָבוֹא בִבְרִית אֹתָךְ of Ezek. 16: 8 and the וָאֶרְחָצֵךְ בַּמַּיִם of Ezek. 16: 9 is paralleled by the τῷ λουτρῷ τοῦ ὕδατος of Eph. 5: 26b. Even the order is the same in Ephesians as it is in Ezekiel.

Thus Eph. 5: 25-7 has close affinity to Ezek. 16: 8 ff. in that both reflect a hieros gamos (YHWH–Jerusalem, Christ–church) in which the groom cleanses his bride by a washing with water and in which the result is a strong emphasis on the beauty and purity of the bride. Here is the first clear evidence that behind the Ephesian verses is the pattern of YHWH's marriage to Israel–Jerusalem as the basis for the understanding of the relation of Christ and the church.

It should be observed that the elements of Ezekiel's formulation that correspond so clearly with the Ephesian hieros gamos – namely, the assertion of the beauty and purity of the bride, the washing of purification, and the betrothal – are clearly not his own creation. S. N. Kramer has collected and translated some Sumerian texts having to do with the hieros gamos of Dumuzi and Inanna that exhibit some features later found in Ezekiel and Ephesians. Kramer generalizes about the nature of the texts:

The available Sumerian literary material, new and old, concerned with the sacred marriage, consists of (1) poems pertaining to the premarital courting and wooing of Dumuzi and Inanna; (2) poetic compositions relating to the marriage ritual, and stressing its importance for the welfare of the king and the prosperity of Sumer, and its people; and (3) rhapsodic love songs uttered by the goddess Inanna to Dumuzi or by one of the temple hierodules to the king in the role of Dumuzi.[2]

---

[1] Zimmerli, *Ezechiel*, p. 351.

[2] Samuel Noah Kramer, 'Cuneiform Studies and the History of Literature: The Sumerian Sacred Marriage Texts', *Proceedings of the American Philosophical Society* (Philadelphia), vol. **107**, 1963, p. 490. I am here

Though there are several passages that might be considered,[1] one is especially noteworthy and is here presented in full. The text, though marred by lacunae and difficulties of translation, opens with a description of Inanna's birth, moves through an account of her preparation for marriage with Dumuzi, and closes with the conjugal embrace.

1. The hierodule...
2. Directed her feet to the mother who gave birth to her.
3. 'Your...,
4. Lo, the youth (?)...,
5. L[o, the you]th...
6. Lo, the [youth], he...for you,
7. Lo, the youth, he is your father,
8. Lo, the youth, he is your mother,
9. His mother has...like your mother,
10. His father has...you like your father,
11. Open the house, my queen, open the house.'
12. Inanna, at the command of her mother,
13. Bathed, anointed herself with goodly oil,
14. Covered her body with the noble *pala*-garment
15. Took..., her dowry,
16. Arranged the lapis lazuli about (her) neck,
17. Grasped (her) seal in her hand.
18. The lady directed her step,
19. Opened the door for (?) Dumuzi,
20. In (?) the house she came forth to him like the light of the moon,
21. Gazed at him, rejoiced for him,
22. Embraced him...[2]

Each of the elements already identified as shared by Ezekiel and Ephesians is also present here. The pre-marital washing, the adornment of her and the consequent marriage are described. The chief difference is that the Sumerian text shows Inanna as the one who bathes and adorns herself while Ephesians, showing great affinity with Ezekiel, portrays the male figure as the one who is the agent in these actions. In conclusion, it

indebted to Thorkild Jacobsen who, in personal conversation, pointed out the striking parallels and referred me to Kramer's article here cited.

[1] Cf., for example, *ibid.* p. 496, where there is a 'detailed account of Inanna's bedecking the various parts of her body with precious stones, Jewels, and ornaments...'.

[2] *Ibid.* p. 498.

appears that Ezekiel, in his presentation of the YHWH–Jerusalem hieros gamos, draws on a conventional hieros gamos extant in the ancient Near East. To be sure, Ezekiel reforms the tradition to suit his own purposes and the author of Ephesians is indebted to Ezekiel's reformulation.

Along with Ezekiel, Song of Songs provides a configuration of imagery similar to certain elements of Eph. 5: 25 *b*–7 and merits consideration as another of the sources of Ephesians' picture of the relation of Christ and the church.

Apart from the questions of the original *Sitz im Leben* of the love poems that make up the canonical Song of Songs, it must be noted that allegorical interpretations appeared quite early. Probably the best recent single work on Song of Songs, is the translation and commentary produced by A. Robert and R. Tournay and entitled *Le Cantique des Cantiques*.[1] The section devoted to the history of interpretation is instructive.[2] Robert and Tournay cite allegorical interpretations of Song of Songs that arose in Jewish circles and that were later followed among the Christians.[3] Already in 4 Ezra 5: 24–7, probably late first century A.D., there seems to be an allegorical interpretation of some of the images in Song of Songs. If that be accurate, as seems most likely, then 4 Ezra is the earliest extant non-canonical evidence of allegorical interpretation of Song of Songs. Akiba is reported to have fought to preserve an important place for Song of Songs: 'All the ages are not worth the day on which the Song of Songs was given to Israel, for all the Writings are holy, but the Song of Songs is the Holy of Holies.'[4] Thus, Song of Songs was early understood to speak of the relationship of Israel, the bride, to YHWH, the lover.

By the time of some of the more prominent church fathers, such as Hippolytus, Origen, Jerome and Augustine, the language of Song of Songs had been transferred from YHWH and Israel to Christ and the church. Eph. 5: 21–33 stands in a mediating position between the early church fathers and

[1] *Le Cantique des Cantiques: Traduction et Commentaire* (Paris: J. Gabalda et Cie, 1963).

[2] *Ibid.* pp. 24–8. [3] *Ibid.*

[4] Yadaim 3. 5. All translations of the Mishnah, unless otherwise specified, are from *The Mishnah*, trans. Herbert Danby (Oxford: Oxford University Press, 1933).

Ezekiel–Song of Songs. Ephesians made the allegorical interpretation of Song of Songs easier, not more difficult.

Just as in Ezekiel there was a strong emphasis on the beauty
of the bride, so also in the Song of Songs this theme is recurrent.
Whereas Ezekiel set forth the beauty of the bride so that her
downfall might appear even more dreadful in terms of contrast,
Song of Songs is predominantly cast as the exchange of oaths
between a lover and his beloved, and, like Ephesians, does not
concern itself with harlotry as a later stage of the relationship.

Concerning the beauty of the bride, Song of Songs abounds
with references that show some relationship to the language of
Ephesians concerning the church. These references to the bride's
unsurpassed beauty take on a special significance when attention is paid to the regularity with which love is associated with
beauty in Song of Songs. This is consistent with the way that the
author of Ephesians has framed his reference to the unequalled
splendor and purity of the church. The three clauses that contain the majority of the material associated with the hieros
gamos follow upon the two traditionally related verbs ἠγάπησεν
and παρέδωκεν, so that the importance of Christ's love in
securing and bestowing the church's beauty cannot be overlooked or separated from the purity and beauty itself.

Of central importance in this regard is the bride's statement
about her lover: 'His banner over me was love' (2: 4). Robert
and Tournay take this phrase to speak of YHWH's love being
the rallying sign set forth in view of the nations.[1] Song of Songs
2: 4 establishes the prominence of love in the relationship of
YHWH and Israel. This corresponds to the traditional formulation that was noted in Eph. 5: 25b and in other portions of the
NT: 'Christ loved the church and gave himself up for her.'

Furthermore, one of the appellatives addressed to the bride
on nine different occasions in the Song of Songs is רַעְיָ (1: 9, 15;
2: 2, 10, 13; 4: 1, 7; 5: 2; 6: 4). It is without exception found on
the lips of the lover and spoken of his beloved, and always
carries the first person singular suffix. Brown, Driver, and
Briggs note that apart from Judg. 11: 37 רַעְיָ occurs only in
Song of Songs.[2] They take it in Song of Songs to refer to the

[1] *Le Cantique des Cantiques*, pp. 103–4.
[2] Francis Brown, S. R. Driver and Charles A. Briggs, *A Hebrew and English Lexicon of the Old Testament* (Oxford: Clarendon Press, 1952), p. 946.

'beloved bride' and the RSV in its translation follows a similar line by consistently translating it as 'my beloved'. The contexts of רֵעַ confirm the legitimacy of the RSV translation.[1]

Also, Song of Songs 7: 7 (RSV 7: 6) reads, 'How fair and pleasant you are, o loved one, delectable maiden!' Here the bride is called 'loved one'. The Hebrew reads אַהֲבָה while the LXX reads ἀγάπη. The above evidence leaves no question of the role of love in this relationship between the lover and his beloved in the Song of Songs.

The bride's beauty is emphasized in Song of Songs in a variety of ways. That the bride is fair or beautiful is expressed primarily by the Hebrew word יפה. On three different occasions the bride is called 'fairest among women' (הַיָּפָה בַּנָּשִׁים).[2] (הַיָּפָה is found in 1: 8, 5: 9, and 6: 1. In 1: 15 and twice in 4: 1 the lover is portrayed as saying to the bride, 'you are beautiful' (הִנָּךְ יָפָה). In 4: 7, the lover makes an even more emphatic statement of his beloved's beauty; it must be translated in a way similar to the RSV, 'You are all fair' (כֻּלָּךְ יָפָה). The bride is twice more addressed by her lover as 'my fair one' (יָפָתִי) (2: 10–13). Likewise, the statement in 7: 7 (RSV 7: 6) – 'how fair...you are' – must be read as an exclamatory statement concerning the beauty of the bride (מַה־יָּפִית).[3] Thus far the picture of the bride that consistently emanates from the Song of Songs is one of unsurpassed beauty and splendor.

Not entirely disassociated from the use of יָפֶה in Song of Songs, and yet not simply to be equated with it, is the use of one further appellative addressed to the bride by the lover. On two occasions, the bride is spoken of as 'my perfect one' (תַמָּתִי) (5: 2, 6: 9). These occurrences cast a certain light on the nature of the beauty of the bride in the Song of Songs, and in a sense, restrict the range of meaning of יָפָה or, as it is translated in the

---

[1] Of all questions relating to this study, the commentary by Robert and Tournay was most disappointing in its treatment of this unusual word רֵעַ. Only three lines are devoted to it on p. 82, and it is not mentioned in the remainder of the commentary.

[2] Here the article ה makes it superlative. According to Robert and Tournay, this phrase belongs in every case to the chorus (pp. 79–80), although the occurrence in 1: 8 could be understood as spoken by the bridegroom.

[3] 7: 7 constitutes the only exception to the otherwise consistent pattern of translating יָפָה in the LXX by καλή.

LXX, καλή. The beauty that is spoken of concerning the bride in the Song of Songs is a splendor such that the bride may be called τελεία (5: 2, 6: 9); although τελεία is not used in Eph. 5: 21–33, the sense of perfection is present as the bride is to be sanctified, to be cleansed to be holy, or put negatively, to be without spot or wrinkle, or blemish, or any such thing.

The connection between Ephesians and Song of Songs is made even clearer in the statement added to 4: 7 a, 'You are all fair my love; there is no flaw in you' (וּמוּם אֵין בָּךְ; καὶ μῶμος οὐκ ἔστιν ἐν σοί). In Song of Songs, as in Ephesians, the positive statement 'you are all fair' and the negative statement 'there is no flaw in you' stand side by side. Of course, there can be little question about the relationship of this statement in Song of Songs to that in Eph. 5: 27: 'that the church might be presented before him in splendor, without spot or wrinkle or any such thing, that she might be holy and without blemish (ἄμωμος)'. Particularly the last clause – 'that she might be holy and without blemish' – is very much like Song of Songs 4: 7 b – 'there is no flaw in you' – except that the negative is accomplished in Song of Songs by the particle οὐ, while in Eph. 5: 27 b it is accomplished by the alpha-privative.[1] As in Eph. 5: 25 b–7, considerable attention is paid to the purification of the bride – a purification expressed positively by the insistence that she be holy and presented before Christ ἔνδοξος, and expressed negatively by the insistence that she be 'without spot or wrinkle or any such thing...and without blemish' – so also in Song of Songs, the evidence set forth manifests a similar concern.

The Hebrew word מוּם in Song of Songs 4: 7 and translated by μῶμος in the LXX is noteworthy. The LXX regularly translates מוּם with μῶμος with a single exception, Job 11: 15. According to Brown, Driver and Briggs,[2] its basic meaning is blemish or defect, such that it would bar from the priesthood the one who bore it.[3] In the one instance where מוּם is not translated by μῶμος (Job 11: 15) there is some confusion in the text, so that מַיִם seems to have been read by the LXX

---

[1] Also in Ephesians, the clause is purposive while in Song of Songs it is a simple declarative statement of the present condition of the bride.

[2] Brown, Driver, Briggs, *A Hebrew and English Lexicon*, p. 548.

[3] Note the relationship between the purity required of the wife and that of priesthood; cf. below, pp. 69–74.

translator, instead of מוּם. The resulting LXX translation is ὕδωρ καθαρόν – still a slight step away from מַיִם and sounding more like the λουτρῷ τοῦ ὕδατος of Eph. 5: 26. Of course, there is the possibility of a play on words behind Eph. 5: 26 where being purified by washing with water (מַיִם) leaves one without blemish or defect (מוּם). The suspicion of such a paronomasia is given more credence when it is noted that Jastrow gives for מום first the meaning 'something, anything', and second the meaning 'blemish'.[1] Within Eph. 5: 27b–c, there is such a possible play on words: 'without spot or wrinkle or any such thing (μὴ ἔχουσαν σπίλον ἢ ῥυτίδα ἤ τι τῶν τοιούτων), that she might be holy and without blemish (ἵνα ᾖ ἁγία καὶ ἄμωμος)'. As noted, the last word in v. 27c, ἄμωμος, 'blemish', has, without the alpha-privative, regularly translated מום in the OT. The other meaning for מום, 'something, anything', may be behind the τι τῶν τοιούτων of v. 27b. From this it follows that, if the author of Ephesians knew Hebrew, the occurrence of τι τῶν τοιούτων in v. 27b might have called מום to mind. Once מום was in his thought as 'something' or 'anything', the other use of מום, meaning 'spot' or 'blemish', might have occurred to him and caused him to pen the ἄμωμος of v. 27c. Unfortunately, there seems to be no way to confirm this speculation.

The parallels thus adduced make it clear that a definite relationship of dependence existed between Ephesians and the YHWH–Israel hieros gamos of Ezekiel and Song of Songs. Ezekiel and Song of Songs show greatest affinity to Ephesians in their emphasis on the bride's beauty and the groom's love for the bride, the betrothal of the bride and related washing in water. Song of Songs also exhibited the use of πλησίον as a term of endearment for the wife.

It is much more difficult in this connection to specify the relationship of the Ephesian hieros gamos to Ps. 45. Ps. 45 is a royal song, or, more precisely, one whose contents presuppose a marriage of the king. Apart from an introductory section (v. 1) and a closing section (v. 17) this psalm generally falls into two parts, one having to do with the king (vv. 2–10), and the other directed to his bride (vv. 11–16). This separation is

---

[1] Jastrow, *A Dictionary*, p. 743. I have thus far been unable to discover any such paronomasia involving מום in tannaitic literature.

certainly not alien to the division that prevails in the Haustafel form *per se*, except that, in Ps. 45, the man is addressed first, and the woman second; in Eph. 5: 21 ff. women are addressed first and then men.

At least three observations concerning Ps. 45 have some bearing on Eph. 5: 21–33. First, as was the case in the language of Ezekiel and the terminology of Song of Songs, the beauty of the bride is stated and emphasized. In v. 12, note the use of the word יָפְיֵךְ for beauty ascribed to the bride; this is the same root found in the word יָפָה that was encountered in Song of Songs as a recurrent appellative of the bride. The use of יָפְיֵךְ is reinforced in vv. 14 ff. where the attire and entourage of the bride are described. As in Ezekiel and Song of Songs, the description of her splendor in Ps. 45 is carried out primarily in terms of the clothes that she wore. Both these clothes and the entourage witness to the beauty that belongs to the bride.

Secondly, v. 14 contains the phrase כָּל־כְּבוּדָּה. Brown, Driver and Briggs show extensive OT use of כָּבֵד to speak of honor, glory, splendor.[1] The preposition כָּל extends the compass of כָּבֵד and, in effect, lends a superlative or exclusive quality to the beauty of the bride. The LXX translates this phrase πᾶσα ἡ δόξα. Both in Ps. 45 and in Eph. 5: 27a – 'in order that she [the church] might be presented to him in splendor (ἔνδοξος)' – there is a close connection between the betrothal of the bride to the bridegroom and her being filled with glory. Hatch and Redpath, in the *Concordance to the Septuagint*, show that when δόξα or ἔνδοξος appears in the LXX, it has often been used to translate some form of the Hebrew כָּבֵד such as the case in Ps. 45: 14.[2] Accordingly there may be a connection between Ps. 45 and Ephesians' use of ἔνδοξος in 5: 27.

Thirdly, Ps. 45: 12 encourages the bride to recognize that the king is her lord (אֲדֹנַיִךְ). Since this is true, the bride is to bow to him.[3] This statement in v. 12, 'he is your lord', is alone enough

---

[1] Brown, Driver and Briggs, *A Hebrew and English Lexicon*, pp. 458–9.

[2] Edwin Hatch and Henry A. Redpath, *A Concordance to the Septuagint and other Greek Versions of the Old Testament* (Oxford: The Clarendon Press, 1897), pp. 341–3 and 470–1.

[3] There is some question concerning whether וְהִשְׁתַּחֲוִי־לוֹ is to be taken with the preceding part of v. 12, and thus be ascribed to the new queen, or to be taken with v. 13 which goes ahead to speak of the daughter or people of Tyre.

to make apparent the submission expected of the bride to her new husband, the king. This is consistent with the picture of the relationship between husband and wife that is reflected in Eph. 5: 21 ff., where the basic injunction to the wife is that she be submissive to her husband.[1]

Thus Ps. 45 contains elements and traditions closely parallel to those in Eph. 5: 21-33; and, though canonical Ps. 45 is not explicitly understood with reference to YHWH and Israel,[2] it further confirms the configuration of imagery already identified in Ezekiel and Song of Songs. Israel's own expression of a betrothal of Israel to YHWH provided the author of Ephesians with ready-made formulations to state the relationship of the church to Christ.

D. GEN. 2: 24 (EPH. 5: 31)

In the LXX Gen. 2: 24 reads: ἕνεκεν τούτου καταλείψει ἄνθρωπος τὸν πατέρα αὐτοῦ καὶ τὴν μητέρα αὐτοῦ καὶ προσκολληθήσεται πρὸς τὴν γυναῖκα αὐτοῦ, καὶ ἔσονται οἱ δύο εἰς σάρκα μίαν. Eph. 5: 31 shows: ἀντὶ τούτου καταλείψει ἄνθρωπος [τὸν] πατέρα καὶ [τὴν] μητέρα καὶ προσκολληθήσεται πρὸς τὴν γυναῖκα αὐτοῦ, καὶ ἔσονται οἱ δύο εἰς σάρκα μίαν. Although several allusions to the OT have been noted, Gen. 2: 24 is the only direct quotation of the OT in Eph. 5: 21-33.[3]

As will be seen,[4] the evidence in the context of the quotation

---

[1] Cf. v. 22, repeated in v. 24, and slightly restated at the close of v. 33, 'Let the wife see that she respects her husband.'

[2] The Midrash on Psalms (45: 6) manifests an explicit identification of Israel with the queen in vv. 10 ff. Cf. the translation by William G. Braude in vol. XIII of the Yale Judaica Series (New Haven: Yale University Press, 1959), pp. 449-54.

[3] Verse 30 as presented by Nestle reads: ὅτι μέλη ἐσμὲν τοῦ σώματος αὐτοῦ. At the close of this clause the following MSS show a partial quotation of Gen. 2: 23 ἐκ τῆς σαρκὸς αὐτοῦ καὶ ἐκ τῶν ὀστέων αὐτοῦ: the Koine text, Bezae, Seidelianus, the entire Latin tradition, the Syriac and Irenaeus. This reading may be accounted for as an accommodation to the quotation of Gen. 2: 24 that follows immediately in Eph. 5: 31. This addition is made easier by the reference to σάρξ, present in v. 29 a. This reading is to be understood as an epexegetical expansion of the phrase that it follows in these MSS: τοῦ σώματος αὐτοῦ. The variant reading ἐκ τῆς σαρκὸς αὐτοῦ καὶ ἐκ τῶν ὀστέων αὐτοῦ may, as Heinrich Schlier suggests, be an early Christian gloss directed against gnosticizing attempts. *Der Brief*, p. 261.

[4] Below, pp. 87-96.

indicates that the author of Ephesians understands the OT quotation in a way different from that of his opponent or opponents, and offers his own interpretation. Normally, in such a polemical situation, one would expect certain indications of the position or positions of the opponents. Such clues, if they are present in 5: 21–33, can be adduced, if at all, with great difficulty. Given the context provided by 5: 21–33, we ought to examine a range of possible functions and references for the OT verse. Wherever germane, points of contact with Eph. 5: 21–33 will be noted and assessed.

To be sure, the original context of Gen. 2: 24 should be kept in mind as a possible indication that the opponents could have understood Gen. 2: 24 to speak of that archetypical marriage of Adam and Eve. In the homologoumena, Paul twice relates Christ and Adam. The two explicit occasions are Rom. 5 and 1 Cor. 15. However, according to C. K. Barrett, the relationship of Christ and Adam may be much more subtle and pervasive:

Paul learnt to think in Hebrew, and knew that the name Adam ('ādām) means *man*. The result of this is not only an inevitable (even when subconscious) tendency to interpret the story of Adam anthropologically, but also that whenever in Paul we meet the word *man* (or other words, such as *image*, used in Gen. i–iii), we may suspect that Adam is somewhere in the background, characteristically hiding himself, though now behind the Greek language.[1]

Not only is Gen. 2: 24 located in the heart of the early traditions about Adam and Eve, but, in line with Barrett's suggestion, it also contains the word ἄνθρωπος, and thus may provide a double reference to Adam. To be sure, the problems of identifying the position of the opponents in this case are compounded not only by the lack of apparent clues in 5: 21–33, but also by the nature of the literature itself. Many of the traditions concerning Adam have no doubt been suppressed, especially by the later church in its controversy with gnosticism. Also, there is no reason to suppose that extant documents contain a legitimate sample of the traditions that once circulated concerning Adam.

At this stage in the investigation, the best procedure seems to

---

[1] C. K. Barrett, *From First Adam to Last: A Study in Pauline Theology* (New York: Charles Scribner's Sons, 1962), p. 6.

call for a presentation of the range of interpretation of Gen. 2:24 extant in (1) Philo, (2) tannaitic traditions and (3) intertestamental literature. Such a knowledge of the range of explication of Gen. 2:24 may give occasion at a later point in this study for illumination of the position or positions held by the opponent or opponents of the author of Ephesians.

Philo treats Gen. 2:24 in a variety of ways. It would be difficult to imagine a more thoroughly allegorical exposition of this OT verse than *Legum Allegoriae* II, 49:

'For this cause shall a man leave his father and his mother, and shall cleave unto his wife, and the twain shall be one flesh' (Gen. 2: 24). For the sake of sense-perception the Mind, when it has become her slave, abandons both God and the Father of the universe, and God's excellence and wisdom, the Mother of all things, and cleaves to and becomes one with sense-perception and is resolved into sense-perception so that the two become one flesh and one experience. Observe that it is not the woman that cleaves to the man, but conversely the man to the woman, Mind to Sense-perception. For when that which is superior, namely Mind, becomes one with that which is inferior, namely Sense-perception, it resolves itself into the order of flesh which is inferior, into sense-perception, the moving cause of the passions. But if Sense the inferior follow Mind the superior, there will be flesh no more, but both of them will be Mind. The man, of whom the prophet speaks is such as has been described; he prefers the love of his passions to the love of God. But there is a different man, one who has made the contrary choice, even Levi, who 'said to his father and his mother "I have not seen thee," and knew not his brethren, and disclaimed his sons' (Deut. 33: 9). This man forsakes father and mother, his mind and material body, for the sake of having as his portion the one God, 'for the Lord Himself is his portion' (Deut. 10: 9). Passion becomes the portion of the lover of passion, but the portion of Levi and the lover of God is God. Do you not see again that he prescribes that on the tenth day of the seventh month they should bring two goats, 'one portion for the Lord, and one for the averter of evil'? (Lev. 16: 8). For in very deed and portion of the lover of passion is a passion that needs an averter.[1]

Gen. 2:24 as used in Eph. 5:21–33 clearly has not served as the basis for such an allegorical interpretation as here for Philo.

Philo is able to interpret Gen. 2:24 apart from the kind of

---

[1] Unless otherwise specified, the translations of Philo come from the volumes of the Loeb Classical Library.

allegory just reflected and much more in line with Eph. 5: 21–33. In *Quaestiones et Solutiones in Genesin*, I, 29, Philo interprets Gen. 2: 24 as clarifying the relationship of a man to his wife:

Why does [Scripture] say, 'Wherefore man shall leave his father and mother, and cleave to his wife and they shall be two in one flesh'? [Scripture] commands man to act toward his wife with the most extreme exaggeration in partnership, so that he may endure to abandon even his parents. Not as though this is proper, but as though they would not be causes of goodwill to the wife. And most excellent and careful was it not to say that the woman should leave her parents and be joined to her husband – for the audacity [of man] is bolder than the nature of woman – but that for the sake of woman man is to do this. Since with a very ready and prompt impulse he is brought to a concord of knowledge. Being possessed and foreseeing the future, he controls and stills his desires, being fitted to his spouse alone as if to a bridle. And especially because he, having the authority of a master, is to be suspected of arrogance. But woman, taking the rank of servant, is shown to be obedient to his life. But when Scripture says that the two are one flesh, it indicates something very tangible and sense-perceptible, in which there is suffering and sensual pleasure, that they may rejoice in, and be pained by, and feel the same things, and much more, may think the same things.

There is one point of affinity here with Eph. 5: 21–33. Both authors recognize in Gen. 2: 24 the authority of the husband and the subservience or obedience of the wife. Philo speaks of the difference in rank between master and servant, and compares husband and wife to this, whereas the author of Ephesians is prevented from this identification because of the separation between wives–husbands and slaves–masters inherent in the Haustafel form.

There is no obligation in Jewish exegesis to treat a whole verse; a fraction of a verse can be employed if it is all that is required for the discussion. In fact a verse as long as Gen. 2: 24 is not often used in its entirety in Jewish exegesis. Fragments of it may be used instead. Gen. 2: 24 lends itself to such fragmentation rather frequently. Some exegetes deal only with the first part, 'A man shall leave his father and mother and cleave to his wife', while others refer only to the remaining words: 'and the two shall become one flesh'.

Philo quotes the last part of Gen. 2: 24 in *De Gigantibus*, 65, and disregards its natural association with marriage. He under-stands it as giving testimony to what he considers an evil and unfortunate association.

But the sons of earth have turned the steps of the mind out of the path of reason and transmuted it into the lifeless and inert nature of the flesh. For 'the two became one flesh' as says the Lawgiver (Gen. 2: 24). Thus they have debased the coin of truest metal and deserted from their post, left a place that was better for a worse, a place amid their own people for a place amid their foes. It was Nimrod who began this desertion. For the lawgiver says 'he began to be a giant on the earth' (Gen. 10), and his name means 'Desertion'....And so the conclusion would follow which Moses, holiest of men, lays down that, even as the wicked man is an exile without home or city or settle-ment, so also he is a deserter, while the good man is the staunchest of comrades.

These quotations of Philo's treatment of Gen. 2: 24 illustrate his varied use of the OT verse, but offer no especially helpful parallels to Eph. 5: 21–33.

There is variety in the treatment of Gen. 2: 24 in tannaitic materials, too, but the variety is actually not as great as just seen in the materials cited in Philo. In marked contrast to Philo, no allegorical function of Gen. 2: 24 appears in the Talmud. Consistently Gen. 2: 24 serves an halakic purpose in the tannaitic literature. It is curious, in light of the variety of interpretations of Gen. 2: 24 in other writings, that its usage in the Talmud is so clearly restricted to halakic decisions.

The most extended passage incorporating and focusing about Gen. 2: 24 may be seen in BT Sanhedrin 58a. In the midst of a protracted debate concerning marriage between heathen and proselytes on the one hand and Jews on the other, there is inserted the quotation of Gen. 2: 24. At the point of the inser-tion the discussion gradually shifts into a question of who may and may not marry whom. Gen. 2: 24 provides the framework for the whole of BT Sanhedrin 58a, but its usage may be illus-trated by a small part of that section:

For it has been taught: *therefore shall a man leave his father and his mother*; R. Eliezer said: *his father* means 'his father's sister'; *his mother*, 'his mother's sister'. R. Haiba said: *his father* means 'his father's wife'; *his mother* is literally meant. *And he shall cleave,* but not to a male; *to his wife*, but not his neighbour's wife; *and they shall be as one flesh*, applying to those that can become one flesh, thus excluding cattle and beasts, which cannot become one flesh with man.

The discussion continues into 58 *b*, but this much of the passage exemplifies the dominant interpretation of Gen. 2: 24 in the Talmud. It is understood primarily as a means of specifying what marital relationships are prohibited. Thus, a man's leaving his father and his mother is seen as excluding certain marital relationships and his cleaving to his wife rules out the possibility of relationship with another man or with another man's wife. The 'becoming one flesh' rules out relationships with those creatures with which man cannot become one flesh – that is beasts, animals.[1]

It happens occasionally that the important part of Gen. 2: 24 for the problem at hand is 'and the two shall become one flesh'. Such a case is indicated by the editors of the Soncino Press edition of the Talmud in BT Kiddushin 6*a*: 'The scholars propounded: (What if one declares,) "Thou art singled out for me", "Thou art designated unto me", "Thou art my help", "Thou art meet for me", "Thou art gathered into me", "Thou art my rib", "Thou art clothed in to me".' The editors report in a footnote at this point that 'Rashi translates: "Thou art one with me"; cf. Gen. II, 24.'[2] Significantly each of these little clauses is a formula of betrothal – including Gen. 2: 24*b*!

These passages provide a fair sample of the restricted range of interpretation of Gen. 2: 24 in the Talmud. It is quoted frequently and generally is found in a context of problems relating to marriage and sexual practice. Tannaitic traditions reflecting Gen. 2: 24 offer no clarification of the use of Gen. 2: 24 by the author of Ephesians.

'Marriage was regarded not only as the normal state, but as a divine ordinance.'[3] The importance in Judaism of Gen. 2: 24 as

---

[1] Other examples of similar use of Gen. 2: 24 could be cited at length. In Genesis Rabbah, XVIII, 5, Gen. 2: 24 is used as a means of answering the question of who may marry whom. Quite like BT San. 58*a*, PT Quid. 1, 1, interprets the last half of Gen. 2: 24 to rule out sexual relationship with other men and animals.

[2] BT Kiddushin, *The Talmud* (Soncino Press), p. 18, n. 9.

[3] George Foot Moore, *Judaism in the First Centuries of the Christian Era: The Age of the Tannaim* (Cambridge, Mass.: Harvard University Press, 1958), II, 119.

one of the prime texts ordaining marriage should not be over-looked in this context. There is no reason to question the assertion that 'Marriage is ordained in Gen. i, 22 and ii, 24'.[1] The importance of Gen. 2: 24 as an ordination of marriage in NT times is also reflected in Mark 10: 2 ff. and its parallel, Matt. 19: 3 ff., where Jesus uses Gen. 2: 24 in response to a question of the Pharisees concerning divorce.[2]

Apocryphal and intertestamental literature provide note-worthy examples of indebtedness to and interpretation of Gen. 2: 24. Without question, the most significant for this study is found in Sirach 13: 15–16. In the broad context of the problems related to a wise man's association with rich and noble people, Sirach comes to the statement that is the basis upon which he can argue that unlike persons should not associate. The principle is stated in vv. 15–16, translated according to the RSV, 'Every creature loves its like, and every person his neighbor; all living beings associate by species, and a man clings to one like himself.' There is in these two verses a curious parallel to Eph. 5: 21–33. First, if the opening part of v. 15 – πᾶν ζῷον ἀγαπᾷ τὸ ὅμοιον αὐτῷ; 'every creature loves its like' – is not itself constructed on the pattern of Lev. 19: 18 – 'You shall love your neighbor as yourself' – then it clearly brings to the author's mind Lev. 19: 18, because the second part of v. 15 – καὶ πᾶς ἄνθρωπος τὸν πλησίον αὐτοῦ; 'And every person his neighbor' – bears all the marks of dependence on Lev. 19: 18. Further, where the ἄνθρωπος of v. 15b becomes ἀνήρ in v. 16b, there seems reason to suspect that part of Gen. 2: 24 – 'Therefore a man shall leave his father and mother and cleave to his wife, and the two shall become one flesh' – under-lies v. 16b: 'A man [ἀνήρ in place of the ἄνθρωπος of v. 15b] clings [προσκολληθήσεται precisely as in Gen. 2: 24] to one like himself [τῷ ὁμοίῳ αὐτοῦ instead of πρὸς τὴν γυναῖκα as in Gen. 2: 24].' That v. 16b reads τῷ ὁμοίῳ αὐτοῦ instead of πρὸς

---

[1] BT Mo'ed Ḳaṭan, *The Talmud* (Soncino Press), p. 39, n. 1.

[2] Manfred R. Lehmann, in his article 'Gen. 2: 24 as the Basis for Divorce in Halakhah and New Testament', *ZAW*, **31**, 263–7, points out how Gen. 2: 24 was used in questions of divorce and concludes that 'divorce laws of Noahides [i.e., 'Jews prior to the revelation of Mt Sinai', p. 264] and non-Jews are not codified in Deut. 24: 1, but in Gen. 2: 24' (p. 267). Could the author of Ephesians be confronted with a need to reclaim Gen. 2: 24 as a grounds for marriage, not divorce?

τὴν γυναῖκα αὐτοῦ is no doubt determined by the context where v. 15*a* speaks of τὸ ὅμοιον αὐτῷ and not at all of a wife or a woman.

The correlation of Lev. 19: 18 and Gen. 2: 24 in Sirach 13: 15–16 closely parallels the relationship of these two OT verses in Eph. 5: 21–33. Sirach's association of Lev. 19: 18 and Gen. 2: 24 also raises the possibility that the author of Ephesians is not the first to make such an affiliation, but is using a traditional formulation that he adopts and uses for his own purposes by developing it.

At first, 1 Esdras 4: 13–25 seems less significant for the study of Eph. 5: 21-33. It is set in a context of a series of discourses delivered by the three bodyguards of King Darius and by the king himself. The immediate context is the third discourse, the one delivered by the third bodyguard, Zerubbabel. In the debate concerning which one thing should be said to be strongest – whether wine, the king or women – Zerubbabel speaks concerning women. On the whole, it is a rather popular discourse, and not too technical. Here follows, for the sake of understanding, a large part of this discourse.

Then the third, that is Zerubbabel, who had spoken of women and truth, began to speak: 'Gentlemen, is not the king great, and are not men many, and is not wine strong? Who then is their master, or who is their lord? Is it not women? Women gave birth to the king and to every people that rules over sea and land. From women they came; and women brought up the very men who plant the vineyards from which comes wine. Women make men's clothes; they bring men glory; men cannot exist without women. If men gather gold and silver or any other beautiful thing, and then see a woman *lovely in appearance and beauty*, they let all those things go, and gape at her, and with open mouths stare at her, and all prefer her to gold or silver or any other beautiful thing. *A man leaves his own father, who brought him up, and his own country, and cleaves to his wife.* With his wife he ends his days, with *no thought of his father or his mother or his country.* Hence you must realize that women rule over you! *A man loves his wife* more than his father or his mother.' (Italics mine.)

This passage has to do with the relationship between men and women, as does Eph. 5: 21 ff. Further, in v. 25, the love of the man for his wife is mentioned as in Eph. 5: 25 ff. Also, as in other OT passages, the beauty of the wife is of great importance in comparison with gold, silver, and other such objects (1 Esdras 4: 18). There can be no question in 1 Esdras 4: 20 that Gen. 2: 24 has played a formative role. 1 Esdras edits Gen. 2: 24 so that it states only that the man leaves his father, not that he also leaves his mother. This is probably determined by the context in which he discusses the importance of women; therefore it would be unimportant to speak of one's leaving one's mother. The second half of v. 20 – 'and cleaves to his wife' – leaves no room for doubt of the indebtedness of 1 Esdras 4: 20 to Gen. 2: 24.

But the possibility of greater significance in this passage is raised by the elements of vv. 20–1 that also seem to be related to Ps. 45. In Ps. 45: 10 the psalmist begins his instructions to the bride: 'Hear, O daughter, consider, and incline your ear; forget your people and your father's house.' Even though the words of Ps. 45: 10 are addressed to the woman, it seems possible that they have been transferred in 1 Esdras 4: 20–1 to refer, in this context of praising women, to the man, in conjunction with Gen. 2: 24. The quote – 'forget your people and your father's house' of Ps. 45: 10 – may be seen in 1 Esdras 4: 20–1 in the emphasis on the man's leaving his father and his country and having 'no thought of his father or his mother or his country'. If these observations be correct, then 1 Esdras 4: 20–1 provides parallel evidence that confirms the possibility of a traditional relationship of Gen. 2: 24 and Ps. 45 that is taken over by the author of Ephesians.

Tobit offers the third passage to be considered. According to the principles of levirate marriage, Tobias is obligated to marry Sarah, since he is her last living kinsman. She has been married seven times (6: 14) and each time her husband has died on the night of the consummation of the marriage. The passage is located at the end of the conversation between Raphael and Tobias concerning Tobias' fear that his life also will be lost. At the beginning of this passage Raphael is saying:

Now then, when you are about to be with her, rise up both of you first, then pray and supplicate the Lord of Heaven that mercy and deliverance may be vouchsafed unto you. And fear not, for she was set apart for you from the beginning, but you shall save her, and she shall go forth with you. And I suppose you shall have children of her, and they shall be as brothers to me. Now, do not worry. So when Tobias heard the words of Raphael, moreover that she was a kinswoman of the stock of his father's house, he loved her very much, and his heart cleaved unto her. (Tobit 6: 18–19[RSV, 6: 17])[1]

In the context of marriage, it is said of Tobias that 'He loved her [Sarah] very much, and his heart cleaved unto her' (6: 19). There is not sufficient evidence here for a final decision whether Gen. 2: 24 is important in this passage. The formulation – 'his heart cleaved unto her' – employs the basic verb of Gen. 2: 24 without the prefixed preposition πρός. Κολλάω is the verb used here as in Gen. 2: 24 and in Eph. 5: 21–33 in the context of marriage. Of especial interest is the relationship that exists in Tobit 6: 19 between the phrases 'he loved her very much, and his heart cleaved unto her' and the same relationship that exists in Eph. 5: 21–33 where the love of Christ for the church is spoken of in conjunction with the use of the OT verse that speaks of a man leaving his father and mother and cleaving to his wife (Gen. 2: 24). Already in Tobit, there is the conjunction of Gen. 2: 24 and love that is so pronounced in Eph. 5: 21 ff.

In Eph. 5: 23, Christ is spoken of as the head of the church αὐτὸς σωτὴρ τοῦ σώματος. That Christ is understood as savior of the church is stated explicitly nowhere else in 5: 21–33, but it must be understood in the imagery contained in 5: 25b ff. In Tobit 6: 18, Raphael is portrayed as saying that Tobias' marriage to Sarah will save her: καὶ σὺ αὐτὴν σώσεις.

The Book of Jubilees opens with a statement of God's promise to dwell with and redeem Israel (Jub. 1: 23 ff.). The Lord is portrayed as saying to Moses:

They will turn to Me in all uprightness and with all [their] heart and with all [their] soul, and I will circumcise the foreskin of their heart and the foreskin of the heart of their seed, and I will create in them a holy spirit, and I will cleanse them so that they shall not turn away from Me from that day unto eternity. And their souls will cleave to Me and to all My commandments, and they will fulfil My commandments, and I will be their Father and they shall be My children.

As in Ezekiel and Song of Songs, so also Jub. 1: 23 ff. uses language depicting a special relationship between YHWH and

[1] Translation by Frank Zimmermann, *The Book of Tobit* (New York: Harper & Brothers, 1958), pp. 85–7. Versification following Zimmermann.

Israel. This is completely in line with the Ephesian presentation, except YHWH and Israel have been exchanged for Christ and the church. Especially germane for the study of Eph. 5: 25 ff. is the phrase 'their souls will cleave to Me' (v. 24), and its relation to the cleansing (v. 23) that YHWH promises Israel. According to Jubilees, YHWH's cleansing of Israel is designed to preserve her as faithful to him for all time. It is because YHWH has cleansed Israel that she will not turn away from him, or, as it is secondly stated, she will cleave to him. The identical purposive relationship between YHWH's cleansing and the securing of Israel is to be found in Eph. 5: 25 ff., but, in the latter, Christ acts on behalf of the church. The cleansing and the purpose of the cleansing, namely eternal faithfulness, are identical to the cleansing of the church reported in Eph. 5: 26: 'that he might sanctify her, having cleansed her by the washing of water with the word'.[1]

These passages from intertestamental writings confirm both a frequency and an interrelationship of certain traditional formulations that have been noted in Eph. 5: 21–33. Such evidence further verifies the judgment that, in the imagery of marriage in Eph. 5: 25*b* ff., one confronts a mosaic of traditional formulations. The apocryphal materials just examined give a view of the continued reworking of the traditions that root finally in the OT. If there were more extant documents contemporary with Ephesians, it is reasonable to suppose that they would show that these same traditions were often used in an even greater variety of ways than has thus far been demonstrated.

E. THE TERMINOLOGY OF HEAD, BODY AND MEMBER

In Eph. 5: 21–33 there is a rather pervasive use of organic terminology as 'head' (v. 23), 'body' (vv. 23 and 30), and 'member' (v. 30). The use of 'bodies' in v. 28 might be

---

[1] The ultimate promise in the quoted passage from Jubilees is that YHWH will be the father of Israel and Israel shall be his children. Certainly, this is at variance with the point of view of the passage in Eph. 5: 21 ff. The language of Jub. 1, though ultimately turned towards a portrayal of YHWH as father, clearly speaks of him in ways otherwise documented as portraying him as suitor and husband.

considered in this connection as well. In v. 23 it is stated: 'For the husband is the head of the wife as Christ is the head of the church, his body.' In v. 30 it is declared that 'we are members of his body'.

In Eph. 5: 23, the church is explicitly identified as Christ's body: 'Christ, the head of the church, his body.' The same identification may be seen to be at work in v. 30, whose context must be read from v. 29: 'For no man ever hates his own flesh, but nourishes and cherishes it, as Christ does the church, because we are members of his body.' Apart from 5: 21–33, Eph. 1: 23 exhibits the same identification: 'the church, which is his body'. Undoubtedly the same understanding is reflected in Eph. 4: 15 ff.: 'Rather, speaking the truth in love, we are to grow up in every way into him who is the head, into Christ, from whom the whole body, joined and knit together by every joint with which it is supplied, when each part is working properly, makes bodily growth and upbuilds itself in love.' In the same passage (4: 15), Christ is explicitly identified as the head (κεφαλή). Likewise 1: 22, a passage indebted to Ps. 110, speaks of Christ as the 'head over all things for the church'.

The question of the source of this language of head and body has been widely debated as is evidenced in Dahl's treatment of the question in his *Das Volk Gottes*.[1] Basically, it is a question whether the terminology is rooted in the popular philosophy of Hellenism or in gnosticism. No one seems ready to dispute that the language of body, head and member found in Ephesians, Colossians and the homologoumena bears certain affinities to similar terminology in the Greco-Roman writings, most of which may be reasonably dated as pre-Christian.[2]

Whether and how far the language of body, member and head is dependent on gnostic development of this terminology is difficult to assess. As Nils Dahl has observed: 'Ob die Aussagen der älteren Paulusbriefe auch von der gnostischen Vorstellung abhangig sind, ist schon aus chronologischen

[1] Nils A. Dahl, *Das Volk Gottes: Eine Untersuchung zum Kirchenbewußtsein des Urchristentums* (Darmstadt: Wissenschaftliche Buchgesellschaft, 1963), pp. 224 ff. For more recent discussion of this matter cf. Eduard Schweizer's article on σῶμα in *ThWB*, VII, 1024–91, esp. pp. 1025–42 on Greek usage. Cf. also Eduard Lohse, *Die Briefe an die Kolosser und an Philemon*, esp. pp. 93–6.

[2] Schlier *Der Brief*, p. 91, and 'κεφαλή', *TDNT*, III, 673 ff.; Dahl, *Das Volk Gottes*, p. 225.

Gründen schwieriger zu sagen.'[1] Much of the evidence that must be considered in any decision concerning the influence of gnostic thought on the terminology of head, members, body found in Ephesians is set forth and discussed by Schlier[2] and Käsemann.[3] In each case, the possibility of some relationship of the terminology of body, head and member to an Urmensch–Erölser–Mythus is set forth at length.

The present state of the discussion of gnosticism makes the interpreter cautious since there are so many problems with the nature and extent of the present sources for understanding gnosticism. The debate over the very definition of gnosticism itself and, therefore, over the identification of gnostic documents, compounds the problems already mentioned. Further, there is not yet sufficient clarification of methodology for the procedures of dating older gnostic traditions contained in later documents now held to be gnostic. It is possible that, with the publication of further documents – for example, from Nag Hamadi – and with the clarification of methodology of interpreting them, it may finally be possible to make some informed judgment concerning the relationship of the material within Ephesians to these gnostic materials. Ernst Percy's rather dogmatic and overbearing insistence upon the absence of gnostic materials in Ephesians stands as a constant warning against any too facile and hasty decision concerning the role of gnostic thought and understanding of Ephesians.[4] Carsten Colpe's argument that gnostic ideas are not required for an understanding of Ephesians and probably do not play a role in the formulation of its content is cautiously set forth in his article 'Zur Leib-Christi-Vorstellung im Epheserbrief'.[5] Another factor contributing to hesitation is an apparent shift in Käsemann's position. There is indication of an alteration in

[1] Dahl, *op. cit.* p. 225.

[2] *Der Brief*, pp. 91–6; 'κεφαλή', *TDNT*, III, 672–81.

[3] Ernst Käsemann, *Leib und Leib Christi* (Tübingen: J. C. B. Mohr (Paul Siebeck), 1933), pp. 59–97, 137 ff.

[4] Ernst Percy, *Die Probleme der Kolosser- und Epheserbriefe* (Lund: C. W. K. Gleerup, 1946). Percy's unyielding position in this matter raises questions concerning imbalance in his interpretation of Ephesians.

[5] Carsten Colpe, 'Zur Leib-Christi-Vorstellung im Epheserbrief', *Zeitschrift für die neutestamentliche Wissenschaft und die Kunde der älteren Kirche*, **26**, 170 ff.

Käsemann's viewpoint, resulting in a diminution of the importance of gnosticism in interpreting Ephesians.[1]

Pending (1) the publication and assessment of new and fuller gnostic materials, and (2) the refinement of methodology with regard both to understanding of gnosticism and to dating of earlier gnostic traditions reflected in later texts, judgment is reserved concerning the importance of gnostic materials for understanding the language of head, member and body in Ephesians.

The following quotation from W. L. Knox is probably representative of the best of the traditional interpretation prior to interpreters such as Käsemann and Schlier:

The Church as a body, of which the individuals were members, was derived from the Stoic commonplace of the state as a body in which each member had his part to play; in this form, Paul had already worked out the parallelism in the same way in which it is worked out in the later rabbinical literature, no less than in the classical writers. Naturally, it was also a commonplace of Hellenistic Judaism; Stoic commonplace was more easily adapted in view of the metaphors from the body found in such passages as Deut. 28: 13. But the political developments of the Hellenistic age had changed the conception of the state from the body in which each member played its part into a body in which the head was the all-important matter; it is likely enough the transition was accomplished in Alexandria in favour of the Ptolemies before it became a convenient method of flattering the Roman Emperors; it is possible that the headship descended from the wise man of the Stoics to the more or less deified ruler and from him to the High Priest at Jerusalem. The transference of the conception of the 'headship' of the state to the 'headship' of the cosmos was an easy matter for Paul, since the cosmic headship of the Lord was the headship not so much over the planets as over the living beings who ruled them; but in any case, the transference is already a commonplace of popular theology.[2]

Knox thus argues that the organic language of head, members and body had permeated the thought world of the time of the writing of the Pauline correspondence. Knox notes that it was

[1] Reports from students in his seminars, and his refusal to allow a republication of an unmodified version of *Leib und Leib Christi*.

[2] W. L. Knox, *St Paul and the Church of the Gentiles* (Cambridge: Cambridge University Press, 1939), p. 161.

not only a commonplace among the Stoics, but it was also rather pervasive in hellenized Judaism and could be found in rabbinic traditions.[1]

Though the church is nowhere in the homologoumena explicitly identified as the body of Christ,[2] language close to that of Ephesians is current in the world and may be observed in several passages from popular Hellenistic philosophy.

To cite evidence from just one author, Seneca uses such organic terminology quite often. In his *Epistulae Morales*,[3] he declares how to deal with men: 'I can lay down for mankind a rule, in short compass, for our duties and human relationships: all that you behold, that which comprises both god and man, is one – we are the parts of one great body [membra sumus corporis magni]' (95, 51 ff.). In this context Seneca further states that nature works through men as its members.

In *De Clementia*, Seneca uses similar organic terminology in an address to Nero: 'For if...you [Nero] are the soul of the state and the state your body [corpus], you see, I think, how requisite is mercy: for you are merciful to yourself when you are seemingly merciful to another. And so even reprobate citizens should have mercy as being the weak members [membris] of the body' (i. 5. 1).[4]

These quotations from Seneca are offered as examples of a usage of organic terminology that was widespread in NT times. The author of Ephesians avails himself of rich and pervasive traditions of organic terminology in order to express in detail

---

[1] Knox gives references to supporting evidence in the Stoics, hellenized Judaism and rabbinic literature; *ibid.* pp. 160–3.

[2] The closest approximation to such an identification may be seen in the two passages where Paul uses the analogy of the body to greatest length: Rom. 12 and 1 Cor. 12.

[3] Translation by R. M. Gummere, The Loeb Classical Library.

[4] In the same tractate Seneca speaks of the empire as a body and Nero is declared to be the head upon which the health of the whole body depends: 'we are pleased to hope and trust, Caesar, that in large measure this will happen. That kindness of your heart will be recounted, will be diffused little by little throughout the whole body [corpus] of the empire, and all things will be molded into your likeness. It is from the head [a capite] that comes the health of the body; it is through it [the head] that all the parts are lively and alert or languid and drooping according as their animating spirit has life or withers' (ii. 2. 1). As Seneca views it, Nero is the head of his body, the empire, and therefore infuses it with life. Trans. J. W. Basore, Loeb.

the relation of husbands and wives and Christ and the church. The author's own creative use of these received traditions will be a subject of later discussion.[1]

F. TRADITIONS OF PURITY

The second part of Eph. 5: 21–33 begins with v. 25 a, the Haustafel injunction to the husbands. Verse 25 b incorporates the traditional formulation that Christ loved the church and gave himself for her. Following upon this construction are the three ἵνα clauses that constitute vv. 26–7.

One of the most striking and often underestimated features of vv. 26–7 is a recurrent, pervasive emphasis on purity ascribed to the church as the bride. Purity is stressed in two ways: (a) by positive statements and (b) by negative statements. Here follows the text of these two verses. Those words and phrases within single brackets are considered positive statements emphasizing the purity of the church. Those words and phrases within double brackets are considered negative statements, emphasizing those characteristics that the church must be without in order to be pure. ἵνα αὐτὴν ⟨ἁγιάσῃ καθαρίσας τῷ λουτρῷ τοῦ ὕδατος⟩ ἐν ῥήματι ἵνα παραστήσῃ αὐτὸς ἑαυτῷ ⟨ἔνδοξον⟩ τὴν ἐκκλησίαν μὴ ἔχουσαν «σπίλον» ἢ «ῥυτίδα» ἤ «τι τῶν τοιούτων», ἀλλ' ἵνα ᾖ ⟨ἁγία⟩ καὶ «ἄμωμος».

Two of the three ἵνα clauses in vv. 26 and 27 open with a similar concern for the holiness or sanctification of the church: ἵνα αὐτὴν ἁγιάσῃ (v. 26 a); ἵνα ᾖ ἁγία (v. 27 c). The first is the verbal form from ἁγιάζω and is the only occurrence of this verb in the letter to the Ephesians. The second is constructed with the third person singular subjunctive form of the verb εἰμί joined with the nominal form ἅγιος. Ἅγιος occurs fifteen times in Ephesians, but nowhere else is it explicitly applied to the church. It is implicitly so applied at several points where the readers of the letter are designated as the saints (1: 1, 5: 3).[2]

---

[1] Occurrences of organic terminology in other Hellenistic philosophers, Philo and tannaitic traditions have been examined and are not detailed here since no especially striking parallels were observed. Reference to further materials relating to the NT use of this language may be found in John A. T. Robinson, *The Body: a Study in Pauline Theology* (London: SCM Press Ltd, 1952), pp. 59–60, n. 1.

[2] Cf. the articles on ἅγιος and ἁγιάζω by Otto Procksch in *TDNT*, I, 100–12.

Verse 26*b* – 'having cleansed her by the washing of water'; καθαρίσας τῷ λουτρῷ τοῦ ὕδατος – was treated in its connection with the imagery from Ezek. 16 of the marriage of YHWH and Jerusalem and is of prime importance for stressing that this purity is bestowed, not achieved.

The remaining positive statement – i.e. one that attributes a quality to the church rather than speaking of its absence – is found in v. 27: 'that the church might be presented before him in splendor (ἔνδοξος)'.[1] The important term in this phrase is ἔνδοξος.[2] Bauer–Arndt–Gingrich have noted that ἔνδοξος in the NT may mean either 'honored, distinguished, eminent' or 'glorious, splendid'.[3] These two shades of meaning are not mutually exclusive but the context of Eph. 5: 27, with its positive and negative concerns for depicting the church as pure, places the emphasis on the latter alternative suggested by Bauer–Arndt–Gingrich, viz., glorious or splendid.[4]

According to Blass–Debrunner–Funk there is evidence within the NT and in classical Greek of a standard form of contrast between a substantive to which the preposition ἐν is prefixed and the same or a similar substantive with an alpha-privative.[5] They cite as an example the ἄνομος–ἔννομος of 1 Cor. 9: 21.[6] Blass–Debrunner–Funk also point to the occurrence of a similar phenomenon in classical Greek in the relationship of the words ἄτιμος–ἔντιμος, without citing specific references.[7] In Eph. 5:

---

[1] παρίστημι will be treated below, pp. 134–7.

[2] This word occurs only four times in the entire NT. Luke uses it twice (7: 25; 13: 17). The former is contained in Jesus' comments about John the Baptist (7: 24 ff.). Ἔνδοξος is used there to describe the soft gorgeous garments worn by those who 'live in luxury...and kings' courts' (v. 25). The second use in Luke is a descriptive statement of the crowd's response to Jesus: 'All the people rejoiced at all the glorious things...done by him.' Ἔνδοξος is used only once in the homologoumena and that in a note of sarcasm directed at the Corinthian Christians who seem to consider that they have already attained their goal. 'You are held in honor (ἔνδοξοι), but we in disrepute (ἄτιμοι)' (1 Cor. 4: 10).

[3] *A Greek–English Lexicon*, p. 262.

[4] There is no occurrence of ἔνδοξος in the LXX that is very helpful either. Cf. Ps. 45: 14.

[5] *A Grammar*, par. 120 (2).

[6] Cf. the Nestle apparatus to Rom. 2: 12 for the same phenomenon. Also, in 1 Cor. 4: 10 ἄτιμοι stands in opposition to ἔνδοξοι; perhaps Paul has substituted ἔνδοξος for ἔντιμος.

[7] *A Grammar*, par. 120 (2).

27, the same pattern is established: in the first part of the verse, ἔνδοξος, and in v. 27c the alpha-privative ἄμωμος. Ἔνδοξος stands over against μῶμος and is brought into conformity only by the addition of the alpha-privative, so that ἔνδοξος now opposes σπίλος and ῥυτίς and agrees with ἄμωνος.[1]

The parts of vv. 26–7 as yet unaccounted for consist of the last two segments of v. 27 and deal with characteristics which the church must lack or be without: 'without spot or wrinkle or any such thing, that she might be...without blemish' (v. 27b and c). We have already treated ἄμωμος in connection with the marital imagery taken over by the author of Ephesians from the Song of Songs, where the bride is said to have no spot: καὶ μῶμος οὐκ ἔστιν ἐν σοί (Song of Songs 4: 7).[2]

The most extended phrase, of course, is that translated by the RSV 'without spot or wrinkle or any such thing' (v. 27b); μὴ ἔχουσαν σπίλου ἢ ῥυτίδα ἤ τι τῶν τοιούτων. Σπίλος has a limited use in the NT, occurring only here in Eph. 5: 27 and in 2 Pet. 2: 13. In 2 Pet. 2, in the context dealing with the actions and fate of the unrighteous or teachers of error, it is said that the

---

[1] One further paronomasia that may be rooted in the Hebrew and play a role in 5: 21–33 would be based on the word רקמה, which means 'embroidered garment', the kind of garment placed upon a regal bride of splendor, such as portrayed in Ezek. 16: 10 and in Ps. 45: 15. Note Zimmerli, *Ezechiel*, p. 352, on this word. This term is used three times in Ezek. 16 (vv. 10, 13, 18) to describe the clothing bestowed upon the bride for her glorification. This provides a further link than those noted previously between the marriage imagery of Ezek. 16 and Ps. 45, because it occurs also in Ps. 45: 15 where once again רִקְמָה is used to describe the resplendent beauty of the bride's clothing, and therefore of the bride herself. These points of contact, however, become even more interesting when it is recognized that רִקְמָה ending in ה has a homonym in Hebrew, ending in an א, רקמא, which means not at all an embroidered garment or a thing of beauty, but on the contrary, a 'checker' or a 'spot' in the sense of blemish, with which we have been dealing in Eph. 5: 27 (Jastrow, *A Dictionary*, p. 1497). We have noted above the dependence of Eph. 5: 21–33 on the imagery of Ezek. 16 and Ps. 45; the possibility must be recognized that the mention of רקמה, as recalled three times in Ezek. 16 and once in Ps. 45, might have called to the mind of the author of Eph. the homophonous term, רִקְמָא, as a means of contrasting the beauty to be desired for the bride, the church, and those things to be avoided as detracting from that beauty. Thus, there develops another possible connection between Eph. 5: 26–7, with its ἔνδοξος, and Ps. 44: 14 (LXX), with its δόξα.

[2] Above, pp. 48–9.

unrighteous ones are σπίλοι καὶ μῶμοι. It is noteworthy that the only other occurrence of σπίλος in the NT occurs in conjunction with another word that means spot or blemish and that the same word, μῶμος, appears in the last part of Eph. 5: 27 with the alpha-privative.[1] Whereas σπίλος does not occur at all in the LXX, it is to be found often in the literature of the first and second century.[2] According to Bauer–Arndt–Gingrich, σπίλος may mean spot or stain or blemish.[3]

'Ρυτίς is found nowhere else in the NT, and appears not at all in the LXX. It does however occur in contemporary literature and means wrinkle, as in the face of one who is aging.[4] The concluding ἤ τι τῶν τοιούτων is an aid to the interpretation of v. 27. This phrase, translated 'or any such thing', makes it clear that, in his use of σπίλος and ῥυτίς, the author is not concerned to catalog the specific characteristics that the church is to avoid. The pleonastic association of nouns or phrases in v. 27b is not expected to impart a greater specificity of detail, but is intended for emphasis. It is, therefore, to be understood as an inclusive statement, not an exclusive one. This observation is confirmed in v. 27c: 'that she might be holy and without blemish'; ἀλλ' ἵνα ᾖ ἁγία καὶ ἄμωμος. In this ἵνα clause the author is able to restate in a short phrase his concern that Christ's love and death – giving of himself – for the church result both in her being pure – ἁγία harking back to ἁγιάσῃ in the first purpose clause (v. 26a) – and also her being without μῶμος, blemish. Thus the entire positive statements are summarized in the last part of v. 27 by the occurrence of ἁγία and likewise all the previous negative statements are summarized there in ἄμωμος.

The preoccupation with purity and holiness reflected in Eph. 5: 26–7 is a very rich and complex phenomenon that has roots reaching back into various concerns and practices of Judaism. As indicated, the interest in purity is, in part, a heritage of the understanding of that purity demanded and provided for Jerusalem/Israel, by her husband/lover YHWH

---

[1] Could the association of σπίλος and μῶμος be conventional?

[2] Cf., for example in Hermas, Sim. 9, 6, 4; 9, 8, 7 and 9, 26, 2.

[3] A Greek–English Lexicon, p. 770. 'Here, beside ῥυτίς, σπίλος means a spot on the body.'

[4] Schlier, Der Brief, p. 259.

(Ezek. 16, Song of Songs and Ps. 45). The purity demanded of Israel before YHWH, her lover, presupposes a set of traditions that stems from older cultic requirements laid down for the purity of the bride. The key OT text for divorce sheds light on part of this background. Only the first verse of that text is of immediate concern for this investigation. It begins: 'When a man takes a wife and marries her, if then she finds no favor in his eyes because he has found some indecency [עֶרְוַה] in her, and he writes her a bill of divorce and puts it in her hand and sends her out of his house, and she departs out of his house' (Deut. 24: 1). עֶרְוַה is a feminine noun which may mean nakedness or pudenda; but it may take on a pejorative sense as it does in Deut. 24: 1 and mean indecency or improper behavior.[1] Any indecency or blemish might give the husband cause for divorcing his wife. Thus, the purity prescribed for brides in ancient Israel's Torah became part of the YHWH–Israel hieros gamos. The author of Ephesians inherited this and developed it in application to the church as Christ's bride.

At some point in the tradition, the requirements for the purity of the bride were joined with the specifications for the purity of the priest. Already in Leviticus any blemish or defect whatsoever (מוּם) in a man would exclude him from service as a priest. Lev. 21: 17 ff. sets forth the regulations for priesthood and states on five different occasions (vv. 17, 18, 21, 21, 23) that no one with a blemish (מוּם/μῶμος) can function as a priest:

Say to Aaron, None of your descendants throughout their generations who has a blemish may approach to offer the bread of his God. For no one who has a blemish shall draw near, a man blind or lame, or one who has a mutilated face or a limb too long, or a man who has an injured foot or an injured hand, or a hunchback, or a dwarf, or a man with a defect in his sight or an itching disease or scabs or crushed testicles; no man of the descendants of Aaron the priest who has a blemish shall come near to offer the Lord's offerings by fire; since he has a blemish, he shall not come near to offer the

---

[1] Brown, Driver and Briggs, *A Hebrew and English Lexicon*, pp. 788–9. In Ezek. 16: 8, it is worth noting that, when the RSV translated 'and I spread my skirt over you and covered your nakedness' 'nakedness' is the translation of the same Hebrew word ערוה. Cf. Moore, *Judaism*, II, 122 ff. For the various interpretations of Deut. 24: 1 in tannaitic literature, cf. H. L. Strack and P. Billerbeck, *Kommentar zum Neuen Testament aus Talmud und Midrasch*, 1922–6, on Matt. 5: 31.

bread of his God. He may eat the bread of his God, both of the most holy and of the holy things, but he shall not come near the veil or approach the altar, because he has a blemish, that he may not profane my sanctuaries; for I am the Lord who sanctify them.

The confluence of priestly traditions and marital traditions concerning the purity of the persons involved is found most clearly in Ketuboth 7. 7:

If a man betrothed a woman on the condition that she was under no vow and she was found to be under a vow, her betrothal is not valid. If he married her making no conditions, and she was found to be under a vow, she may be put away without her Ketubah. (If he betrothed her) on the condition that there were no defects in her, and defects were found in her, her betrothal is not valid. If he married her, making no conditions, and defects were found in her, she may be put away without her Ketubah. *All defects which disqualify priests, disqualify women also.* (Italics mine.)

Thus, the relative sparsity of OT statements concerning the purity demanded of the bride before marriage is greatly expanded by the assimilation of the demands for purity of the priesthood.

Into this already complex picture a further factor comes in consideration of the demands of purity on the part of animals to be sacrificed. By far, the preponderance of occurrences of ἄμωμος in the LXX refer to the ritual requirements for animals without blemish for sacrifice. It may well be asked whether there may not be some more direct connection between the purity demanded of the bride and priest on the one hand, and the spotless nature of the sacrifices demanded before YHWH on the other. Again, there is evidence that confirms such an identification by the time of the codification of the Mishnah, and there is no reason to doubt that the identification reaches back much further. In Bekhoroth, in the context of a discussion of what constitutes blemishes in an animal being considered for sacrifice,[1] there occurs the following statement. 'These same blemishes, whether lasting or passing, likewise render [priests] unqualified [to serve in the Temple]' (Bekhoroth 7. 1). The remainder of Bekhoroth 7 sets forth what blemishes disqualify a priest from priestly service.

[1] Cf. especially 6. 1 f.

Although it is impossible to supply a date for this confluence of various traditions of purity in Judaism, there is no reason to doubt that such an identification is at work in the strong concern for purity reflected in Eph. 5: 26–7. The author of Ephesians calls for a purity nothing less than that described of the bride, the priest, and sacrificial animals. In effect what is to be presented must be without spot or wrinkle or any such thing; it must be without blemish as befits the Lord, whose name shall be glorious (τὸ ὄνομα κυρίου ἔνδοξον ἔσται, LXX Isa. 24: 15). Moreover, the connection between 5: 25*b* and 5: 2*b* informs the reader that the sacrificial character of the earlier part of the chapter (vv. 1–2) ought not to be excluded in the emphasis on the purity expected of the church (v. 27).

The pervasive concern for purity manifest in many writings from the Qumran community also gives evidence for the confluence of Israel's traditions for purity. While the Mishnah extends the requirements of purity for the priests to include all specifications pertaining to sacrificial animals, it is apparent that Qumran goes one step further. All who would enter the Qumran community are expected to meet the requirements of purity previously reserved for the priests.

No one who is afflicted by any form of human uncleanness is to be admitted to the community, nor is anyone who becomes so afflicted to maintain his position within it. Similarly, no one who is afflicted with a bodily defect, who is stricken in hands or feet, who is lame or blind or deaf or dumb, or who has any visible bodily defect [או מום מנוגע בבשרו], is to be admitted to a place among the 'dignitaries' for 'holy angels are in the congregation' (1 QSa II, 3–9*a*).[1]

The word מום found in the OT to be so important for the purity expected of brides, priests, and sacrificial animals is in Qumran stated in the Manual of Discipline as the final criterion for judging whether one may be admitted to or remain within the community. Anyone with a מום is excluded. This prescription is no longer restricted to priests or brides alone. The specific requirements formerly limited to a distinct group within

---

[1] English translation from *The Dead Sea Scriptures in English Translation* (2nd ed. rev., trans. T. H. Gaster, New York: Doubleday & Company, Inc.; Anchor Books, 1964). Hebrew text from *Die Texte aus Qumran: Hebräisch und deutsch* (ed. and trans. Eduard Lohse; München: Kösel-Verlag, 1964).

the community of Israel are now generalized and applied uniformly to all members of the community. Such a generalization of the requirements for purity is also to be found, of course, in Eph. 5: 25 ff., expressed there for the church. One of the specific emphases of the epistle to the Ephesians is found in the assertion that God's purposes are not restricted to Israel. The author insists that Gentiles now stand before God along with his chosen nation Israel (2: 11 ff.). The requirements for purity that formerly pertained to Israel are now required of all men, whether Jew or Gentile. In this respect, Qumran's insistence on purity for all of its members is quite analogous to the purity expected on the part of all members of the church in Ephesians.

Similar requirements of purity are expressed in the War Scroll (1 QM VII, 4–5) for those entering the final conflict.

And no lame man, nor blind, nor crippled, nor having in his flesh some incurable blemish [אוֹ אִישׁ אֲשֶׁר מוּם עוֹלָם בִּבְשָׂרוֹ], nor smitten with an impurity in his flesh; none of these shall go with them into battle. They shall all be volunteers for the battle and shall be perfect in spirit and body [וּתְמִימֵי רוּחַ וּבָשָׂר] and prepared for the Day of Vengeance.[1]

Again מוּם is used to express a defect that would disqualify one from participating in the eschatological war. Then the War Scroll states that the ones who enter the battle will be perfect (תָּמַם).[2] As in Ephesians, so also in Qumran, the purity that is desired can be spoken of negatively – the people must be without blemish – as well as positively – the people must be pure or perfect. Thus, in Qumran, there is explicit evidence of the confluence of Jewish traditions for purity of priests and sacrificial animals – and this purity is demanded of all who desire to gain or retain a place within the community.

Although the primary emphasis in Eph. 5: 26–7 has to do with marriage, and not the priesthood or the quality of animals to be used in sacrifice, it remains true that the qualifications for the purity of the wife gradually came to assimilate ideas in purity from those of the priesthood and sacrificial animals. One further point of contact between Eph. 5: 26–7 and the levitical requirements for priestly purity may be found in Lev. 21.

---

[1] Ibid.

[2] Ephesians, like Qumran, portrays the life of the believer as an eschatological battle. Cf. Eph. 6: 10 ff.

Concerning the man who has a blemish, the Lord directs Moses to say: 'he shall not come near the veil or approach the altar, because he has a blemish, that he may not profane my sanctuaries; for I am the Lord who sanctify them' (Lev. 21: 23). Neither the priest (Lev. 21) nor the church (Eph. 5) is sanctified on its own; for both, sanctification is bestowed.

The purity and sanctity that the church is to attain rest on the initiative and action of Christ in behalf of the church. To declare positively what the church is to be, the author of Ephesians twice uses forms of the word ἁγιάζω. In this same category fall the statement that Christ has purified the church by washing of water (v. 26b) and the use of the word ἔνδοξος in the phrase that constitutes v. 27a. Interspersed with these statements that inform the reader of the positive demands upon the church is a set of words that characterizes what the church must not exhibit in terms of its appearance and action.

Two of these latter words – ἅγιος and ἄμωμος – already occur in 1: 4 and provide occasion for further observation. 1: 3 opens the section that begins as a blessing of God and the 'Father of our Lord Jesus Christ who has blessed us... even as he chose us in him before the foundation of the world, that we should be holy and blameless before him' (1: 4): εἶναι ἡμᾶς ἁγίους καὶ ἀμώμους κατενώπιον αὐτοῦ. Here in the opening statement that must be considered somewhat programmatic for the entire epistle, the author of Ephesians sets over against one another the same dual characteristics that later dominate his concern in Eph. 5: 26–7, viz., that the readers be holy and spotless or blameless before God. Eph. 1: 4 and 5: 26–7 share a distinct eschatological note which calls for the completion in the reader of something that is begun but not yet finished. As it is stated in Eph. 1: 4, election before the foundation of the world has as its purpose the perfection of those chosen. The presentation of the church before Christ in a state of splendor, that is, without spot, wrinkle or blemish, is clearly something yet incomplete; but the expectation of completion is clearly intimated.

In all three strands of traditions concerning purity – those related to marriage, to the priesthood and to sacrificial animals – the blemishes that are mentioned both in the OT and in tannaitic traditions are of two sorts: first, there are those that must strictly be considered bodily blemishes, such as leprosy or some deformity, whether natural or inflicted; and second, there are those that consist of immoral or otherwise wrong behavior. The predominance of the usage both in the OT and tannaitic literature gives evidence of the former interpretation, i.e., that blemishes are considered to be primarily those of bodily deficiencies or illnesses. It is not surprising to find in Eph. 5: 21–33 the combination of marriage imagery with the concern for purity, and both of these linked together with terminology of body, member, and head. This observation, however, need not be understood as determinative that Ephesians likewise stresses bodily blemishes *per se*, while ignoring those blemishes that are 'wrong behavior'. In fact, in Ephesians the concern for bodily blemishes or physical defects has entirely been transposed into concern with ethical behavior. This shift or transposition is made manifestly clear in the way Ephesians treats the notion of the body. Eph. 4: 15–16 is a part of the evidence: 'Rather, speaking the truth in love, we are to grow up in every way into him who is the head, into Christ, from whom the whole body, joined and knit together by every joint with which it is supplied, when each part is working properly, makes bodily growth and upbuilds itself in love.' There is no question in these verses of any merely physical understanding of the body and its desired condition.

The Ephesian transposition from purely bodily blemishes and defects to ethical behavior is also manifested in language of vestment that occurs in 4: 17 ff. The author's interest lies in putting off the 'old nature' (v. 22) and putting on the 'new nature' (v. 24). Likewise in 5: 25 ff. the interest in purity of the church is directed toward the very nature of the church and her faithfulness to her calling. Only when the church is faithful to the one who nourishes and sustains her can she be truly pure.

In summation, Eph. 5: 21–33 incorporates some important OT traditions.

Lev. 19: 18 is, of course, a very prominent verse in Torah. Rabbi Akiba was not advocating an original idea when he suggested that Lev. 19: 18 – 'Love your neighbor as yourself' – might be understood as the greatest principle of all Torah. In similar fashion, Jesus, as portrayed by the gospels, represented a rather standard Jewish interpretation of Torah when he listed

Lev. 19: 18 as one of the great commandments in summary of the whole Torah (Mark 12: 31 and par.). In the homologoumena, Paul is clear about the importance of Lev. 19: 18: 'For the whole law is fulfilled in one word, "you shall love your neighbor as yourself"' (Gal. 5: 14). Given such a role of Lev. 19: 18 as a hallmark of Torah, it is of signal importance that the author of Ephesians should draw upon it in his statement of the relationship that should persist between a man and his wife.

The importance of Gen. 2: 24 in Eph. 5: 21–33 has not yet been assessed. But it must be borne in mind that Gen. 2: 24 – 'and a man shall leave his father and mother and cleave to his wife and the two shall become one flesh' – is not only the passage understood in Jewish tradition to ordain marriage; as is clearly manifested in talmudic traditions, it is also a verse used as a guideline for many marital problems.

Therefore an examination of the traditional materials incorporated in Eph. 5: 21–33 reveals that two crucial verses from the OT – one a summary of all of Torah (Lev. 19: 18), the other the prime OT verse ordaining marriage (Gen. 2: 24) – have been interwoven with the hieros gamos of Christ and the church. As the investigation has shown, the sacred marriage between Christ and the church portrayed in 5: 21–33 is thoroughly informed by the author's dependence upon traditions grounded in Ezekiel, Song of Songs and Psalm 45 concerning the marriage of YHWH and Israel.

Furthermore, the author has focused upon the idea of the purity of the bride and expanded it by means of an infusion of sacrificial and priestly concerns with purity also rooted deeply in Israel's traditions. Completing the traditional materials incorporated in Eph. 5: 21–33 is the organic terminology of body, head and member, known to be prevalent in extant literature of the Near East prior to and in the time of the writing of Ephesians.

The identification of traditional and conventional formulations in 5: 21–33 is the first step necessary in interpreting this complex passage. Such minute examination of traditions and their sources only lays the foundation for the interpreter to evaluate the author's creative association of these materials for his own purposes. Such a clarification must await the elucidation to be gained by examination of certain related passages.

CHAPTER IV

THREE PASSAGES FROM THE HOMOLOGOUMENA ESPECIALLY RELATED TO 5: 21–33

There are in the homologoumena three passages that bear a certain relationship to Eph. 5: 21–33, especially with regard to similar formulations and associations of terminology and ideas. The first of these is 1 Cor. 6: 12–20.

'All things are lawful for me', but not all things are helpful. 'All things are lawful for me', but I will not be enslaved by anything. 'Food is meant for the stomach and the stomach for food' – and God will destroy both one and the other. The body is not meant for immorality, but for the Lord, and the Lord for the body. And God raised the Lord and will also raise us up by his power. Do you not know that your bodies are members of Christ? Shall I therefore take the members of Christ and make them members of a prostitute? Never! Do you not know that he who joins himself to a prostitute becomes one body with her? For, as it is written, 'The two shall become one.' But he who is united to the Lord becomes one spirit with him. Shun immorality. Every other sin which a man commits is outside the body; but the immoral man sins against his own body. Do you not know that your body is a temple of the Holy Spirit within you, which you have from God? You are not your own; you were bought with a price. So glorify God in your body.

This passage is set in the context of Paul's discussions of the Corinthians' practice. The segment opens with what seem to be two slogans probably circulating among the Corinthians. Paul takes them up as representative of one aspect of their thought. The first slogan is 'All things are lawful for me'; it occurs twice in v. 12. Paul punctuates these slogans with his own retorts: 'but not all things are helpful...but I will not be enslaved by anything'. Then in v. 13, Paul relates another slogan, translated by the RSV: 'Food is meant for the stomach and the stomach for food.'[1] Paul responds that 'God will destroy both

---

[1] In the Greek, it reads: τὰ βρώματα τῇ κοιλίᾳ καὶ ἡ κοιλία τοῖς βρώμασιν, leaving the impression that the RSV presents a modest translation.

77

one and the other'. In the last part of vv. 13 ff. Paul shifts his discussion to the believer's proper use of his body.[1]

There are certain points of contact between this passage and Eph. 5: 21–33. Most of the similarity seems to be of the general nature of shared traditional material in the early church. For example, the formulation in 1 Cor. 6: 14 – 'and God raised the Lord and will also raise us up' – closely parallels the formulation of the first two chapters of Ephesians, where the end of chapter 1 speaks of Christ being raised and the opening section of chapter 2 tells about the believers being raised with Christ.

For the purposes of this investigation, however, there are certain clear patterns of formulation in 1 Cor. 6: 12 ff. that are also present in Eph. 5: 21–33. First there is the presence of a partial quote from Gen. 2: 24. 1 Cor. 6: 16 contains Gen. 2: 24 b: ἔσονται οἱ δύο εἰς σάρκα μίαν. That Paul is consciously dealing with Gen. 2: 24 is made clear by his insertion of γάρ φησίν at the opening of v. 16. It would be hasty to state that the first part of Gen. 2: 24 plays no role in this passage from 1 Corinthians. The unquoted part of Gen. 2: 24 – 'For this reason a man shall leave his father and mother and be joined to his wife' – uses προσκολλάω as the verb there translated 'joined to' and informs 1 Cor. 6: 15 ff. Twice in 1 Cor. 6: 15 ff. participial forms of κολλάω, the same root verb, are found, but without the prefixed preposition πρός. They are located one on either side of the quotation of the last part of Gen. 2: 24.[2] Κολλάω is used in 1 Cor. 6 to speak of the possibility of a person uniting himself either with a prostitute or with the Lord. In any case, Paul asserts that a person becomes one body with the one to whom he cleaves. The context – that is not at all concerned with a man leaving his father and mother or cleaving to his wife – determines that only the last half of Gen. 2: 24 is explicitly quoted and one main verb of the first part of Gen. 2: 24 used. In 1 Cor. 6 the relationship between the believer and the Lord is

---

[1] In a sense, Paul is answering here for the Corinthians a question also dealt with in Rom. 6, viz., whether there may be sin in the believer. Whereas the question is answered in Rom. 6 in terms of death and resurrection, in 1 Cor. 6 it is dealt with in a context of marital or sexual behavior. Associated with this terminology is that of body and member.

[2] That the verb κολλάω here does not have the prefixed preposition as found in Gen. 2: 24 is not a problem. Note that the occurrence of Gen. 2: 24 in Matt. 19: 5 reads κολλάω, not προσκολλάω.

set forth primarily in the terminology of body and member as in Eph. 5: 21–33.

The alternatives of cleaving to a prostitute or cleaving to the Lord are clearly conventional. Paul has appropriated them, perhaps directly from Sirach where the alternatives are set forth. In Sirach 19: 2 it is said: 'The man who cleaves to a prostitute is reckless.' There κολλάω is used just as it is in 1 Cor. 6: 12 ff. Also in Sirach 2: 3 the other alternative is stated: 'Cleave to him [the Lord].' There, also, κολλάω is the main verb. Ps. 72 (73): 27 (28) sets forth the same alternatives.

It must be finally noted that the σῶμα–μέλος terminology used in 1 Cor. 6: 12 ff. is slightly different in purpose from the use of the same language in Eph. 5: 21–33. The difference in context accounts for much of this change, since in Eph. 5: 21–33 σῶμα becomes equated with the church in the development of thought there (and is Christ's), whereas in 1 Cor. 6: 12 ff., the individual σῶματα of the believers are said to be members of Christ. What is important for this study, however, is that in 1 Cor. 6: 12 ff. the σῶμα–μέλος terminology is closely related to Gen. 2: 24 as it is in Eph. 5: 21–33. Thus, such an association is not highly unusual, but may reflect a convention in the early church.

In this conjunction, it is important that the σάρκα μίαν of Gen. 2: 24 is used by Paul to support the argument about the ἕν σῶμα of 1 Cor. 6: 16. In this context, then, σάρξ and σῶμα are interrelated in such a way that there is no awkwardness in supporting the argument concerning σῶμα with a reference to the σάρξ of the OT quotation.

This observation accounts for two features of the formulation of Eph. 5: 21–33. First, it ties together, even more closely than was formerly realized, the σάρξ of the quotation of Gen. 2: 24 (Eph. 5: 31), not only with the σάρξ of v. 29, but also with the σῶμα mentioned in vv. 28–9. Eph. 5: 28 ff. may then again be said to be an exposition of Gen. 2: 24 along the lines of Lev. 19: 18. Second, it also helps to account for the ease with which the popular language or terminology κεφαλή, σῶμα, μέλος is introduced even earlier in the passage (v. 23).[1]

[1] The differences in the use of common terminology between 1 Cor. 6:12 ff. and Eph. 5: 21–33 as well as the basic differences in purpose in the two passages – despite the shared materials – prevent any facile decision

The organic terminology of 'head', as discussed above, is also found in a related passage in 1 Cor. 11: 2 ff., the second of the three basically related Pauline passages. The most pertinent verses are 2 and 3: 'I commend you because you remember me in everything and maintain the traditions even as I have delivered them to you. But I want you to understand that the head of every man is Christ, the head of a woman is her husband and the head of Christ is God.' The point of greatest correspondence is found between 1 Cor. 11: 3 b κεφαλὴ δὲ γυναικὸς ὁ ἀνήρ and Eph. 5: 23 a ἀνήρ ἐστιν κεφαλὴ τῆς γυναικός.

Similar also is the description of Christ as ἡ κεφαλή in 1 Cor. 11: 3 and Eph. 5: 23. The similarities end at this point, however, since in 1 Corinthians Christ is the head not of the church, as in Ephesians, but of every man. Furthermore, in 1 Cor. 11: 3, it is stated that God is the head of Christ, and this is nowhere explicitly stated in Ephesians. The basic terminology, however, is the same and the description of the man as the head of the wife is identical. These similarities become even more significant in view of 1 Cor. 11: 2, the verse immediately preceding the sentence so full of organic terminology: 'I commend you because you remember me in everything and maintain (κατέχετε) the traditions (παραδόσεις) even as I have delivered (παρέδωκα) them to you' (11: 2). Immediately after he mentions their holding fast the traditions that he has delivered to them, Paul embarks on a statement that, given the context of v. 2, may be considered either as a tradition that he has already conveyed to them, or as one that he now adds to those that he has communicated in the past. In large measure, this same tradition has been incorporated by the author of Ephesians into the Haustafel form in Eph. 5: 21–33.

In Ephesians, however, the purposes of the author govern what parts of the tradition, reflected also in 1 Cor. 11: 3, he chooses to focus upon. In the context of his discussion of marriage, the author of Ephesians has no need to speak of God's headship over Christ. In fact, to do so would be out of place.

concerning dependence of Ephesians on 1 Corinthians at this point. There is evidence in 1 Cor. 6: 12 ff., as we have noted, that Paul has taken over traditional materials and terminology, and there is no *a priori* reason to assume that the author of Ephesians, if he be not Paul, lacked access to those same materials and terminology.

The first two parts of the traditional formulation, however, are quite apt. 'The head of every man is Christ, the head of a woman is her husband.' Just as Paul uses this tradition in his letter to the Corinthians as a tradition he passes on to them for the governance of their lives, so also in Eph. 5, in the context of the discussion of marriage, the tradition of the headship of Christ over man and the headship of a man over his wife is developed in a creative, new way.

The third, and one of the passages most frequently considered in connection with Eph. 5: 21–33, is 2 Cor. 11: 1–6, especially 11: 2–3.

I wish you would bear with me in a little foolishness. Do bear with me! I feel a divine jealousy for you, for I betrothed you to Christ to present you as a pure bride to her one husband. But I am afraid that as the serpent deceived Eve by his cunning, your thoughts will be led astray from a sincere and pure devotion to Christ.

In the fragment of a letter that may consist of chapters 10–13 in which Paul seems to be on the defensive, Paul's purpose in the opening verses of chapter 11 is not so much to say anything about Christ and the church as to establish clearly his own authority. Certainly, Paul's modesty is not at stake in this passage! Twice in chapters 10–13, Paul claims that he is 'not in the least inferior to these superlative apostles' (11: 5, 12: 11). The tone of this part of the letter is rather heated, and the statements border on hyperbole. At the opening of chapter 11, Paul asks the reader to bear with him in a little foolishness.[1]

The imagery of the marriage of Christ and the church reflected in 2 Cor. 11 is actually limited to one-half of one verse (11: 2*b*): ἡρμοσάμην γὰρ ὑμᾶς ἑνὶ ἀνδρὶ παρθένον ἀγνὴν παραστῆσαι τῷ χριστῷ; 'For I betrothed you to Christ to present you as a pure bride to her one husband.' This is a very compact,

---

[1] It is difficult to see how Francis W. Beare can maintain about vv. 2 f. as he does: 'It is only in v. 16 that Paul carries out his just expressed intention to boast. Here he turns aside to explain why he is so concerned for the Corinthians' ('The Epistle to the Ephesians', *The Interpreter's Bible*, x, 392). The whole statement of Paul's betrothing the Christians to Christ gives not only the basis for his concern with the Corinthian Christians, but also already points unquestionably to the importance of his role. How else can 11: 5–6 be understood?

laconic statement which presupposes on the part of the readers a background of knowledge arising out of Paul's earlier relationship with them. It is clear that, in Paul's view, the Corinthians are understood as the bride, and Christ is understood as the bridegroom to whom the church is to be presented. That presentation is not yet complete. But Paul is concerned that the Corinthians maintain their purity, a purity which is best understood, as Hauck suggests, in terms of 'a pure devotion to Christ' (11: 3).[1] Ἁρμόζομαι, the word translated by the RSV in 11: 2 as 'betrothed', is found nowhere else in the NT,[2] but its usage is widely witnessed in the literature of the times.[3] It may be translated as 'fit together, join' or 'join or give in marriage, betroth'.[4]

That ἁρμόζομαι in 2 Cor. 11: 2 means betrothal, or joining in marriage and not some more general sense of joining, is made apparent by the remainder of 11: 2b in the reference to one husband (ἑνὶ ἀνδρί) and pure bride (παρθένον ἁγνήν). These words being associated with the verb ἁρμόζομαι make it abundantly clear that the latter must be understood as a marriage between Christ and the Corinthian Christians.

Apart from its celebrated use in the birth stories, and in the parable of the ten virgins (Matt. 25: 1 ff.), παρθένος is not widely found in the NT. In fact, apart from 2 Cor. 11: 2, Paul uses it only six other times, and all of those are to be found in 1 Corinthians. In the NT this word is generally used simply to mean 'virgin'. In this context, it functions as a means of expressing the purity of the church.

Purity is further stressed by the adjective ἁγνός that is used to modify παρθένος.[5] As Hauck notes, ἁγνός is related to ἅγιος: 'ἁγνός, like ἅγιος, is a verbal adjective of ἅζομαι'.[6] Ἁγνός,

---

[1] *TDNT*, I, 122.

[2] This verb is found here in the middle instead of the active, but is to be understood in an active sense, according to Blass–Debrunner–Funk, *A Grammar*, par. 316 (1).

[3] Bauer–Arndt–Gingrich, *A Greek–English Lexicon*, p. 107.

[4] *Ibid.*

[5] Ἁγνός also is not used often in the NT; it occurs three times in the homologoumena and five other times, all of which are to be found in the later writings in the NT.

[6] *TDNT*, I, 122. Cf. also R. C. Trench, *Synonyms of the New Testament*, 9th ed. (Grand Rapids, Michigan: W. B. Eerdman's Publishing Company, 1963), pp. 331–3.

then, reinforces and emphasizes the purity and devotion that are demanded of the Christians.[1]

Paul states the purpose for which this betrothal was undertaken in the phrase παραστῆσαι τῷ χριστῷ. By far the closest explicit direct parallel to Eph. 5: 21–33 may be found in this phrase: 'to present you to Christ'. Παρίστημι may be translated, as it is by the RSV, by 'present', but as Bauer–Arndt–Gingrich noted, '"Present" becomes almost equivalent to *make, render*.'[2] Translated in the latter way, Paul would be understood as saying to the Corinthians that he betrothed them to Christ in order to make or render them a pure bride to their husband. But παρίστημι may also mean 'put at someone's disposal', or 'yield' to someone.[3] In the latter sense, one would understand Paul as saying that he betrothed the Corinthian Christians in order to put them at Christ's disposal or to cause them to yield to Christ, as a pure bride to her one husband. This same verb, παρίστημι, is used in a similar context in Eph. 5: 27: 'that the church might be *presented* before him in splendor'.

The use of παρίστημι in 2 Cor. 11: 2 clearly pertains primarily to the formal presentation of the bride to her husband. Paul's apprehension, as expressed in v. 3, is that the bride will be deceived into insincerity and lack of devotion to Christ, and he uses a general reference to Eve's deception by the serpent (Gen. 3: 4) as a means of giving voice to this fear that the church's fate will be the same as Eve's. Both 2 Corinthians and Ephesians refer to Genesis and the marriage of Adam and Eve as an illustration from which to admonish the church. Therefore there is an early connection between Christ and the church and Adam and Eve. In 2 Cor. 11 the connection is more explicit between the church and Eve than it is in Ephesians. In Ephesians, Gen. 2: 24 falls in the section addressed to the man and is primarily a connection there between Christ and Adam. In 2 Cor. 11 and in Eph. 5 the historian is allowed a glimpse into a popular speculation that may have been much more pervasive than the extant early Christian literature indicates.

Elsewhere in Paul, παρίστημι is used in the sense 'to put

---

[1] In some contexts ἀγνός is basically negative and indicates the lack of defects in the object in question. 'This gives rise to the meaning "chaste"' (Hauck, *TDNT*, I, 122).

[2] *A Greek–English Lexicon*, p. 633. [3] *Ibid.*

at someone's disposal'. The most extended occurrence in this sense may be found in Rom. 6 where it is used five times (Rom. 6: 13, 16, 19). 'Do not yield (μηδὲ παριστάνετε) your members to sin as instruments of wickedness, but yield (ἀλλὰ παραστήσατε) yourselves to God' (v. 13). 'For just as you once yielded (παρεστήσατε) your members to impurity, and to greater and greater iniquity, so now yield (παραστήσατε) your members to righteousness for sanctification' (6: 19).[1] In Rom. 6, it is not a question *whether* someone puts himself at someone else's disposal or some other power's disposal; it is simply a question of *how* and to *what* or *whom*.

Thus there are several affinities between 2 Cor. 11: 2 and Eph. 5: 21–33. In general, the overall portrayal of Christ as the bridegroom and the church as the bride is the same, although ἁρμόζομαι and παρθένος are nowhere mentioned in Eph. 5: 21–33. The emphasis on the purity of the bride seen in 2 Cor. 11: 3 in the use of παρθένος and observed most clearly then in the adjective modifying the latter, ἁγνός, is present and greatly emphasized in 5: 21–33. The explicit mention of Eve in 2 Cor. 11: 3 and the reference to her seduction is paralleled explicitly only in the sense that Adam and Eve are reflected in Gen. 2: 24, quoted in Eph. 5: 31. Only one relationship between 2 Cor. 11: 2 and Eph. 5: 21–33 is greater than that having to do with the insistence on the purity of the bride. That is the related idea reflected in the verb παρίστημι discussed above.

The three passages just considered from the homologoumena – 1 Cor. 6: 12–20, 11: 2 ff. and 2 Cor. 11: 1–6 – are each especially related to one another and to Eph. 5: 21–33. These texts show that in Paul's own writings there is an identifiable complex of terms and ideas associated with marriage and drawing on a hieros gamos of Christ and the church. The language of Gen. 2: 24 and the terminology of head, body and member are found very naturally associated with one another. Since it is apparent that Paul, in none of these passages, sets forth the full detail of

---

[1] The use of παρίστημι in Rom. 6 is three times related to the term μέλος, and otherwise related to 'yourselves' (ἑαυτός). Cf. the relationship in Eph. 5: 21–33 of the language of body, member and head to the use of παρίστημι in v. 27 of the church. Also, note in Rom. 6: 19, the last occurrence of παρίστημι in the chapter, that the readers are urged to yield their members 'to righteousness, for sanctification'. This conjunction of παρίστημι and ἁγιασμός parallels Eph. 5: 26–7a.

the tapestry he has in view, the interpreter may surmise that this language and its patterns of association are familiar to the readers. From 1 Cor. 11: 2 it is clear that the idea of the head-ship of a man over his wife is part of a conventional statement that speaks of this relationship under the broader rubric of Christ's relationship to the man. It becomes increasingly apparent that the author of Ephesians has expressed his originality not in the Christ–church hieros gamos but in the way that he has related various other traditional formulations to that one.

CHAPTER V

HERMENEUTICAL PROBLEMS
IN 5: 31-2

At several points in this investigation references have been made to the appearance of Gen. 2: 24 in Eph. 5: 21–33 as well as to the occurrence of that OT quotation in other related passages. Apart from what may be said about Gen. 2: 24 in Jewish traditions and in other NT documents, its occurrence in Eph. 5: 31 must be examined in its own context. Its function in 5: 21–33 has been a matter of considerable debate. In 5: 21–33, Gen. 2: 24 (v. 31) must be considered with v. 32 since a special set of problems clusters around those two verses. They consist of the quotation of Gen. 2: 24 and one other verse: '"for this reason a man shall leave his father and mother and be joined to his wife, and the two shall become one flesh." This is a great mystery (μυστήριον), and I take it to mean Christ and the church.'

What is the function of μυστήριον in 5: 32? There are several clues in its context that should be considered. The demonstrative pronoun οὗτος in the phrase, τὸ μυστήριον τοῦτο, modifies μυστήριον and limits the reference of μυστήριον to something 'comparatively near at hand'[1] or 'immediately present to the thinking of the writer'.[2] Thus, τοῦτο does not designate the specific referent of μυστήριον, but could conceivably refer to any part or parts of the section beginning with 5: 21.

The adjective μέγα has variously been taken as standing in an attributive and predicative relationship to μυστήριον. True, the adjective does not need an article for it to be considered attributive in the phrase τὸ μυστήριον τοῦτο μέγα ἐστίν,[3] but 'the predicate adjective occurs invariably without the article' as is the case here.[4] Also, the presence of the copula

---

[1] Bauer–Arndt–Gingrich, *A Greek–English Lexicon*, p. 600.
[2] H. E. Dana and Julius R. Mantey, *A Manual Grammar of the Greek New Testament* (New York: The Macmillan Company, 1927), par. 136 (5).
[3] *Ibid.* par. 131 (1). [4] *Ibid.*

ἐστίν necessitates the consideration of μέγα as a predicate adjective in this context. The difference at stake in the understanding of 5: 32 is whether μέγα ascribes a quality to μυστήριον – as attributive – or whether it makes an assertion concerning μυστήριον – as predicative. The RSV followed the KJV by translating μέγα as attributive – 'this is a great mystery' – and has attracted several commentators. This translation lends itself to the qualitative interpretation that the greatness of the mystery has to do with its difficulty or obscurity.[1] Schlier, possibly following Bauer,[2] states: 'Μέγα meint dabei, wie 1 Tim. 3, 16, das Gewicht des Geheimnisses, nicht etwa seine Dunkelheit.'[3] Properly taken as a predicate adjective, μέγα allows its immediate context and the use of μυστήριον in the remainder of the epistle to determine what it asserts about μυστήριον here.

But it must be said that the best evidence for understanding μυστήριον in this context comes from 5: 32 b: ἐγὼ δὲ λέγω εἰς χριστὸν καὶ [εἰς] τὴν ἐκκλησίαν. The postpositive particle δέ provides the link between v. 32 b and what has gone before.[4] Of the various functions of δέ described by Blass–Debrunner–Funk, two seem most appropriate in this context: 'Δέ may introduce a parenthesis' or give 'an explanation or an intensification.'[5]

In spite of the widespread recognition that the ἐγώ is intensive,[6] there is considerable disagreement among scholars concerning how ἐγὼ δὲ λέγω should be understood. Many interpreters maintain that the author of Ephesians is thereby emphatically stating his own position in opposition to others. As is often the case with his work on Colossians and Ephesians, Dibelius is rather cautious as he asserts: 'Perhaps one can gather from ἐγὼ δὲ λέγω that others also interpreted the OT quotation

---

[1] Cf. Masson, L'Épître, p. 215.

[2] Cf. Bauer–Arndt–Gingrich, A Greek–English Lexicon, p. 499.

[3] Der Brief, p. 262.

[4] Δέ is an adversative particle serving as a conjunction and usually indicates general contrast instead of sharp contrast, for which ἀλλά is most commonly used. Blass–Debrunner–Funk, A Grammar, par. 447.

[5] Ibid. par. 447 (7, 8).

[6] As Blass–Debrunner–Funk note: 'the nominatives ἐγώ, σύ, ἡμεῖς, ὑμεῖς are employed according to the standards of good style as in classical Greek for contrast or other emphasis'; ibid. par. 277 (1).

[Gen. 2: 24 in Eph. 5: 31] as "mysterious", but in a different sense.'[1] Bornkamm is less reserved: 'The interpretation introduced by ἐγὼ δὲ λέγω is in express opposition to other interpretations which also find a μυστήριον in the text but different from Eph. in exposition.'[2] Schlier concurs:

V. 32 b, through the emphasis of ἐγώ, leaves possible scarcely no other understanding than that the apostle defines his interpretation against another. 'But *I* speak with regard to Christ and the church' means: I explain (the OT passage) of Christ and the church. Paul thus cites the formerly quoted passage, Gen. 2: 24, in order to wrest it from his opponents to the acknowledgement of his interpretation.[3]

To be sure, there are dissenting opinions. Raymond E. Brown states: 'When Paul says egō de legō, he need not be opposing some other interpretation; he may simply mean that he himself is going beyond the obvious meaning of the passage.'[4] But this seems to be begging the question, since even this 'going beyond the obvious meaning' is contraverting a standing interpretation, namely, 'the obvious meaning of the passage', as Brown states it. Also, regarding a verse so clearly related to Adam and Eve, and knowing as we do only certain points of what seems to have been rich variety of traditions about that primeval pair, one might experience considerable difficulty in determining what constitutes this 'obvious meaning'. A glance at the history of the interpretation of Gen. 2: 24[5] would almost force one to despair of looking for 'the obvious meaning'.[6]

Scholarship on this problem has so far not considered Morton Smith's careful and illuminating work, *Tannaitic Parallels to the*

[1] Dibelius, *An die Kolosser Epheser an Philemon*, p. 95.
[2] Günther Bornkamm, Μυστήριον, *TDNT*, iv, 823. In this immediate context Bornkamm continues: 'Opponents have been sought among champions of a Gnostic syzygy teaching.'
[3] *Der Brief*, p. 262. Cf. also Masson, *L'Épître*, p. 215, n. 3.
[4] Raymond E. Brown, 'The Semitic Background of the New Testament Mysterion', *Biblica*, **40**, 83, n. 2.
[5] Cf. above, pp. 51–61.
[6] Brown raises this objection in the context of his discussion of Bornkamm's just cited position concerning the interpretation of Eph. 5: 32. One suspects that Brown's reaction is primarily an objection to Bornkamm's declaration that the opponent is gnostic, rather than an objection to seeing the author as opposing some other interpretations.

Gospels.[1] In a chapter entitled 'Parallels of Idiom' he examines the occurrences of ἐγὼ δὲ λέγω in the [so-called antitheses of Matt. 5. Smith notes that the use of this phrase in Matt. 5 functions 'to introduce a legal opinion contradicting that generally accepted'.[2] There follow five examples from tannaitic materials where a similar formula is used to supplant dominant positions of the time: these texts provide evidence for Smith's judgment. Ἐγὼ δὲ λέγω, therefore, appears to have been a rather standard form, derived ultimately from Judaism, for use in opposing established interpretations of scripture. Since the ἐγὼ δὲ λέγω in 5: 32 occurs with a quotation from the OT, it would seem that, in part, Smith's position would hold true here as well: at stake is the interpretation of the OT verse, and the author of Ephesians sets forth his own interpretation εἰς χριστὸν καὶ [εἰς] τὴν ἐκκλησίαν.

There remains the question of the meaning of εἰς χριστὸν καὶ [εἰς] τὴν ἐκκλησίαν. If, indeed, the author is setting his own interpretation over against one or more current interpretations, then v. 32b must be understood not at all as the author's full statement of his position – since that would be so cryptic as to approach nonsense – but as the clue to what, in fact, has taken place within the context provided by the Haustafel form. In and of itself ἐγὼ δὲ λέγω εἰς χριστὸν καὶ [εἰς] τὴν ἐκκλησίαν would convey little or no specific meaning and would therefore be no way for the author of Ephesians to make any clear demarcation between his own interpretation and those offered by others. Considering v. 32b alone, one would not be sure what the author's position was with regard either to Christ and the church or to the just cited OT verse. But the author has already – prior to the quotation of the OT in v. 31 – set forth his own interpretation in some detail. That is why the phrase εἰς χριστὸν καὶ [εἰς] τὴν ἐκκλησίαν is neither nonsensical nor unclear; that is why such shorthand is possible after the OT quotation. In vv. 21–30, the readers have already encountered his own interpretation of the disputed OT verse.

The crucial verse (v. 31) is introduced near the end of the exposition. Eph. 5: 21–33 is not unique in this regard; Paul

---

[1] *The Journal of Biblical Literature Monograph Series*, vol. VI (Philadelphia: The Society of Biblical Literature, 1951).

[2] *Ibid.* p. 28.

Meyer pointed out a similar case in 1 Cor. 2: 10–16.[1] There Isa. 40: 13 – 'who has directed the Spirit of the Lord, or as his counselor has instructed him?' – probably functions as a means of associating 'spirit' and 'mind' throughout 2: 10 ff. Isa. 40: 13 finally comes to the surface in 2: 16 and enables Paul to cap off his argument: 'But we have the mind of Christ.'

Furthermore, there is in 5: 21–33 itself evidence that Gen. 2: 24 is playing a role even before it is cited in v. 31. As noted below,[2] it is often conceded by modern scholarship that v. 29a – 'For no man ever hates his own flesh' – reads 'flesh' (σάρκα) instead of the just mentioned 'bodies' (σώματα) of v. 28a or 'himself' (ἑαυτῶν) of v. 28b in view of the upcoming quotation from Genesis. Already in v. 29a, Gen. 2: 24 (v. 31) informs what the author states. The quotation from Genesis ends, even though it is obscured by the RSV, as follows: 'and the two shall become one flesh'; καὶ ἔσονται οἱ δύο εἰς σάρκα μίαν (5: 31). Internal evidence confirms the suggestion that the author of Ephesians is offering his interpretation of Gen. 2: 24 before he actually quotes it.

Against the background provided by these observations, attention must be turned once again to the meaning of μυστήριον and to the function of the OT quotation. Most scholars still see the problems connected with the understanding of μυστήριον in 5: 21–33 much as von Soden stated them in 1911:

Die Exegese hat zwei Möglichkeiten. Man kann das Mysterium sehen in der altestamentlichen Schriftstelle, die dann als parabolische Weissagung zu behandeln und zu allegorisieren wäre; und man kann es sehen in der Ehe selbst, die ihrerseits ein parabolische, typologische Institution des vergehenden Äons uber sich selbst hinausweisen soll.[3]

According to this position, τὸ μυστήριον τοῦτο μέγα ἐστίν refers either to the immediately preceding quotation from Genesis or to the 'institution of marriage'. Just as most interpreters have accepted von Soden's alternatives, so also the majority of them have chosen to say with him: 'Der Zusammenhang scheint mir das erstere [reference to the OT verse] zu fordern.'[4]

---

[1] Private conversation in 1963.　　　　[2] Below, pp. 143–5.

[3] Hans von Soden, 'ΜΥΣΤΗΡΙΟΝ und sacramentum in den ersten zwei Jahrhunderten der Kirche', *ZNW*, **12** , 194.　　[4] *Ibid.*

Dibelius, for example, sets up the alternatives in the same way:

fraglich scheint zunächst, ob man bei μυστήριον...an die Ehe oder an die Schriftstelle denken soll. Für das letztere spricht die Beobachtung, dass unsere Stelle ja nicht die Institution der Ehe auf den ἱερὸς γάμος zwischen Christus und der ἐκκλησία deuten, sondern umgekehrt Regeln für die Ehegatten vom ἱερὸς γάμος herleitet.[1]

The alternative – either the OT quotation or the institution of marriage – as set forth in great clarity by von Soden and followed by Dibelius must be qualified by another observation brought to prominence by Dibelius himself. As is well known, Dibelius was the first to note the formal characteristics of the NT Haustafeln.[2] If the function of the Haustafel form in this passage be taken into account, it alone accounts for a large percentage of what is said about the 'institution of marriage' and greatly lessens the possibility that μυστήριον refers to marriage *per se*. This would indicate that, from the beginning, the alternatives suggested by von Soden were not of the same class of possibility.[3]

Does the use of the term μυστήριον in the remainder of Ephesians provide any guidelines that might inform the interpretation of 5: 21–33? To be sure, Brown's statement must serve as a healthy warning to refrain from reducing the possibility of a variety of usage for one word by any artificial constriction enforced arbitrarily. As Brown asserts: 'We have seen too much variation of meaning in the history of the word "mystery" to argue that the word cannot have two different shades of meaning in one writer.'[4] However, when a substantive like μυστήριον is used six times[5] in such crucial places as it is in Ephesians, there is considerable probability of some lines of continuity of meaning between the uses in the different contexts.

[1] *An die Kolosser Epheser an Philemon*, p. 95.
[2] Above, p. 18.
[3] Von Soden's alternatives must divorce the understanding of μυστήριον in 5: 32 from all other occurrences of the word in Ephesians.
[4] Brown, 'Mysterion', *Biblica*, **40**, 84.
[5] No other single writing in the NT exhibits a greater numerical use of μυστήριον than does Ephesians. Here it appears six times. Only 1 Corinthians uses it as many times; the other writings in the homologoumena use it considerably less.

The frequency of μυστήριον in Ephesians allows some judgments concerning its function. Here follow all the occurrences:

For he [God] has made known to us in all wisdom and insight the mystery of his will (τὸ μυστήριον τοῦ θελήματος αὐτοῦ), according to his purpose which he set forth in Christ as a plan for the fulness of time, to unite all things in him, things in heaven and on earth (1: 9–10).

For this reason I, Paul, a prisoner for Christ Jesus on behalf of you Gentiles – assuming that you have heard of the stewardship of God's grace that was given to me for you, how the mystery (τὸ μυστήριον) was made known to me by revelation, as I have written briefly. When you read this you can perceive my insight into the mystery of Christ (ἐν τῷ μυστηρίῳ τοῦ χριστοῦ), which was not made known to the sons of men in other generations as it has now been revealed to his holy apostles and prophets by the Spirit; that is, how the Gentiles are fellow heirs, members of the same body, and partakers of the promise in Christ Jesus through the gospel...To me, though I am the very least of all the saints, this grace was given, to preach to the Gentiles the unsearchable riches of Christ, and to make all men see what is the plan of the mystery (ἡ οἰκονομία τοῦ μυστηρίου) hidden for ages in God who created all things; that through the church the manifold wisdom of God might now be made known to the principalities and powers in the heavenly places. This was according to the eternal purpose which he has realized in Christ Jesus our Lord (3: 1–6, 7–11).

This is a great mystery (τὸ μυστήριον) and I take it to mean Christ and the church (5: 32).

Pray at all times in the Spirit, with all prayer and supplication. To that end keep alert with all perseverence, making supplication for all the saints, and also for me, that utterance may be given me in opening my mouth boldly to proclaim the mystery of the gospel (τὸ μυστήριον τοῦ εὐαγγελίου), for which I am an ambassador in chains; that I may declare it boldly, as I ought to speak (6: 18–20).

The first occurrence of μυστήριον is found in the thanksgiving section that opens the letter; the last use of it is located in the summation of the letter, just prior to the note about Tychicus and the benediction. At the midpoint of the epistle is to be found the greatest concentration of occurrences of the term in the NT. There the word appears three times. Without parallel in the homologoumena, these verses contain an explicit specification of the content of the mystery: 'that is, how the Gentiles are fellow heirs, members of the same body, and partakers of the promise in Christ Jesus through the gospel' (3: 6).

Since 3: 1–11 presents the most extensive treatment of μυστήριον in the epistle, it is not surprising to find there many of the facets of the term as it is used in the other verses of Ephesians. First, this μυστήριον has not always been known – 'which was not made known to the sons of men in other generations' (3: 5) – 'was made known...by revelation' (3: 3), 'it has now been revealed' (3: 5).[1]

Secondly, the μυστήριον that formerly was hidden but is now disclosed concerns God's plan (1: 10, 3: 9), or, as it is stated again, his 'eternal purpose' (3: 11). Thirdly, though it is finally God's initiative and God's plan, it is also clear that the accomplishing of God's purpose is inextricable from what took place in Christ. Twice, even though in slightly different language, the author gives evidence for this: the disclosure of the μυστήριον 'was according to *the eternal purpose which he has realized in Christ Jesus* our Lord' (3: 11); 'For he [God] has made known...the mystery of his will, according to *his purpose which he set forth in Christ*' (1: 9). It is *in Christ* that God's purpose is disclosed; there what has been hidden is revealed.

In fact there is such a complete identification between Christ as the locus of the disclosure and the disclosure itself that the μυστήριον is even once called τῷ μυστηρίῳ τοῦ χριστοῦ 'the mystery of [or about] Christ' (3: 4). The same association may account for a similar genitival construction in 6: 19: τὸ μυστήριον τοῦ εὐαγγελίου, 'the mystery of the gospel'.

Fourthly, as is stated in the opening section of the epistle, God's ultimate purpose is an eschatological and cosmic one: 'to unite all things in him [Christ], things in heaven and things on earth' (1: 10). The bringing of the Gentiles into a position of being 'fellow heirs, members of the same body, and partakers of the promise' (3: 6) is the first sign of the final fulfilment and unification: 'that in the coming ages he [God] might show the immeasurable riches of his grace in kindness toward us in Christ Jesus' (2: 7).

Fifthly, according to Ephesians the locus of God's work in

[1] Cf. Rom. 16: 25 ff.

93

Christ is to be found in the church, itself an eschatological body. It is in fact the church whose task now is to carry out God's purpose in the entire cosmos; God's 'plan of the mystery hidden for ages' is 'that *through the church* the manifold wisdom of God might now be made known to the principalities and powers in the heavenly places' (3: 9–10). In its use of μυστήριον, Ephesians combines eschatology, ecclesiology and cosmology.

In this connection, it should be noted that οἰκονομία occurs three times in Ephesians (1: 10, 3: 2, 9), but always in conjunction with μυστήριον. According to Bauer–Arndt–Gingrich this term in the NT was to do with the administration of apostolic office, or with 'arrangement, order, plan' or with 'training'.[1] According to them, the occurrence in 3: 2 – 'assuming that you have heard of the stewardship of God's grace (τὴν οἰκονομίαν τῆς χάριτος τοῦ θεοῦ) that was given to me for you' – is best translated as the RSV does by 'stewardship' since it has to do with the execution of apostolic commission.[2] The other two occurrences – 'as a plan (εἰς οἰκονομίαν) for the fulness of time' (1: 10); 'and to make all men see what is the plan of the mystery (ἡ οἰκονομία τοῦ μυστηρίου) hidden for ages' (3: 9) – Bauer–Arndt–Gingrich understand as dealing with 'God's plan of salvation, his arrangements for man's redemption'.[3] The genitival construction οἰκονομία τοῦ μυστηρίου in 3: 9 shows how closely μυστήριον and οἰκονομία are related.

Do the shades of meaning and similarities of the occurrence of μυστήριον in Ephesians, apart from 5: 32, offer any guidelines for understanding the term there? This can be checked by taking each of the five facets of μυστήριον noted above and asking whether 5: 21–33 as a unit bears any relationship to them.

First, the μυστήριον of the remainder of Ephesians pertained to something that was hidden, but now is revealed. Does this apply to 5: 21–33? What might be at stake in this context is a heretofore undisclosed relationship that now subsists between Christ and his church. In 5: 21–33 that relationship is not only clarified; it is also connected with human marriage.

That μυστήριον in 5: 32 has to do with God's plan or purpose

[1] *A Greek–English Lexicon*, p. 562. [2] *Ibid.*
[3] *Ibid.*

is nowhere explicitly stated in 5: 21–33. Indeed, God is not mentioned at all in the passage. However, the third observation about μυστήριον in Ephesians – that God's purposes are inextricable from what happened in Christ – shows the fallacy in the assumption that failure to mention God indicates the presence of a different use of μυστήριον. At no other point in Ephesians can one find in so few verses such a comprehensive rehearsal of Christ's relationship to the church and vice versa. This, of course, ties in directly with the fifth observation above: the locus of God's continuing work is in the church, Christ's body. The church is called 'his body' in vv. 23 and 30. Christ is spoken of as the church's 'Savior' in v. 23, and it is said that he 'nourishes and cherishes' (v. 29) the church, thus implying a continuing relationship whose details shall be discussed in what follows.

Uniquely connected with the use of μυστήριον in chapters 1 and 3 was the notion that the mystery had to do specifically with God's purpose in uniting all things, both in heaven and on earth, in Christ. In broad scope, that unification was seen in chapters 1 and 2 to focus upon the joining of Jew and Gentile in the church. In 5: 21–33, the focus is upon marriage and the concern for unity again comes to the fore as it did with the earlier occurrences of μυστήριον, in chapters 1 and 3. The content that the author inserts within the Haustafel form speaks in different ways for the unity that should subsist between husband and wife as well as between Christ and his body, the church.

Many features of μυστήριον in the earlier sections of Ephesians are also associated with the use of the term in 5: 32. Therefore it may be concluded that μυστήριον in 5: 32 partakes of much the same range of meaning already noted in earlier sections of Ephesians.[1] It follows that μυστήριον does not refer, as Brown would take it, 'to a scripture passage which contains a deeper meaning than that which appears at first sight'.[2] Brown finds this use of μυστήριον in the apostolic fathers, and is inclined to think it fits Eph. 5: 32 as well. This would make μυστήριον a sort of exegetical flagstaff raised by the author to

---

[1] Contra Brown, who judges the occurrence of μυστήριον in 5: 32 as different from its other appearances in Ephesians. 'Mysterion', *Biblica*, **40**, 83–4.

[2] *Ibid.* p. 83.

indicate a bit of strained interpretation. Brown asks: 'Can mystery then be used of any such deeper meaning of an OT passage?'[1] This question misses the mark because it fails to recognize that in Ephesians μυστήριον does not refer to 'any such deeper meaning', but it is precisely this and no other deeper meaning of Christ and the church that constitutes the mystery for the author of Ephesians. This interpretation not only has the merit of being fairly consistent with the scope of meaning of μυστήριον in the remainder of the epistle, but it also points more clearly to the relationship of v. 32b – ἐγὼ δὲ λέγω εἰς χριστὸν καὶ [εἰς] τὴν ἐκκλησίαν – and v. 31 – 'For this reason a man shall leave his father and mother and cleave to his wife, and the two shall become one flesh'.

Apart from the background provided by other occurrences of μυστήριον, the best clue to the understanding of μυστήριον in Eph. 5: 21–33 must be v. 32b – ἐγὼ δε λέγω εἰς χριστὸν καὶ [εἰς] τὴν ἐκκλησίαν – in which the author sets his own interpretation apart from that of others. The author of Ephesians, by means of the λέγω εἰς χριστὸν καὶ [εἰς] τὴν ἐκκλησίαν, informs the reader that he has before him the OT quotation and that his interpretation of it precedes the OT verse and, in fact, has to do with Christ and the church – the whole of which relationship may indeed be called τὸ μυστήριον as he has used the term before in his epistle. Such a mystery is by definition of great import, not only for understanding the relationship of the church to Christ, but also for the understanding of the relationship that should subsist between husbands and wives. The unification of all things is thus extended by the author of Ephesians even to man and wife as one flesh.

It is legitimate for one to ask why a quotation from the OT occurs in this context and it is furthermore appropriate to ask why Gen. 2: 24 occurs. It is easy to understand why Gen. 2: 24 might be introduced in such context of discussion of marriage since in the OT it appears as a cardinal passage ordaining marriage. It may well have been included in Eph. 5: 21–33 for that very reason. Undoubtedly that consideration played a role in determining that Gen. 2: 24 instead of some other OT passage was inserted here. But there still remains the further question why the author introduced an OT quotation at

[1] *Ibid.* pp. 83–4.

all. The answer comes in an early Christian conventional formulation.

There is an identifiable pattern in the NT whose elements include: (1) a statement that women should be submissive, and (2) a reference to Torah as a means of supporting the concern with the subordination of women. In the first element, the verb is consistently ὑποτάσσομαι and is always related to women. It is in the second element that the author has freedom to adapt the form to his own purposes, but there is a common element that sets some limits to that freedom: the reference ought, in some way, to ground the subordination in Torah. The author is at liberty to choose whatever verse or allude to whatever story in the law that would best serve his needs at the moment. The latitude exercised within the NT in the second element of this pattern probably accounts for its having escaped the notice of scholars in the past.[1]

In 1 Tim. 2: 8 requirements are laid down for the action expected of the man. There follows a rather extended statement of the requirements expected of the woman (vv. 9–15). This disproportionate treatment in the conduct of men and women in 1 Timothy gives occasion for the author to set forth rather extensively the behavior expected of the woman and the reasons for this expectation. Both 1 Tim. 2: 8 ff. and Eph. 5: 21 ff. manifest, as a shared framework, Haustafel addresses to wives and husbands. With v. 11, 1 Timothy comes as close as possible to the actual wording of Eph. 5: 22a, the Haustafel address to women. 1 Tim. 2: 11 reads: 'let a woman learn in silence with all submissiveness'. Verse 12 expounds this understanding and states clearly that no woman is 'to have authority over men'. But vv. 13–14 are the verses of interest at this point: 'For Adam was formed first, then Eve; and Adam was not deceived, but the woman was deceived and became a transgressor.' By a general reference to different parts of the Genesis accounts of Adam and Eve, the author is able to adduce two different grounds for the submissiveness of women to men and for men having authority over women. First, the author of

---

[1] For example, Barrett, *The Pastoral Epistles*, p. 55, notes some kinship between 1 Tim. 2: 11 f. and 1 Cor. 11: 3 ff., 14: 34 f., but he fails to recognize a pattern of ὑποτάσσομαι plus a reference to the OT in all three. He overlooks also the connection with Eph. 5: 22 ff. and 1 Pet. 3: 1 ff.

1 Timothy points out that Adam was created before Eve, thus giving a temporal priority. Second, Adam has authority over Eve since it was Eve, not Adam, who was deceived. So, in 1 Tim. 2 the exhortation of submission directed to the women is supported by a reference to Adam and Eve and the stories about them.

Examples of this form may be found within the homologoumena. In 2 Cor. 11: 2 f., a passage already considered in some detail for some striking features shared in common with Eph. 5: 21–33,[1] are found (1) subordination urged upon the Corinthian Christians as the bride and (2) the reference to the story about Eve's deception as grounds for that subordination. 'I feel a divine jealousy for you, for I betrothed you to Christ to present you as a pure bride to her one husband. But I am afraid that as the serpent deceived Eve by his cunning, your thoughts will be led astray from a sincere and pure devotion to Christ' (2 Cor. 11: 2–3). The context makes clear that what is at stake is a 'sincere and pure devotion to Christ' which for Paul is identical with submission to his gospel. In an effort to secure that submission, Paul reminds the Corinthians of his special role in their relationship to Christ. It was he who betrothed the Corinthian Christians to Christ in order to present them as a 'pure bride to her husband'. The Christians are portrayed as the wife from whom purity is expected, but Paul is afraid that this wife is about to be led astray into a misplaced submission to 'another' gospel. The point of correspondence between 2 Cor. 11 and 1 Tim. 2 on this matter is noteworthy: both passages deal with the question of submission on the part of wives. Of further interest is the presence of the second element of the pattern in the reference to Eve: 'but I am afraid that as the serpent deceived Eve by his cunning, your thoughts will be led astray' (2 Cor. 11: 3). In 2 Cor. 11, in the context of submission fully expected of a wife, there is an explicit reference to that first wife, Eve. There is no mention of Adam, because Paul, in 2 Cor. 11, is not concerned to make any statement about Christ or the husband, as was the author of 1 Timothy in the passage discussed just above.

One further example of the pattern just detected in 1 Tim. 2 and 2 Cor. 11 is found in 1 Cor. 14: 33 b–4: 'As in all the churches of the saints, the women should keep silence in the churches.

---

[1] Above, pp. 81–4.

For they are not permitted to speak, but should be subordinate, *as even the law says*.' There is no specific reference to Adam or Eve as has been the pattern in the other texts examined. There is, however, a reference to the law, and it is assumed that the reader will be able to supply the verse or verses in question in support of the subordination of women to their husbands.

1 Pet. 3: 1–6 shows the same pattern. First, it opens with an admonition of submission to the wives (3: 1). Then, after some brief comments about behavior and adornment, there follows the expected reference to the pentateuch: 'So once the holy women who hoped in God used to adorn themselves and were submissive to their husbands, as Sarah obeyed Abraham, calling him lord. And you are now her children if you do right and let nothing terrify you' (3: 5–6). Whereas 2 Cor. 11 had referred to a story about the deception of Eve, 1 Pet. 3 uses Gen. 18: 12 (LXX) where Sarah called Abraham 'lord'. For 1 Peter, this reference provides the grounds for understanding the submission of wives to their husbands. Of further import for the study of Eph. 5: 21–33 is the recognition that this early paraenetic form takes place within the Haustafel in 1 Peter just as it does in Ephesians.

These verses from 1 Cor. 14, 2 Cor. 11, 1 Tim. 2 and 1 Pet. 3 share basic similarities, but the differences in broad contexts and focuses are sufficient to prohibit any claims of direct dependence of any one passage on another. Each of these passages manifests a widespread early Christian convention of a reference to the pentateuch pattern or lesson to be applied to the understanding of the position of women in marriage in early Christian times. The stories and accounts that constituted earliest Christian scriptures, the OT, were varied enough so that one might be chosen for the purposes or needs of a particular situation.

This pattern, once established in the NT, may also be observed in 1 Clement. The clearest case is 1 Clem. 57: 2 ff.: 'Learn to be submissive...for the excellent wisdom says...' Then begins the quotation from Prov. 1: 23–33, which, being lengthy, runs through the remainder of chapter 57.[1] In 1

---

[1] 58: 1 then opens with ὑηακούσωμεν οὖν so that ὑποτάσσομαι stands on one side of the OT text while ὑπακούω is to be found on the other. These same verbs are also related within the total Haustafel in Ephesians (5: 21, 6: 1, 5).

Clement, the potential reference to scripture has been broadened to include much of the OT.[1] Also, in 1 Clem. 57 it is not a question of submission of wives alone, but of those 'who laid the foundation of the sedition'. However, it is still the NT pattern adapted for different circumstances.

Once committed to the Haustafel form that opens with the admonition of submission to the wives, the author of Ephesians follows the pattern current in the early church by associating an account concerning Adam and Eve with the question of submission as a mark of the behavior of the wife. Since the purposes and concerns of the author of Ephesians are not identical with those of the authors of 1 Cor. 14, 2 Cor. 11, 1 Tim. 2 and 1 Pet. 3, it is not the deception of Eve by the serpent or Adam's being formed prior to Eve that is of moment for this author, but instead a story or account concerning the relationship of Adam to Eve. The author of Ephesians has chosen for his purposes one verse that not only refers to the primordial marriage of Adam and Eve, but that also by his time has its own independent history as an ordination of marriage.[2] Thus, the author of Ephesians not only employs a pattern given him by the early church, but also chooses one that may equally well be related to Christ and the church. ἐγὼ δὲ λέγω εἰς χριστὸν καὶ [εἰς] τὴν ἐκκλησίαν (v. 32b).

In 5: 32 the author of Ephesians contests contemporary interpretations of Gen. 2: 24 and in so doing sets himself in opposition to his readers or at least to part of his readers. The author is not opposing the traditional practice of relating the accounts dealing with Adam and Eve to the relationship of the marriage partners. This he clearly supports, and, in fact, carries out in 5: 21–33.

There are perhaps two ways in which the author of Ephesians modifies the traditional pattern. First, the reference to Adam and Eve is not one of contrast as it was in 2 Cor. 11, where the

[1] In this regard, cf. another appearance of the form in 1 Clem. 34: 5 where the OT verse used to provide the foundation for submission comes either from Isaiah or from Daniel.

[2] It is possible that it is the recipients of Ephesians who have chosen Gen. 2: 24 and have drawn conclusions either about the relationship between a husband and a wife or perhaps about the relationship between Christ and the church. If such be the case, the author contests their conclusions as dangerous and worthy of refutation.

church was to avoid the kind of deception that resulted from Eve's discussion with the serpent. Second, the author of Ephesians departs from the traditional pattern by affirming that the primordial marriage spoken of in Gen. 2: 24 is also prototypically true in an eschatological way of the relationship that does and should exist between Christ and his church (εἰς χριστὸν καὶ [εἰς] τὴν ἐκκλησίαν). It may be precisely this additional factor of taking the reference to Adam and Eve to speak also of the relationship of Christ and the church that constitutes the author's opposition to the traditional pattern and to his readers.[1] Gen. 2: 24 – 'therefore a man shall leave his father and mother and cleave to his wife and the two shall become one flesh' – is ideally suited to the author's purpose in 5: 21-33. For the author of Ephesians, a thoroughgoing traditionalist himself, the injunction of submission to the wives recalls a pattern of reference to the law or Adam or Eve in such a context. Gen. 2: 24 meets the author's needs quite well by suggesting not only the relationship that should subsist between husband and wife but also the relationship of Christ and the church; and since the latter is no minor concern of this particular author, the resulting emphasis on the relationship between Christ and the church is strong.

Since the author's use of the basic pattern just delineated has not heretofore been recognized, studies of Eph. 5: 21-33 have found themselves suggesting rather limited roles for the OT quotation. The past alternatives for interpreting Eph. 5: 31-2, such as those suggested by von Soden, are, on the grounds of the identification of the formal pattern just described, inadequate and in some cases even misleading.

The formal pattern is set in movement in 5: 21-33 by the

---

[1] It does not follow from what has just been said that the right hand of the chart shown below on p. 104 alone is the contribution of the author of Ephesians to an expanded Haustafel that he has inherited from the church in its present form. The major reason that this does not follow as a consequence is that, with a few exceptions, what is said of the man and the wife is in the right column applied to Christ and the church and vice versa. In this sense the left-hand column and the right-hand column for the most part share too many elements in common to make credible any assumption that column A or column B as they now stand ever had any separate history as a literary unit. To be sure, certain elements have in large part been traced in the earlier parts of this study.

occurrence of the Haustafel address to the wives: 'Wives be submissive (ὑποτάσσομαι) to your husbands' (v. 22a). A pentateuchal story or verse then follows (v. 31) as the grounds for the injunction of submission to the wives. One of the chief OT verses used for ordination of marriage is chosen. Since it applies equally well to husbands and to wives, it may be set toward the conclusion of the section to the husbands. Furthermore, husbands and wives are really 'one flesh' according to Gen. 2: 24. Therefore, we must conclude that Gen. 2: 24 informs the development of the first section of the Haustafel beginning from the opening admonition of submission to the wives. It is accordingly not inserted as an afterthought, and it does not function as an intrusion or digression.

The recognition of this pattern also makes much more compelling the interpretation of 5: 32 – ἐγὼ δὲ λέγω εἰς χριστὸν καὶ [εἰς] τὴν ἐκκλησίαν – as controverting previous expositions of Gen. 2: 24. The recognition of the function of Gen. 2: 24 in Eph. 5: 21-33 clears the way for an explanation of the movement or train of thought in the whole passage.

CHAPTER VI

THE MOVEMENT OF THOUGHT
IN 5: 21–33

Former treatments of Eph. 5: 21–33 have overlooked or under-estimated the importance of the train of thought in the passage. Even studies of 5: 21–33 as important as Schlier's do not treat the movement of thought,[1] but focus exclusively on other problems such as the hieros gamos.

Since this investigation has shown that 5: 21–33 must be considered as a literary unit, any effort to set forth the train of thought must reflect that unity. Such a clarification of the movement of thought should provide a framework in which to see further relatedness of the diverse traditions within 5: 21–33.

On the basis of subject-matter alone, it is possible to separate those parts of 5: 21–33 most directly concerned with husband and wife on the one hand from those parts most specifically related to Christ and the church on the other hand. This separation is not to be considered distinction, since there is a definite interplay and relatedness that will be examined later. Apart from judgments made on the basis of subject-matter, there is also grammatical corroboration for such a separation. Comparative particles such as ὡς, οὕτως, and καθώς as well as the somewhat adversative conjunction πλήν provide a grammatical basis for confirming the separation suspected on the basis of an analysis of the subject-matter.

Apart from the quotation of Gen. 2: 24 in Eph. 5: 31, the remainder of Eph. 5: 21–33 falls readily into two groupings: the one having primarily to do with the relationship between husbands and wives (column A), the other treating more directly the relation of Christ and the church (column B). The following tabulation of the text illustrates this separation.

---

[1] *Der Brief.* Ernst Käsemann refers to Schlier's treatment of 5: 21–33 as the zenith of the commentary ('Das Interpretationsproblem des Epheser-briefes', p. 261).

Column A   *Column B*

(21) ὑποτασσόμενοι ἀλλήλοις ἐν φόβῳ χριστοῦ

(22a) Αἱ γυναῖκες τοῖς ἰδίοις
ἀνδράσιν (22b) ὡς τῷ κυρίῳ
(23a) ὅτι ἀνήρ ἐστιν κεφαλὴ τῆς
γυναικός

(23b) ὡς καὶ ὁ χριστὸς κεφαλὴ
τῆς ἐκκλησίας. (23c) αὐτὸς σωτὴρ
τοῦ σώματος. (24a) ἀλλὰ ὡς ἡ
ἐκκλησία ὑποτάσσεται τῷ χριστῷ

(24b) οὕτως καὶ αἱ γυναῖκες τοῖς
ἀνδράσιν ἐν παντί. (25a) Οἱ
ἄνδρες, ἀγαπᾶτε τὰς γυναῖκας

(25b) καθὼς καὶ ὁ χριστὸς
ἠγάπησεν τὴν ἐκκλησίαν
(25c) καὶ ἑαυτὸν παρέδωκεν ὑπὲρ
αὐτῆς, (26a) ἵνα αὐτὴν ἁγιάσῃ
(26b) καθαρίσας τῷ λουτρῷ τοῦ
ὕδατος ἐν ῥήματι, (27a) ἵνα
παραστήσῃ αὐτὸς ἑαυτῷ
ἔνδοξον τὴν ἐκκλησίαν, (27b) μὴ
ἔχουσαν σπίλον ἢ ῥυτίδα ἤ τι τῶν
τοιούτων (27c) ἀλλ᾽ ἵνα ᾖ ἁγία
καὶ ἄμωμος.

(28a) οὕτως ὀφείλουσιν [καὶ] οἱ
ἄνδρες ἀγαπᾶν τὰς ἑαυτῶν
γυναῖκας ὡς τὰ ἑαυτῶν σώματα.
(28b) ὁ ἀγαπῶν τὴν ἑαυτοῦ
γυναῖκα ἑαυτὸν ἀγαπᾷ (29a)
οὐδεὶς γάρ ποτε τὴν ἑαυτοῦ
σάρκα ἐμίσησεν, (29b) ἀλλὰ
ἐκτρέφει καὶ θάλπει αὐτήν,

(29c) καθὼς καὶ ὁ χριστὸς τὴν
ἐκκλησίαν (30) ὅτι μέλη ἐσμὲν τοῦ
σώματος αὐτοῦ.

(31a) ἀντὶ τούτου καταλείψει ἄνθρωπος [τὸν] πατέρα καὶ [τὴν]
μητέρα καὶ προσκολληθήσεται πρὸς τὴν γυναῖκα αὐτοῦ, (31b) καὶ
ἔσονται οἱ δύο εἰς σάρκα μίαν. (32a) τὸ μυστήριον τοῦτο μέγα ἐστίν

(32b) ἐγὼ δὲ λέγω εἰς χριστὸν
καὶ [εἰς] τὴν ἐκκλησίαν.

(33a) πλὴν καὶ ὑμεῖς οἱ καθ᾽ ἕνα
ἕκαστος τὴν ἑαυτοῦ γυναῖκα
οὕτως ἀγαπάτω ὡς ἑαυτόν,
(33b) ἡ δὲ γυνὴ ἵνα φοβῆται τὸν
ἄνδρα.

With the exception of the quotation from Genesis and the half-verse immediately after it, the remainder of 5: 22–33 falls clearly into two columns.

Confirmation that the above chart does no violence to 5: 22–33 may be found in the function of ὡς and the combined forms, οὕτως and καθώς. These comparative particles appear at every shift from either side of the chart to the other prior to 5: 31, the quotation from Genesis. Ὡς is to be found at v. 23 b and introduces the expansion that treats of Christ and the church (vv. 23 b–4 a). Verse 24 b uses οὕτως for a return to a concluding statement to the wives. After the Haustafel injunction to the husbands (v. 25 a), καθώς marks the transition to a long statement about Christ and the church (vv. 25 b–7). In v. 28 a, οὕτως is the comparative particle that enables a return to some comments about husband and wife. As was the use in v. 25 b, so also in v. 29 c καθώς is the particle used in returning to a final statement about Christ and the church prior to the OT quotation. It should be noted that the admonition to the husbands in v. 25 a has no particle or conjunction at its beginning since it continues the basic familial concern that dominates column A.

After the OT quotation in 5: 31 and the ensuing τὸ μυστήριον τοῦτο μέγα ἐστίν (v. 32 a), 5: 32 b opens with the postpositive particle δέ in the phrase ἐγὼ δὲ λέγω. In this context δέ may be considered an adversative conjunction used to introduce 'an explanation or an intensification' even though Blass–Debrunner–Funk do not list its occurrence in this verse as an example.[1] In the next verse (5: 33), the concluding statement of this section of the Haustafel and the closing remark in column A of the above table, πλήν is the introductory adverb functioning as a conjunction.[2] The pattern of transition established prior to the OT quotation would have given cause to expect some compound of ὡς at this point of movement. Πλήν is more appropriate for at least two reasons. First, ὡς and its compound forms are basically particles of comparison, and since the coordination between familial relations and the relationship of Christ and the church does not extend beyond the OT quotation there is no call for such a particle. Second, according to Bauer–Arndt–Gingrich

[1] Blass–Debrunner–Funk, *A Grammar*, par. 447 (8).
[2] Bauer–Arndt–Gingrich, *A Greek–English Lexicon*, p. 675.

πλήν may be concessive or may serve to close off a discussion.[1] To be sure, v. 33 is a concluding statement in which the admonitions both to the wives and to the husbands are recapitulated. Verse 33 does close off the whole section 5: 21–33 and allows the author to return to the next set of relationships in the Haustafel form.

On the basis of this analysis of some features of the chart presented above, the movement or train of thought of 5: 22–33 is as follows: (1) an exhortation to the wives (provided by the Haustafel form) combined with a statement about the pre-eminence of the husband (column A), (2) a descriptive statement of the relationship of Christ and the church (column B), (3) a closing injunction to the wives (almost an exact parallel of v. 22 a) (column A), (4) an exhortation to the husbands (given in the Haustafel form), followed by (5) an extended rehearsal of what Christ did for the church (column B), (6) a return to a discussion of the duties of the husband with regard to the wife (column A) and (7) a closing statement concerning Christ and the church (column B). At this point the author introduces the OT quotation and the statement, 'this mystery is great'.

The pattern seen so clearly prior to the OT quotation in 5: 31 is continued in the last part of v. 32 with (8) the statement ἐγὼ δὲ λέγω εἰς χριστὸν καὶ [εἰς] τὴν ἐκκλησίαν (column B), followed by (9) a concluding double admonition, including the duties of both husbands and wives (column A).

Two observations can be made about the passage as it has been recast in the chart above. First, it is not surprising in Ephesians to see the author's attention focused clearly on Christ and the church – even within the Haustafel form. In fact, it would almost seem in 5: 21–33 that this concern has nearly eclipsed the Haustafel itself. However, the role of the church and its relationship to Christ have come to the fore

---

[1] *Ibid.* Also, Blass–Debrunner–Funk, par. 449 (2), say: 'Πλήν means more nearly "only, in any case" in Paul, used to conclude a discussion and emphasize what is essential.' In 5: 21–33 caution must be exercised in determining in what sense v. 33 contains 'what is essential', lest by implication one be found asserting that part or all of the verses prior to v. 33 are not essential. Cf. also A. T. Robertson, *A Grammar of the Greek New Testament in the Light of Historical Research* (Nashville: Broadman Press, 1934), p. 646: 'πλήν is an adversative conjunction at the beginning of a clause'.

in Ephesians with a consistency unparalleled in the homologoumena.[1]

Second, the representation of the basic pattern of the movement of thought of the author that Dahl has elucidated in
other parts of the letter on a grand scale also describes quite
accurately what the above tabulation shows about 5: 22–33.
Everything listed in column A clearly is concerned with the
conduct of the readers (stage 1); likewise, everything found in
column B pertains to the relationship of Christ and the church
(stage 2). Thus, in 5: 22–33 the pattern of alternation suggested
as typical of most of the thought of Ephesians may be seen very
clearly as ABABABA or 1 2 1 2 1 2 1.

Even though a separation such as the above table represents
can be established, it must also be noted how closely related
these two columns are. The comparative particles do fall at the
major breaks prior to the quotation of Gen. 2: 24. Although
the position of these particles supports the legitimacy of such a
separation into tables, the fact that the particles are *comparative*
presupposes some essential interrelationship. Such a connected-
ness is itself confirmed by the smoothness and regularity of the
transition from the familial situation (column A) to the
Christ–church concern (column B) and back again. If there
were no such relatedness, repeated transition would at best be
awkward.

Also, the ways in which verbs are supplied or assumed from
the immediate context as well as repeated point up the limita-
tions of any attempt to make a radical distinction between the
two sides of this table. On three occasions, verbs that are explicitly stated in a phrase or clause in one column are assumed
for the phrase or clause that follows in the other column. Verse 23 b
(ὡς καὶ ὁ χριστός...) begins the first segment of the text to be
found in column B; for the sake of understanding, it requires a
verb, but has none of its own. Of course, some form of εἰμί can
be assumed in such a clause without any consideration of context, but since the immediately preceding clause (v. 23 a)

---

[1] Note for one example the unique role ascribed to the church in carrying
out God's plan: it is given to the author 'to make all men see what is the
plan of the mystery hidden for ages in God who created all things; that
through the church the manifold wisdom of God might now be made known to
the principalities and powers in the heavenly places' (3: 9–10).

shows not only ἐστιν but also other significant parallels to v. 23*b* there is no reason to think that the verb of v. 23*b* is other than assumed from v. 23*a*. Similarly, v. 24*b* (οὕτως καὶ αἱ γυναῖκες...) appears as the first clause after a return to column A and has no verb of its own, but assumes the verb (ὑποτάσσεται) of v. 24*a* in column B. Finally in vv. 28 ff. the author is once again concerned with love between husband and wife. Verse 29, beginning in column A, declares that 'no man ever hates his own flesh, but nourishes and cherishes it, as Christ does the church'. The verbs ἐκτρέφει and θάλπει belong first of all and explicitly to a descriptive statement about what a husband does to his own flesh, his wife, but they are also understood in the following statement that returns to a concern for Christ and the church (column B); καθὼς καὶ ὁ χριστὸς τὴν ἐκκλησίαν. In the same way the repetition of the same verb (ἀγαπάω) in v. 25*a* and v. 25*b*, even though these parts of verses are found in different columns, illustrates the interrelationship suggested above in the use of assumed verbs.

The general function of Gen. 2: 24 in its context has been clearly identified as a traditional construction. However, the detailed specification of the function of Gen. 2: 24 (Eph. 5: 31) in Eph. 5: 21–33 can be observed more fully in the following verse by verse explication of the passage. Only in the examination of such details can the extent of its role be appreciated.

CHAPTER VII

DETAILED ANALYSIS OF 5:21–33

As may readily be seen from the preceding chapters, the author of Ephesians is well acquainted with a variety of traditions that circulated in the early church. He is a master of these formulations and has brought them together in almost shorthand fashion in the brief compass of 5:21–33. As apparent from the preceding work there is no verse or part of a verse in Eph. 5:21–33 that is devoid of traditional formulations. The author's own contribution, however, must be seen not only in his collecting these particular traditions, for any historian could do this, but also in the way in which he associates these materials one with another.

The author of Ephesians, in absence of traditions that he personally has communicated to the readers, draws heavily on traditions that he presumes to have some currency among them, possibly from their early training as catechumens within the church. The nature of catechetical instruction and liturgical practice in the life and worship of the early church is of increasing concern in NT studies. Ephesians offers a valuable source for determining the content of these catechetical and liturgical formulations.

It is the nature of written traditional materials and formulations to lend themselves to fractional or laconic treatment as a means of referring to the entire construction. When the author alludes to information he shares with his hearers or readers, he need not repeat the entire set of materials. In fact, it is only by virtue of the author's ability to introduce larger configurations of traditional formulations by means of seemingly cryptic allusions that such extensive traditional materials can be identified and explicated in so few verses as Eph. 5:21–33.

That the author of Ephesians could have incorporated so many traditions in so few verses is even more striking in view of his tendency towards repetition or a bunching together of related words. This proclivity has been noted in the reproduction of the Haustafel admonition to the wives (v. 22) in v. 24

and in a similar repetition of the Haustafel admonition to the husbands (v. 25) in v. 33. A less formal case of such collection of related words may be found in v. 27 *b–c* where the spotless character that the church is to display is expressed by various terms, any one of which would have communicated the basic point: σπίλος, ῥυτίς, μῶμος and τι τῶν τοιούτων. One might also cite as further cases such epexegetically related verbs as ἠγάπησεν and παρέδωκεν in v. 25 and ἐκτρέφει and θάλπει in v. 29. In a similar way, the three related and somewhat repetitious short statements that compose vv. 28–9*a* might also be cases in point, even though there is some development of the flow of thought within these three statements. There is one further contributing factor to the sense of iteration in this passage. The author often makes a statement concerning the wife or the husband and then applies it also to Christ or the church and vice versa. For example, the first part of v. 23 opens 'for the husband is the head of the wife'. The second part of that verse then continues with a statement about Christ and the church: 'as Christ is the head of the church'.

Eph. 5: 21–33 has as its framework the Haustafel admonitions to the wives and the husbands. Into the framework supplied by these exhortations, the author of Ephesians inserts the quotation of Gen. 2: 24 – 'therefore a man shall leave his father and mother and cleave to his wife, and they shall become one flesh' – as the foundation for his understanding of the relationship that should subsist between wives and husbands, the church and Christ.

A. THE HAUSTAFEL FORM AND THE QUOTATION OF GEN. 2: 24

The Haustafel governs the form of 5: 21–33 and, when isolated, accounts for a considerable amount of the material in that passage. On the basis of the evidence examined earlier, the Haustafel injunction to the wives required the use of ὑποτάσσομαι. In that regard the author of Ephesians functions within the bounds of the tradition. In the injunction to the husbands, however, there is no prescription concerning which verb must be used. Whether the author of Ephesians has chosen ἀγαπάω or inherited it along with the Haustafel form cannot be readily determined on the evidence at hand. However, ἀγαπάω manifestly serves his purposes. It is possible that ἀγαπάω was suggested to the author by the Lev. 19: 18 – 'You shall love your neighbor as yourself.' One further possible source suggested by the examination of the traditions incorporated within Eph. 5: 21–33 would be the conventional christological association of a ἠγάπησεν and παρέδωκεν.

It is more likely, however, that the Haustafel injunction to the husbands, by using the verb ἀγαπάω, triggers immediately (vv. 25b ff.) an extended reference to Christ and the church in which the dominant verb must be considered ἠγάπησεν. Caution must be exercised against the facile conclusion based on the widespread use of the term 'love' in Eph. 5: 25–33 that the verb ἀγαπάω in the Haustafel admonition is the author's own insertion or choice. It could just as well be that ἀγαπάω was the main verb in the Haustafel form received by the author and provided the occasion for him to speak in various ways concerning the nature and extent of this love. The presence of ἀγαπάω in the parallel form in Col. 3: 19 seems to confirm the latter.

There is some question in 5: 22b concerning the relationship of the phrase ὡς τῷ κυρίῳ to 5: 22a, the Haustafel injunction. The question centers on the problem whether ὡς τῷ κυρίῳ was transmitted to the author along with the Haustafel admonition to the wives. There is in the Colossian parallel also a ὡς phrase immediately following the Haustafel injunction to the wives: ὡς ἀνῆκεν ἐν κυρίῳ (Col. 3: 18). The wording of the Colossian phrase is sufficiently different to call into question the assumption of the borrowing of one by the other. Since there is no recurrence of the Ephesian phrase ὡς τῷ κυρίῳ in any NT Haustafel address to the wives, the only remaining basis for decision is internal evidence within the expanded Haustafel form within Eph. 5: 21–33. In other words, the only possible way to determine whether ὡς τῷ κυρίῳ in v. 22b is an addition by the author of Ephesians is to ask whether the other material within the expansion of the injunction to the women yields enough information concerning the author's purpose to allow some probability claim concerning this short phrase. On the basis of formal and stylistic characteristics evident in vv. 23–4, the author of Ephesians shows a proclivity towards comparative statements in which he uses the particle ὡς or some compound form of ὡς. On this basis, the use of ὡς in v. 22 b in the phrase ὡς τῷ κυρίῳ is entirely consistent with the development in the immediately following verses which can be attributed in their present form to the author of Ephesians. Also, in the section encompassing vv. 22–4 there is, apart from v. 22, a consistent pattern of movement on the part of the author where one statement about the relationship of a man to his wife (v. 23a) leads to a statement about similar relationships existing between Christ and the church (v. 23b). These two are connected consistently with the comparative particle ὡς. For this reason as well it is not surprising to find that the author of Ephesians states the Haustafel admonition to the wives and follows it with a comparative particle ὡς and a phrase that relates what is said of wives and husbands to 'the Lord'.

There is, however, one further curious feature concerning the phrase ὡς τῷ κυρίῳ in v. 22b. There can be no certainty whether κύριος in this context refers simply to the lordship of the husband over the wife, or whether κύριος refers already to Christ and the lordship that he has over all things. If the phrase ὡς τῷ κυρίῳ is read with v. 22a immediately preceding it, then the interpretation would lean towards understanding κύριος in v. 22b on a human level; if it is taken with the material that follows (vv. 23 f.), then the lordship of Christ over all things is the resulting emphasis. There is nothing explicit within the passage that requires the exegete to reduce the ambivalence to a single meaning, which seems reason enough to allow the two-sidedness of its potential understanding to remain.

Into the Haustafel, the author inserts the quotation of Gen. 2: 24 (Eph. 5: 31). With the inclusion of this verse from the OT the author of Ephesians places himself fully in line with the pattern of the early church, whereby a reference to the law or OT is commonly associated with a concern for submission of wives to their husbands.

Within 5: 21–33, Gen. 2: 24 is used to reinforce both of the admonitions found in the Haustafel. Gen. 2: 24 suggests a posture of passivity for the wife. At no point in Gen. 2: 24 is the wife the subject of the action; she is instead the object. The wife is the recipient of the action undertaken by the husband; she is never the actor. This is thoroughly consistent with the admonitions to the wives in 5: 21–33 and indeed with the tone of the whole passage in which the wives are consistently expected to be submissive.

Similarly, Gen. 2: 24 can be taken as supporting the basic Haustafel admonition to the husbands – husbands, love your wives. Gen. 2: 24 speaks of the activity of the husband in leaving his father and mother and in cleaving to his wife. It is this same kind of activity and preeminence that is expected of the husband throughout Eph. 5: 21–33, and Gen. 2: 24 can be understood as the basis of it.

What becomes apparent through the above observations is the double function of Gen. 2: 24 in Eph. 5: 21–33. On a human level it explicates the mutual relationship that should subsist between a man and his wife. On another level the OT quotation sets forth in some detail the reciprocal relations that must obtain between Christ and the church. Underlying these observations concerning the role of Gen. 2: 24 is the presence of a clear and definite correlation of the church and the wife in 5: 21–33, so that any statement made about the wife has a certain appropriateness also about the church, and conversely, any statement made about the church may also be applied to the wife. In the same way statements made about the husband also have a certain relevance when applied to Christ, and statements about Christ may also be applied to the husband. In Eph. 5: 21–33, therefore, the author has chosen to speak of two marriages: (1) the marriage of the husband and his wife set forth initially in the Haustafel admonition and (2) the marriage of Christ and the church. As the foundation for explicating his understanding of both these marriages, the author has chosen the chief OT text ordaining marriage, namely Gen. 2: 24. Of course, Gen. 2: 24, located in the heart of the narratives about Adam and Eve, introduces that prototypical marriage. The marriage of Christ and the church, however, seems to supplant the marriage of Adam and Eve, so that the latter alliance never explicitly comes to the surface in 5: 21–33.

The function of Gen. 2: 24 in Eph. 5: 21–33 is, however, not one strictly limited to the introduction of marriage imagery. The last clause of Gen. 2: 24 – 'and the two shall become one flesh' – can be understood not only of the uniting of two marriage partners, but also can be seen as the occasion for the introduction of organic terminology. For example, since Gen. 2: 24

states that 'the two shall become one flesh', it is possible for the author to speak of the man as the head of the wife (v. 23 a) and Christ as head over the church, his body (v. 23 b). The language of head, body and members is imported by the author and can be understood as brought in on the basis of the last clause of Gen. 2: 24.

B. VERSE-BY-VERSE ANALYSIS OF 5: 21-33

For closer examination, the material in 5: 21-33 may be divided conveniently into the following units: (1) Eph. 5: 21; (2) Eph. 5: 22-4; (3) Eph. 5: 25-7; (4) Eph. 5: 28-30; (5) Eph. 5: 31-2; and (6) Eph. 5: 33.

1. *Eph. 5: 21*

The first set of problems focuses about v. 21: ὑποτασσό-μενοι ἀλλήλοις ἐν φόβῳ χριστοῦ. How does the plural participle ὑποτασσόμενοι relate to its context? It has generally been easier to answer this question concerning the matter following v. 21 than about the material prior to v. 21. Verse 22 – αἱ γυναῖκες τοῖς ἰδίοις ἀνδράσιν – understands as its verb the ὑποτασσόμενοι of v. 21, and thereby provides a clear connection. There is, however, a much more complex question of the relationship of v. 21 to the verses immediately preceding it. Scholarship has formerly resolved the matter in one of two ways: either ὑποτασσόμενοι is understood as a participle dependent on the previous finite verb (namely πληροῦσθε in v. 18) or it is asserted that participles in a paraenetic section such as this can take on an imperative function without reference to any other finite verb.[1]

---

[1] That the participle can function as imperative such scholars as Blass–Debrunner–Funk, Moulton and Daube, among others, agree; but they do not all agree in the ways that they account for it. Blass–Debrunner–Funk (*A Grammar*) treat this matter under anacoluthon. In par. 468 (2) they state: there is 'the peculiar use of a participle in place of a finite verb and without any connection to one, usually in a long series and in an imperatival sense . . . ἐστέ may be supplied throughout'. J. H. Moulton, *A Grammar of New Testament Greek* (Edinburgh: T. and T. Clark, 1908, 3rd ed.), I, 180 ff. and 232 ff., refers to several occurrences in papyri and generalizes from these to the hypothesis that participles functioning as imperatives were a rather standard

In his article 'Die Hodajot-Formel in Gebet und Hymnus des Frühchristentums',[1] James M. Robinson identifies a traditional, conventional association and sequence that may be seen in patristic writings. The formulation relates to church order and brings together some reference to thanksgiving – whether by hymns, tongues or prophecy – and an associated concern for submission.

Once he has established the existence and character of this traditional formulation in patristic literature, Robinson examines 1 Cor. 14 and finds the same pattern.[2] He claims: 'Dass aber diese Verbindung, nicht nur äusserlich-zufällig ist, geht aus einem Vergleich mit den beiden bekannten Stellen über das Singen im NT, Col. 3: 18 f. Eph. 5: 19 f. hervor.'[3] With detailed and compelling arguments Robinson finds that the association of ecstatic utterance with the submission of women was a convention in ethical instruction. Of course, that is precisely the sequence found in the movement from Eph. 5: 18 ff. to 5: 22. In 5: 18 ff. the author is concerned with 'ecstatic utterance' and proceeds to speak of the submission expected of wives:

And do not get drunk with wine, for that is debauchery; but be filled with the spirit, addressing one another in psalms and hymns and spiritual songs, singing and making melody to the Lord with all your heart, always and for everything giving thanks in the name of our Lord Jesus Christ to God the Father. Be subject to one another out of reverence for Christ. Wives be subject to your husbands...

characteristic of Hellenistic Greek. David Daube's appended note in E. G. Selwyn's classic commentary, *The First Epistle of St Peter* (London: Macmillan and Co., Ltd, 1961, 2nd ed.), pp. 467–88, is entitled 'Participle and Imperative in I Peter' and addresses itself to the question of the participle functioning as imperative. Daube concludes that an imperatival use of the Greek participle is most closely related to the use of the Hebrew participle in similar literature of the Talmud. The object of his appended note is 'to shew that underlying that strange use of the participle in Romans, Ephesians, Colossians, Hebrews, and I Peter may be the participle of Hebrew rules, of Mishna, Tosefta and so on; the participle expressing a duty, positive or negative, with the person or class concerned sometimes named, and sometimes omitted, and other imperative forms employed in the same context, as on the same level' (p. 484).

[1] *Apophoreta: Festschrift für Ernst Haenchen* (Berlin: Alfred Töpelmann, 1964), pp. 194–235.

[2] *Ibid.* p. 223.　　　　　　　　[3] *Ibid.* p. 224.

It is just this conventional movement that accounts for the lack of a finite verb between v. 18 ('be filled with the spirit') and v. 23, the verse following the injunction for submission of wives. Robinson's study makes clear that what has seemed to some interpreters an awkward insertion of the Haustafel[1] is in fact the author's movement through a conventional sequence from ecstatic utterance to an injunction of submission to wives. The author chooses as the form of this call for submission of women the opening admonition of the Haustafel. From 5: 21 through 6: 9, then, the author works out his concerns through the framework provided by the Haustafel form.

It must be noted that v. 21 is not itself a part of the Haustafel but stands immediately prior to the introduction of the Hausta-fel form of admonition to the wives. As it stands, it is a general admonition calling for the submission of each one to the other ἐν φόβῳ χριστοῦ. As such, it may be a slight counterbalance to the Haustafel form that follows. As might be expected, the Haustafel reflects the sociological patterns of the time that formulated it, in that wives were to be submissive to the husbands and thereby relegated to a thoroughly secondary role. When viewed as a superscription for the entire Haustafel, Eph. 5: 21 – ὑποτασσόμενοι ἀλλήλοις ἐν φόβῳ χριστοῦ – seems more appropriate for the admonitions to the wives, the children and the slaves than it does for the husbands, the fathers and the masters. The husbands are nowhere in 5: 22–33 exhorted to submission or to anything like submission. The admonition to the fathers in 6: 4 likewise partakes not at all of the notion of submission. The admonition to the masters in 6: 9 qualifies the notion of absolute authority on the part of the masters by the statement 'knowing that he who is both their Master and yours is in Heaven, and there is no partiality with him'. Thus 5: 21 is not in complete harmony with the Haustafel injunctions to the husbands and fathers and retains only a qualified appropriateness with regard to the masters. Quite to the contrary, it would be entirely appropriate to the tone of the admonitions to the wives, the children and the slaves.

[1] Cf. Abbott, *Epistle to the Ephesians*, p. 164: 'To suppose a direct connection with πληροῦσθε ἐν πν. does not yield a suitable sense. The connection with the preceding context is, in fact, only in form, that with what follows is in substance.'

The possibility arises that 5: 21, in relation to the material following it, belongs only to 5: 22 f., namely, the Haustafel admonition to the wives. If this be so, then 5: 21 could not be considered a general heading for the entire Haustafel. Such a solution would relieve the exegete of any concern to show how submission is appropriate for those classes of individuals for which there is no submission recommended by the Haustafel form. This solution, however, will encounter difficulty in interpreting the ἀλλήλοις of 5: 21, since ἀλλήλοις suggests some reciprocal relationship between two individuals or two classes of individuals.

The resolution of this exegetical dilemma is possible if 5: 21 is understood as the author's critique of the basic stance of the Haustafel form wherein one group is ordered to be submissive to another group vested with authority over it. By means of 5: 21, the author introduces the entire Haustafel form in such a way that the absolute submission and the absolute predominance of one or the other class is qualified from the very start by a mutual submission ἐν φόβῳ χριστοῦ. Once the author has established the necessity for a mutual submission of Christians, he can then take over a Haustafel form that will serve many of his purposes but with the posture of which he does not entirely agree. Further evidence of this interpretation will be seen in the exegesis of 5: 22–33, where, within the framework provided by that Haustafel admonition to the wives and husbands, the author will in other ways qualify both the absoluteness of the submission of the wives to the husbands and the completeness of the authority of the husbands over the wives. Eph. 5: 21 is to be understood not only as a specific injunction to be followed by all Christians but it is also a general introduction to the entire Haustafel form and therefore a rubric under which all of 5: 22–6: 9 is to be interpreted.[1]

The prepositional phrase ἐν φόβῳ χριστοῦ[2] that constitutes

---

[1] Cf. 1 Pet. 5: 5 for another example of admonition to mutual subordination.

[2] In v. 21 the witnesses are divided concerning whether χριστοῦ, θεοῦ or κυρίου should be read as the last word of the verse: ὑποτασσόμενοι ἀλλήλοις ἐν φόβῳ...The evidence for κυρίου is the weakest since it is supported only by K. θεοῦ stakes a stronger claim, having as its MSS the Koine text, a great number of other MSS and Clement. Significantly absent from confirming the reading of θεοῦ, however, are the family of texts often designated Hesychian and including such important witnesses as Sinaiticus and

the latter half of Eph. 5: 21 is important since it specifies the grounds of the mutual subordination called for in the first half of that verse.[1] The other occurrence of φόβος is in 6: 5: 'Slaves, be obedient to those who are your earthly masters, with fear and trembling.' It qualifies the verb ὑπακούετε, paralleling its relation to ὑποτασσόμενοι in 5: 21. The slaves are to be obedient to their earthly masters with fear and trembling as to Christ (ὡς τῷ χριστῷ). The use of φόβος and the phrase ὡς τῷ χριστῷ in this admonition no doubt reflect the superscription (5: 21): 'be obedient to one another in the fear of Christ'.[2]

Apart from the two occurrences of φόβος (6: 5 and 5: 21), the root word appears only one other time in the epistle to the Ephesians, in 5: 33 ἡ δὲ γυνὴ ἵνα φοβῆται τὸν ἄνδρα. In 5: 33 the subjunctive φοβῆται with the conjunction ἵνα takes an hortatory function and is directed to the wife. Φόβος is what is demanded of the wife towards her husband. The φόβος expected of the wife to her husband shares in large part with the φόβος called for from all Christians (the church) to Christ. Divine and secular, sacred and profane are not to be distinguished in arriving at the root meaning of φόβος as it occurs in 5: 21 and in 5: 33.[3] That the φόβος required of the wife toward her husband is not absolutely identical with the φόβος required of all Christians towards Christ will become apparent as the exegesis of 5: 22–30 proceeds.

Alexandrinus. The latter MSS support the reading that Nestle has incorporated as the chosen reading: χριστοῦ. On the basis of internal evidence also, χριστοῦ may be considered the probable reading since χριστός is a much used title in Ephesians and since it predominates in the verses that are to follow (vv. 22–33).

[1] The nominal form φόβος does not appear in Colossians, but the verbal form may be found in Col. 3: 22: φοβούμενοι τὸν κύριον. It must be noted that in Colossians, the use of φοβέομαι is found within the Haustafel but is not associated with the admonition to the wives and husbands, as in Ephesians. Instead, it appears in the expanded section dealing with slaves.

[2] This occurrence of ὡς τῷ χριστῷ in 6: 5 in conjunction with φόβος gives further credence to the reading of χριστοῦ in 5: 21 instead of the other alternatives: θεοῦ and κυρίου.

[3] The material that stands between v. 21 and v. 33 correlates Christ with the husband in that what is said of Christ is also in a large extent applied to the husband and, conversely, what is said of the husband is in large part applicable to Christ. This reciprocity should cause the interpreter to hesitate in making such a distinction within the material of this passage.

In the homologoumena the phrases 'fear of the Lord', 'fear of God' and 'fear of Christ' seem to be interchangeable and the choice of one over another depends largely on the author's own purposes in a given passage. That 'fear of the Lord' has roots in the OT and in the Jewish understanding of God is clear enough. Such an instance is even quoted by Paul in Rom. 3: 18 οὐκ ἔστιν φόβος θεοῦ ἀπέναντι τῶν ὀφθαλμῶν αὐτῶν (Ps. 35: 2 (36:1)).

The two NT passages that best illuminate the ἐν φόβῳ χριστοῦ of Eph. 5: 21 are found in 2 Corinthians. The first is in 5: 11, the second in 7: 1. Schlier finds most helpful the passage in 2 Cor. 5: 11 – εἰδότες οὖν τὸν φόβον τοῦ κυρίου ἀνθρώπους πείθομεν.[1] It provides a verbal parallel and has as its point of reference the description of the judgment of all Christians by Christ: 'For we must all appear before the judgment seat of Christ, so that each one may receive good or evil, according to what he has done in the body. Therefore, knowing the fear of the Lord. . .' (5: 10–11 a). The fear of God in v. 11 is known by Paul and is the basis for his admonishing or persuading men. The fear of the Lord in 2 Cor. 5 pertains primarily to a question of the kind of life lived by the Christians in which good or evil is meted out according to what one has done. The importance of the purity of the body in Eph. 5: 21–33 is indeed clear enough, but there is no explicit notion of judgment or of punishment and reward as seen in 2 Cor. 5: 10 f.

There are further problems in taking 2 Cor. 5: 10 f. as the key to understanding the occurrence of φόβος in Eph. 5: 21. Although σῶμα is important in both places, the direction and intent of its importance seem to be different. In 2 Cor. 5 it is a matter of what a person has done in the body and judgment that will result from a computation of these deeds. In Eph. 5: 21 ff., body has come to be almost equivalent with wife on the one hand (v. 28) and with the church on the other (v. 23). In Ephesians it is not a question whether someone in the body has done good or evil, it is instead a question of the purity of the body *per se* and of the love for it.

Actually, the occurrence of the phrase 'fear of God' in 2 Cor. 7: 1 makes a stronger claim as a parallel than does 2 Cor. 5: 10 f. 7: 1 is a part of the section that begins in 6: 14

[1] Schlier, *Der Brief*, p. 252.

and that has been suspected of being either a fragment of another letter from Paul to the Corinthian Christians or non-Pauline.[1] The major part of the fragment follows:

> Do not be mismated with unbelievers. For what partnership have righteousness and iniquity? Or what fellowship has light with darkness? What accord has Christ with Belial? Or what has a believer in common with an unbeliever? What agreement has the temple of God with idols? For we are the temple of the living God;...Since we have these promises, beloved, let us cleanse ourselves from every defilement of body and spirit, and make holiness perfect in the fear of God.[2]

This passage opens with the injunction, 'Do not be mismated with unbelievers.' There follows a series of rhetorical questions given in support of Paul's position regarding the marriage of Christians to unbelievers. The citation of OT verses that forms the middle section of this pericope actually begins as proof of the statement that 'we are the temple of the living God'. The OT verses themselves, however, soon range beyond support of this statement; by the second verse quoted from the OT it seems that the author has returned to the question of Christians being married to unbelievers; 'therefore come out from them, and be separate from them, says the Lord, and touch nothing unclean'. The last verse in the pericope (7: 1) is then the important one for this investigation. The OT verses are understood as promises that God has made to the Christians. Having cited these promises the author exhorts his readers: ταύτας οὖν ἔχοντες τὰς ἐπαγγελίας, ἀγαπητοί, καθαρίσωμεν ἑαυτοὺς ἀπὸ παντὸς μολυσμοῦ σαρκὸς καὶ πνεύματος ἐπιτελοῦντες ἁγιωσύνην ἐν φόβῳ θεοῦ (7: 1 b). The similarity between 2 Cor. 7: 1 b and Eph. 5: 21–33 is readily apparent. In both places a cleansing is of utmost importance. In Ephesians, the cleansing is of the church, the bride of Christ, and is done by Christ himself. In 2 Corinthians the cleansing is incumbent upon the Christians as a consequence of the promises of God. The sentence structure of 2 Cor. 7: 1 gives reason to believe that the cleansing to be

---

[1] For detailed bibliographical references to the discussions of the authenticity of 2 Cor. 6: 14–7: 1, cf. Paul Feine, Johannes Behm and W. G. Kümmel, *Introduction to the New Testament*, trans. A. J. Mattill, Jr (14th ed. rev.; Nashville: Abingdon Press, 1965), pp. 205, 211.

[2] The section omitted is a series of OT quotations with the introductory phrase 'as God said'.

undertaken by the Corinthian Christians is tantamount to the perfecting of holiness (ἐπιτελοῦντες ἁγιωσύνην) ἐν φόβῳ θεοῦ. The ἐν φόβῳ θεοῦ of 2 Cor. 7: 1 is precisely like ἐν φόβῳ χριστοῦ of Eph. 5: 21, the χριστοῦ in the latter standing instead of θεοῦ in the former. In 2 Cor. 7: 1, the cleansing, the perfecting of holiness, is done ἐν φόβῳ θεοῦ. In Eph. 5: 21 ff. ἐν φόβῳ θεοῦ stands – with the substitution of χριστός for θεός – as the heading of the section of the epistle to the Ephesians that admonishes and gives directions to all the members of the family concerning how they should relate as Christians to other members of the family.

In these contexts φόβος does not mean fright; neither is it to be taken, it would seem, in a mystical self-centered sense of reverence. Rather, in both 2 Cor. 7 and Eph. 5: 21 ff. the point of the φόβος refers primarily to an initiative taken by God (2 Cor. 7: 1) or by Christ (Eph. 5: 21–33). It is because of previous action in both cases, by God or Christ, that the Corinthian Christians and the Christians addressed by the epistle to the Ephesians find themselves called upon for a thorough, consistent response – a response in view of what has been done for them. That response is further characterized in 2 Cor. 6: 14–7: 1 and in Eph. 5: 21–33 as holiness.

2. Eph. 5: 22-4

Αἱ γυναῖκες τοῖς ἰδίοις ἀνδράσιν ὡς τῷ κυρίῳ, ὅτι ἀνήρ ἐστιν κεφαλὴ τῆς γυναικὸς ὡς καὶ ὁ χριστὸς κεφαλὴ τῆς ἐκκλησίας, αὐτὸς σωτὴρ τοῦ σώματος. ἀλλὰ ὡς ἡ ἐκκλησία ὑποτάσσεται τῷ χριστῷ, οὕτως καὶ αἱ γυναῖκες τοῖς ἀνδράσιν ἐν παντί.

With the brief introduction provided by 5: 21, the author of Ephesians, in these three verses, sets forth his treatment of the Haustafel address to wives. Immediately upon the completion of the Haustafel address to wives – αἱ γυναῖκες (some form of ὑποτάσσομαι assumed) τοῖς ἰδίοις ἀνδράσιν – he mentions ὁ κύριος. It soon is apparent that the phrase ὡς τῷ κυρίῳ (v. 22 b) is no passing remark made casually by the author.[1] Rather, by v. 23 b, introduced by ὡς καί, it is clear that the author's assertions about wives and their relationship to husbands will

---

[1] The introduction of such phrases characterizes early Christian adaptation of Haustafeln. Cf. Col. 3: 18 b: ὡς ἀνῆκεν ἐν κυρίῳ.

be alternated with comments about the relationship between Christ and the church. This oscillation takes place until v. 24 *b* repeats the Haustafel form that opened the section. Therefore, the structure of vv. 22–4 is as follows: basic Haustafel admonition to the wives, short comparative statement ὡς τῷ κυρίῳ, a declaration about the relationship of a woman to her husband (23 *a*), and an application of this same statement to Christ and the church (23 *b*). There follows the phrase αὐτὸς σωτὴρ τοῦ σώματος (v. 23 *c*). Verse 24 *a* opens with a statement about Christ and the church and returns in v. 24 *b* to the Haustafel admonition as a conclusion to the section.

Of what significance is the shift from the plural in the Haustafel address (v. 22 *a*) to the singular in the comparative phrase ὡς τῷ κυρίῳ? On one level κύριος may be understood to refer to husbands as masters. This cannot be ruled out on any consideration, but the development in vv. 23–4 makes clear another possible level of meaning. Κύριος may refer to Christ. If the meaning of ὡς τῷ κυρίῳ were restricted to the one level of referring to the husband (v. 22 *a*) as the lord or master, then the phrase might read ὡς τοῖς κυρίοις. However, immediately after the author states the Haustafel injunction – given in the standard form, the plural – he reverts to a use of the singular and everything that follows remains in the singular until v. 24 *b*, the restatement of the Haustafel admonition which is rightfully in the plural. By the shift from the plural to singular, the author gives the first major clue that his concern lies not with general classes of individuals and general admonitions to those classes but with the individual man and woman, with Christ and the church. For this reason, vv. 23–4 *a* provide the best evidence for the author's concerns in this first section.

When v. 23 *c* – αὐτὸς σωτὴρ τοῦ σώματος – is set aside and the remaining material is arranged in the following way, certain observations can be made.

ὅτι   ἀνήρ ἐστιν κεφαλὴ τῆς γυναικὸς
ὡς καὶ ὁ χριστὸς κεφαλὴ τῆς ἐκκλησίας
ἀλλὰ ὡς ἡ ἐκκλησία ὑποτάσσεται τῷ χριστῷ
οὕτως καὶ αἱ γυναῖκες   τοῖς ἀνδράσιν

In v. 23 the two masculine nouns ἀνήρ and χριστός are correlated, as are the two feminine nouns γυναικός and ἐκκλησίας.

Considered alone, these verses would tend to identify the husband and Christ and the wife and the church since the statements are reciprocal. Further, it is clear that within the section formally addressed to the wives, the author of Ephesians has constructed a chiasmus that, in the first element, moves from masculine to feminine and, in the second element, changes the sequence to feminine and masculine.

The first line of this expansion – namely v. 23a, ὅτι ἀνήρ ἐστιν κεφαλὴ τῆς γυναικός – is introduced by the causal conjunction ὅτι and may here be translated 'because'.[1] As a causal conjunction meaning 'because' or 'for', the entire statement of v. 23a – a man is the head of his wife – is introduced as the reason why wives should be submissive to their husbands. Because a husband is the wife's head, the wife is to be submissive. This reasoning is not part of the Haustafel form itself but is introduced here as a justification by the author. While v. 23a provides a basis upon which one can justify the demand placed upon women by the Haustafel injunction to them, it also provides the occasion for the author of Ephesians to move, by means of the correlative conjunction ὡς and the emphatic καί to a similar statement about Christ's headship of the church.

Twice within one verse (v. 23) the author of Ephesians uses the word κεφαλή. In both he speaks of the authority of the male figure over the female. The author portrays the wife as the body of which the husband is the head and the church as the body of which Christ is the head. Such an understanding is presupposed by the author about the church and Christ precisely because the epistle has twice touched on this subject previously. The first occurrence is in 1: 22–3. In 1: 22b–3a (1) the church is identified as Christ's body and (2) it is claimed that Christ has been made head (κεφαλή) over all things for the church. Here we find κεφαλή and σῶμα applied respectively to χριστός and ἐκκλησία.[2] To speak of Christ as the κεφαλή in v. 22b is to speak of Christ as the one who exercises authority and power. The statement that opens 1: 22 – 'and he has put all things under his feet' – is paralleled with καὶ αὐτὸν ἔδωκεν κεφαλὴν

---

[1] Blass–Debrunner–Funk, *A Grammar*, par. 456.
[2] In 5: 23, where κεφαλή occurs twice along with χριστός and ἐκκλησία, σῶμα is clearly to be understood. Cf. v. 23c.

ὑπὲρ πάντα τῇ ἐκκλησίᾳ (v. 22 b). Such an association of diverse images reinforces the picture of the absolute authority conveyed to Christ over all things, including the church. This same association informs the use of κεφαλή as applied to Christ in 5: 23.

At the close of 4: 15 the author of Ephesians returns to the theme of the authority and lordship of Christ. Once again, Christ is identified explicitly as ἡ κεφαλή. Furthermore, the language about Christ as κεφαλή elicits a comment about τὸ σῶμα (v. 16) and the way it is related to Christ the head.

When the reader encounters 5: 23 a – 'for the husband is the head of the wife' – and then sees in v. 23 b the parallel statement – 'as Christ is the head of the church' – he knows, from what has been said before about Christ as κεφαλή, what is now being asserted about the headship of Christ over the church and by analogy about the headship of the husband over his wife. Even if there were no mention of σῶμα, the reader, because of his knowledge of the earlier parts of the letter, could understand precisely what is at stake.[1]

At this point, the reader finds the phrase that has troubled interpreters: αὐτὸς σωτὴρ τοῦ σώματος (v. 23 c). The use of κεφαλή and ἐκκλησία has possibly brought σῶμα to mind for the author because of their association in 1: 22 and 4: 15.

This phrase – αὐτὸς σωτὴρ τοῦ σώματος – was not included in the delineation of vv. 23–4 because it obstructed the visualization of the neat four line chiasmic structure. The RSV has forced the translation of this phrase into an immediate connection with what precedes it: 'For the husband is the head of the wife as Christ is the head of the church, his body, and is himself its Savior.' Perhaps the RSV has adopted this translation to avoid the seeming awkwardness and resulting parenthetical nature of the Greek phrase αὐτὸς σωτὴρ τοῦ σώματος (v. 23 c) that would result if a period were placed after v. 23 b as follows: 'For the husband is the head of the wife as Christ is the head of the church.' Then v. 23 c would be translated by assuming the presence of the copula, according to standard Greek practice. The resulting reading would be: 'He himself is savior of [his]

---

[1] Τὸ σῶμα is probably not used explicitly in 5: 23 a–b because its neuter gender would disrupt the parallelism of masculine–feminine, masculine–feminine.

body.' To take it thus would in fact make it seem almost a parenthetical statement.

How is one to account for the presence of v. 23c at this point? A comment about σῶμα comes to the surface after having been understood in v. 23 and v. 23b. That in itself might be ample cause for its presence. However, one further purpose must be suggested as even more essential and more likely to elucidate its function and significance within Eph. 5: 21-33. The statements about the man and his headship or lordship over his wife and the claims concerning the headship and lordship of Christ over the church are parallel in form and content. The intensive pronoun αὐτός that opens the statement in v. 23c may function not only as emphasizing but also as contrasting. It may differentiate the last subject mentioned (Christ) from the earlier subject (the husband). As a parenthetical statement, v. 23c distinguishes between the husband and Christ and makes clear in this context what the author has stated earlier: there is no power or authority co-extensive with that of Christ. Thus, though the husband may be said to be the head of the wife as Christ is the head of the church, there is a significant difference that the author of Ephesians now states before he completes the chiasmus: Christ, unlike the husband, is the savior of his own body.[1]

The noun σωτήρ occurs nowhere else in the epistle to the Ephesians. It functions in 5: 21-33 as a way of differentiating between the Christ–church and the husband–wife relationship. What is meant by Christ being the savior of his body, the church, is explicated more fully by the author in his expansion of the section of the Haustafel addressed to the husbands (vv. 25 ff.). On the basis of what has been said in the chapters prior to 5: 21, the author of Ephesians can rest his case by simply inserting the parenthetical statement (v. 23c) as a means of qualifying the correlation of Christ and the husband.

Since v. 24 actually relates more closely to v. 23a–b than it does to v. 23c the use of the adversative conjunction ἀλλά serves

---

[1] Dibelius, *An die Kolosser Epheser an Philemon*, p. 93, maintains that there is no 'Parallele in der irdischen Ehe' to v. 23c. Schlier, *Christus und die Kirche im Epheserbrief* (Tübingen: J. C. B. Mohr (Paul Siebeck), 1930), p. 66, concurs. Tobit 6: 18 (RSV, 6:17) qualifies as a parallel (καὶ σὺ αὐτὴν σώσεις), but the author of Ephesians sets himself in opposition to any such claim of a husband saving his wife.

to contrast v. 24 with the immediately preceding v. 23 c. Verse 23 c has interrupted the train of thought and the chiasmic form of the expansion that constitutes the bulk of vv. 23–4. The ἀλλά that introduces v. 24 a is the author's way of returning to the completion of the chiasmic form that he began in v. 23 a.[1] The ὡς following the adversative conjunction ἀλλά in v. 24 a is directly related to the οὕτως καί that begins v. 24 b: οὕτως καί αἱ γυναῖκες τοῖς ἀνδράσιν ἐν παντί. With the comparative particle ὡς at the beginning of v. 24 the author returns to his statement about Christ and the church.[2]

There remain two words in the section of the Haustafel addressed to the wives that have not been examined. They form the prepositional phrase ἐν παντί that may be found in v. 24 b, at the conclusion of the restatement of the Haustafel admonition to the wives. The function of this prepositional phrase is to modify the verb assumed in v. 24: ὑποτάσσομαι. Though the husband is not the savior of his wife, namely his body, and therefore does not have the same authority over his wife that Christ has over the church, the wife is nevertheless to be obedient to him 'in all things'. The qualification of his authority seen in v. 23 c does not at all qualify the submission expected from the wife to her husband. In v. 24 b the author makes clear that what he has said within the Haustafel admonition to the wives does not delimit the basic admonition to the submission found in the Haustafel. The limitation of the husband's authority (v. 23) does not limit the wife's submission (ἐν παντί, v. 24 b).

3. Eph. 5: 25–7

With v. 25, the address to the husbands, the second formal section of the Haustafel begins. The Haustafel injunction to the

---

[1] Further confirmation of our question concerning the RSV translation of v. 23 c may be seen in their opening translation of v. 24 where ἀλλά is not reflected at all. The movement of thought and formal structure of vv. 23–4 are obscured by the RSV translation; in the Greek the train of thought and the chiasmic form are evident.

[2] The omission of ὡς, as read in B, would deemphasize the correlation of v. 24 a and v. 24 b. Apart from the weight of textual evidence for its inclusion such correlation has been shown to be typical of the structure of 5: 22–30; cf. above, pp. 103–7.

husbands (v. 25a) requires no further analysis. The section relating the marriage of Christ and the church (vv. 25b–7) may now be considered.

Οἱ ἄνδρες ἀγαπᾶτε τὰς γυναῖκας, καθὼς καὶ ὁ χριστὸς ἠγάπησεν τὴν ἐκκλησίαν καὶ ἑαυτὸν παρέδωκεν ὑπὲρ αὐτῆς, ἵνα αὐτὴν ἁγιάσῃ καθαρίσας τῷ λουτρῷ τοῦ ὕδατος ἐν ῥήματι, ἵνα παραστήσῃ αὐτὸς ἑαυτῷ ἔνδοξον τὴν ἐκκλησίαν, μὴ ἔχουσαν σπίλον ἢ ῥυτίδα ἤ τι τῶν τοιούτων, ἀλλ' ἵνα ᾖ ἁγία καὶ ἄμωμος.

In the development of vv. 25–7, the author of Ephesians has clearly taken his cue from the occurrence of the verb of the Haustafel admonition to the men (ἀγαπάω) and turns, by means of the common comparative conjunction καθώς, to set forth a statement concerning Christ's love for the church. What follows in v. 25b ff. may be understood as a development of the Haustafel admonition. Καθώς, introducing v. 25b, may be translated 'because'.[1] The occurrence of καί in v. 25b and again in v. 25c may serve to emphasize the correlation of these two clauses. As noted earlier,[2] v. 25b–c is a traditional formulation widespread in the early church as a means of speaking of the significance of Christ's death for the believers. Whereas generally the occurrence of the two verbs ἠγάπησεν and παρέδωκεν has been a means of focusing on the death of Christ, in Eph. 5: 21–33 the author's major concern is to speak of a continuing relationship between Christ and the church that is founded on an understanding of them as husband and bride or wife. For this reason there is no explicit development of the death motif. It is clear, however, that the author, by this particular traditional formulation, brings to bear on the Christ–church hieros gamos a perspective informed by an understanding of the significance of Christ's death for the life of the church. Thus, when the author speaks of the love of Christ for the church (v. 25b) he makes it clear that his love is measured by Christ's giving up of himself for that church. It must be noted that the two verbs in v. 25b–c, ἠγάπησεν and παρέδωκεν, both portray Christ as the subject; they both have the church as their object.

Once again the connection of 5: 21–33 with 5: 1–2 becomes apparent. The conventional association of ἠγάπησεν and

[1] Blass–Debrunner–Funk, *A Grammar*, par. 453.
[2] Above, pp. 35–7.

παρέδωκεν in 5: 2b provides the framework for interpreting its reappearance in 5: 25b. There can be no question that the statement at the opening of chapter 5 focuses on the death of Christ as a sacrifice made to God on behalf of the believers. However, it is apparent that, in a discussion of marriage, the emphasis on the traditional formulation shifts to the verb 'love', but such an alteration of emphasis is not to be considered a rejection of the understanding of the importance of Christ's death. Rather, the death functions as a definition of the love. Indeed, much of the entire epistle prior to 5: 21 has concerned itself with an illumination of Christ's death and its significance: 'he [God] raised him [Christ] from the dead and made him sit at his right hand in heavenly places' (1: 20). Likewise, in chapter 2, the assertion that the believers are made alive together with Christ and raised up with him (2: 5–6) presupposes that a new situation of the believers is defined by and made possible by the death and resurrection of Christ. The theme continues later in chapter 2 when the readers are described as being 'alienated from the commonwealth of Israel, and strangers to the covenants of promise' (2: 12). The readers who were once far off 'have been brought near in the blood of Christ' (v. 13). In various ways the death of Christ and its import for the believers is discussed throughout the epistle prior to the concern with marriage evidenced in the Haustafel, and this emphasis is presupposed by the author in his presentation of Christ's love for the church (5: 27b ff.).

Verses 26–7a are composed of two parallel clauses that must be taken as dependent on both the verbs in v. 25b–c. They are translated by the RSV: 'that he might sanctify her, having cleansed her by the washing of water with the word, that the church might be presented before him in splendor'.

In the two ἵνα clauses (vv. 26a and 27a) Christ is clearly understood as the subject acting upon the church. A third ἵνα clause (v. 27c) has as its subject the church: 'in order that she might be holy'. The first two ἵνα clauses are coordinate, final clauses resulting from and explaining the significance of Christ's love and giving up of himself for the church.

In the first ἵνα clause (v. 26), the verb ἁγιάζω raises, to be sure, a range of meanings that has to do with sanctification or purification. It means to set apart, to make holy, or to purify;

but, as a technical term, it may mean to separate out for oneself, namely in the sense of marriage.[1] Ἁγιάζω (v. 26a) retains the breadth of meaning from a sense of purity or sanctity to an understanding of marriage or selecting a wife.

The object of ἵνα ἁγιάσῃ is αὐτήν, clearly the feminine pronoun standing for τὴν ἐκκλησίαν. There is some concern among commentators for the position of αὐτήν since the object occurs prior to the verb ἁγιάσῃ. Schlier, for example, has suggested that the author wants to emphasize that the church and the church alone is the object of Christ's sanctification.[2] This does not seem to be the only, or even the best, explanation for the position of αὐτήν. Perhaps it precedes the verb ἁγιάσῃ so that the participle καθαρίσας and ἁγιάσῃ may be related more closely to one another as a means of emphasizing that Christ is subject of both the verb and the participle. Also its pre-position ties together more closely the range of meanings in ἁγιάζω and in καθαρίζω, a connection that is to be verified by the author's own development in v. 27.

The participial phrase that constitutes v. 26b – καθαρίσας τῷ λουτρῷ τοῦ ὕδατος ἐν ῥήματι – has a circumstantial or adverbial function with regard to Christ's sanctifying or betrothing the church to himself. There seems to be a temporal relationship between the participle καθαρίσας and the finite verb ἁγιάσῃ. Blass–Debrunner–Funk have the following general comments on this problem:[3]

Participles originally had no temporal function, but denoted only the *Aktionsart*; their temporal relation to the finite verb was derived from the context. Since, however, a participle expressing the notion of completion often preceded the finite verb so that the sequence was: the completion of the action denoted by the participle, then the action of the finite verb, the idea of relative past time became associated to a certain degree with the aorist participle coming after the verb.

Normal procedure calls for the participial phrase to precede the verb but the structure of the coordinate ἵνα clauses probably causes it to be placed after the verb. Since it is an aorist participle, its translation should convey punctiliar, completed action: having cleansed her.

---

[1] Above, pp. 42–3.   [2] *Der Brief*, p. 256.
[3] *A Grammar*, p. 339.

The conjunction of παρέδωκεν (he gave himself) with a purpose ἵνα clause that constitutes the structure of 5: 25f. is not unique in the NT. A very close parallel may be seen in Titus. In 2: 13 there is a mention of Jesus Christ that provides the occasion for the relative clause that constitutes v. 14: 'who gave himself for us to redeem us from all iniquity and to purify for himself a people of his own.' The Greek reads: ὃς ἔδωκεν ἑαυτὸν ὑπὲρ ἡμῶν ἵνα λυτρώσηται ἡμᾶς ἀπὸ πάσης ἀνομίας καὶ καθαρίσῃ ἑαυτῷ λαὸν περιούσιον. The opening phrase of v. 14 – ὃς ἔδωκεν ἑαυτὸν ὑπὲρ ἡμῶν – is an instance of the traditional formulation that the early church used in speaking of the death of Christ and its significance. The chief difference is that the verb in Ephesians is παρέδωκεν, while it appears in Titus 2: 14 without the prefixed preposition: ἔδωκεν. It is especially noteworthy that the remainder of Titus 2: 14 is also formed by a ἵνα clause with two purposes effected as a result of Christ's giving himself up. The first purpose is of no great relevance for the study of Eph. 5: 21–33, but the second, coordinated by the use of the conjunction καί, is germane. It states (ἵνα understood) καθαρίσῃ ἑαυτῷ λαὸν περιούσιον. Both in Eph. 5: 25b and in Titus 2: 14 there results a cleansing or a purification of a people. The basic difference is that in Titus 2: 14 the author makes no application of the notion of purity to a marriage between Christ and the church. In Ephesians, the interest in purification is overlaid by a wider set of concerns, related to the pre-marital cleansing of the bride. The purity of the bride is rooted in the hieros gamos of YHWH and Israel.[1]

Following the participle καθαρίσας in 5: 26b is the phrase τῷ λουτρῷ τοῦ ὕδατος. Τὸ λουτρόν is used only twice in the NT; apart from Eph. 5: 26 it is found in Titus 3: 5: ἀλλὰ κατὰ τὸ

---

[1] This same connection of traditions found already in Eph. 5: 25bf. and in Titus 2: 14 is very possibly also reflected in Heb. 9: 14: 'how much more shall the blood of Christ, who through the eternal Spirit offered himself without blemish to God, purify your conscience from dead works to serve the living God'. As in Eph. 5: 25bf. and in Titus 2: 14, Christ's death is understood as an offering of himself for purification of others. The author of Hebrews has taken the purification to be one of conscience, a matter inconsequential in this study. Here as in the other two cases just examined the death results in purification. It must be noted that ἄμωμος, a very important word in Eph. 5: 27, occurs in this similar context in Heb. 9: 14.

αὐτοῦ ἔλεος ἔσωσεν ἡμᾶς διὰ λουτροῦ παλιγγενεσίας καὶ ἀνακαι-
νώσεως πνεύματος ἁγίου. In Titus 3: 4 ff. the author talks
of salvation coming not because of good works but by the
mercy of God, 'by the washing of regeneration and renewal in
the Holy Spirit'. Baptism of believers is clearly in view in
Titus 3: 4 ff. as the means and occasion for the renewal and
regeneration imperative for the Christian life. The washing of
baptism is connected with the death of Christ. There is no
reason to suppose that in Ephesians the washing is unrelated to
baptism.[1] However, in view of the connection of 5: 25 b f. to
Ezek. 16 and YHWH's washing of the bride-to-be Israel,[2] one
could not possibly assume that τὸ λουτρόν has reference only to
early Christian baptism. The remainder of v. 26 may provide
the needed basis upon which to reach some interpretive
decision concerning τὸ λουτρόν.[3]

The closing words of v. 26, and therefore the last phrase of the
first ἵνα clause, are the prepositional phrase ἐν ῥήματι. This
phrase has for a long time troubled interpreters of Ephesians. It
is indeed difficult to find any concrete evidence to aid in understanding it. The word ῥῆμα occurs only one other time in
Ephesians (6: 17) where it is ῥῆμα θεοῦ: 'and take the helmet of
salvation and the sword of the Spirit, which is the word of
God'. In itself, Eph. 6: 17 offers no great help for interpreting
the occurrence of ῥῆμα in v. 26 b.

There is little agreement among scholars concerning the
syntactic relationship of ἐν ῥήματι to the material that precedes
it. Dibelius states that the significance of ἐν ῥήματι cannot be
settled by grammatical arguments.[4] Dibelius contents himself
with the listing of alternative ways of understanding ἐν ῥήματι.[5]
It might refer, he maintains, to a statement made in conjunction with baptism such as the trinitarian formula 'in the name of

---

[1] Such a connection of τὸ λουτρόν with baptism may also be the best way
of understanding the last phrase in v. 26 (ἐν ῥήματι) which will be discussed
hereafter.

[2] Above, pp. 41–2.

[3] Whether related to baptism or not, the author of Ephesians takes τὸ
λουτρόν as the means by which the church is cleansed by Christ. The author
of Titus takes τὸ λουτρόν as a bath of regeneration. Heb. 10: 22 – καὶ
λελουσμένοι τὸ σῶμα ὕδατι καθαρῷ – shows a phrase with some similarities
to that in Eph. 5: 26 b.

[4] *An die Kolosser Epheser an Philemon*, p. 94.   [5] *Ibid.* pp. 94–5.

the Father and of the Son and of the Holy Spirit'. Or, it might be a further restriction of the meaning of the participle καθαρίσας in the sense of 'wasser tut's freilich nicht'; and that would bring it closer to the occurrence in 1 Pet. 1: 25: 'but the word of the Lord abides forever. That word is the good news which was preached to you.' The context of 1: 25 requires a reference to 1: 23 'You have been born anew...through the living and abiding word of God' (διὰ λόγου ζῶντος θεοῦ καὶ μένοντος). For 1 Peter λόγος and ῥῆμα are interchangeable (1: 23–5). In 1: 25 ῥῆμα is clearly connected with baptism and the being born anew (cf. 1: 3), and is equated with τὸ εὐαγγελισθέν (1: 25). Dibelius suggests one other meaning but does not pursue it: the prepositional phrase might pertain to ἁγιάσῃ along the lines of John 17: 17 – 'Sanctify them in truth; thy word is truth.'

Schlier finds difficulties in understanding ἐν ῥήματι as dependent on either ἁγιάζω or καθαρίζω and maintains that ἐν ῥήματι belongs much better with τῷ λουτρῷ.[1] He would understand it in the same way as ἐν ἐπαγγελίᾳ is generally taken by exegetes in Eph. 6: 2: 'unter Begleitung von'. Without supporting argumentation, Schlier rules that ῥῆμα is not to be considered a 'word' in general or an 'Einsetzungswort' or a rule or regulation from Christ. Also, he declares that it is not a word of God or word of Christ or the gospel itself or even a confession of faith. According to Schlier, ῥῆμα is in all probability to be taken as referring to a baptismal formula, specifically in the name of Christ. Schlier's position is as follows: 'Die Reinigung der Kirche also, die ihre Heiligung bewirkt, geschicht nach unserer Epheserstelle im Vollzug des Bades mit Wasser, bei dem das ῥῆμα, d. h. der Name Christi (innerhalb der Taufformel), laut wird.'[2]

In Eph. 5: 26 ἐν ῥήματι seems to function in an instrumental manner.[3] Schlier is right; the addition of ἐν ῥήματι at the close of v. 26 is difficult to understand apart from baptism, especially when associated with τὸ λουτρόν, which in later literature is one way of referring to baptism. From such a perspective, it is also

---

[1] *Der Brief*, p. 257. [2] *Ibid.*

[3] Blass–Debrunner–Funk maintain: 'The use of ἐν owes its extension especially to the imitation of Hebrew constructions with ⸱.' *A Grammar*, par. 219.

possible to relate the ἁγιάζω and καθαρίζω of v. 26a–b to baptism.

In view of these claims, should the earlier treatment of Eph. 5: 26 be withdrawn or modified?[1] The previous examination of the backgrounds of the traditions incorporated into vv. 26 f. has established that much of the material here is best understood in terms of the hieros gamos of YHWH and Israel.[2] That includes even the participial phrase καθαρίσας τῷ λουτρῷ τοῦ ὕδατος of v. 26.

It remains clear that the author's predominant concern in vv. 26 f. is an explication of the relationship of the church to Christ in view of the hieros gamos of YHWH and Israel. However, the parallelism between Christ–church and YHWH–Israel is so clearly established that the author can, at the suggestion of the phrase καθαρίσας τῷ λουτρῷ τοῦ ὕδατος from Ezek. 16, allude to baptism by means of the same phrase with the addition of ἐν ῥήματι. In the context of 5: 25 ff. the καθαρίσας τῷ λουτρῷ τοῦ ὕδατος ἐν ῥήματι of v. 26 does double duty: (1) it refers to the purification of the church as the bride of Christ by analogy from the cleansing of Israel; and (2) it is made relevant to the reader by turning it to speak of baptism, the means by which each of the readers became incorporated into the church.

It is in v. 26b that the reader first encounters an indication that the author of Ephesians is undertaking a correlation of Christ with YHWH and of the church with Israel. In so doing the author has adumbrated, by means of these slight references, the history of YHWH's relationship with Israel. The author of Ephesians has adapted the YHWH–Israel hieros gamos for his purposes in speaking of Christ and the church. This connection not only ties christology into the history of Israel and her understanding of YHWH, but also links ecclesiology with that same history. By his development in vv. 26–7, the author makes clear a positive continuity between the history of Israel and the history of the church, between YHWH's action for Israel and Christ's action for the church. It is only by such a grounding of the present in terms of the understanding of the past that the author of Ephesians can make any comment about what should carry into the future. The author has not

---

[1] Above, pp. 37–51.   [2] *Ibid.*

yet finished his statement of the relationship of the past to the present, so an explication of what pertains to the future awaits clarification in v. 27b–c.

With v. 27 the author of Ephesians continues the pattern that he has inherited from the early church. Verse 27 is very complex:
(v. 27a) ἵνα παραστήσῃ αὐτὸς ἑαυτῷ ἔνδοξον τὴν ἐκκλησίαν,
(v. 27b) μὴ ἔχουσαν σπίλον ἢ ῥυτίδα ἤ τι τῶν τοιούτων,
(v. 27c) ἀλλ' ἵνα ᾖ ἁγία καὶ ἄμωμος. As in v. 26, Christ is the subject of the ἵνα clause of v. 27a and the church is the object. However, with the naming of τὴν ἐκκλησίαν at the conclusion of v. 27a, there follows a participial phrase of which Christ is no longer the subject. Beginning in v. 27b with μὴ ἔχουσαν, the church becomes the subject and continues to be so through the ἵνα clause that forms v. 27c: ἀλλ' ἵνα ᾖ ἁγία καὶ ἄμωμος. For the purposes of this investigation, therefore, v. 27a must be separated temporarily from v. 27b–c and each must be considered as a unit. Only then can the relationship between the two be examined.

The emphatic personal pronoun αὐτός in v. 27a makes it especially clear that Christ is the one who is the subject of the verb παρίστημι. The emphasis upon Christ's action is expressed further by the occurrence of ἑαυτῷ as the indirect object of the verb παραστήσῃ: in order that he himself might present to himself...The object of παραστήσῃ is clearly τὴν ἐκκλησίαν. To be found in 5: 27a also is the adjective ἔνδοξος, here standing in agreement with τὴν ἐκκλησίαν and describing the latter.

Παρίστημι, the verb of the second ἵνα clause (v. 27a), expresses a result of Christ's loving the church and giving himself for her. In the writings of the early church παρίστημι has a wide range of usage and occurs in the NT forty times, but only once in Ephesians. In the transitive, as it stands in Eph. 5: 27, it is ascribed a breadth of meaning that includes (1) 'place beside' or 'put at someone's disposal'; (2) 'present' or 're-present'; (3) 'make, render'; (4) 'offer, bring, present' as a technical term 'in the language of sacrifice'; (5) 'as a legal technical term bring before (a judge)'; (6) 'prove, demonstrate'.[1] The context of the occurrence of παρίστημι in Eph. 5: 27a must be the prime determinant of the choice to be made among these possible meanings or shades of meaning.

[1] Bauer–Arndt–Gingrich, *A Greek–English Lexicon*, p. 633.

To be sure, the simple sense of 'present' or 'represent' some-one to someone might be understood in Eph. 5: 27a.[1] In this sense Christ would be understood as presenting the church to himself. For this purpose and to this end he loved the church and gave himself for her, that he might present her to himself ἔνδοξος. Or παρίστημι in Eph. 5: 27a might partake of the meaning suggested by Bauer-Arndt–Gingrich: 'place beside, put at someone's disposal' or 'yield'. In a context where the church has been correlated with the wife and where submis-sion or obedience has been urged upon the wife as the hall-mark of her relationship to her husband, it is not difficult to read παρίστημι either of Christ's placing the church along side himself, i.e., in a position of honor – or using παρίστημι as a means of stressing the subservience or obedience of the church to Christ.

The occurrence of παρίστημι in Eph. 5: 27a may also be read as 'almost equivalent to make, render'. Taken with this shade of meaning Eph. 5: 27a could say that Christ makes or renders the church ἔνδοξος to himself or in his presence.[2] Bauer–Arndt–Gingrich suggest the following translation for Eph. 5: 27a: 'that he might render the church glorious before him'.[3] This translation stresses Christ's action on behalf of the church.

It has not been the practice of interpreters of Eph. 5: 21–33 to consider the possibility that παρίστημι as it occurs in 5: 27a might in any sense be considered a technical term in the language of sacrifice meaning 'offer, bring, present' such as is found in the opening of Rom. 12 – παρακαλῶ οὖν ὑμᾶς... παραστῆσαι τὰ σώματα ὑμῶν θυσίαν ζῶσαν ἁγίαν. However, this study has noted the indebtedness of the remainder of v. 27 to language dealing with purity and reflecting the purity that is expected of priests and sacrificial animals in Jewish tradition. Given the remainder of v. 27 and the connections of 5: 21–33 with the sacrificial language of 5: 1–2 such a connotation is quite viable for the occurrence of παρίστημι in Eph. 5: 27a.

[1] Cf. Acts 23: 33.
[2] Bauer–Arndt–Gingrich list Eph. 5: 27 as the first illustration of this meaning for παρίστημι. It is very curious that they do not list the occurrence of παρίστημι in 2 Cor. 11: 2 under the same category with Eph. 5: 27.
[3] *A Greek–English Lexicon*, p. 633.

Therefore, παρίστημι, as it occurs in Eph. 5: 27a, refers to Christ's putting the church at his disposal or making it yield to him, or to his making or rendering her ἔνδοξος before him, or to his bringing her as a sacrifice that is without blemish or spot. These three suggestions are not mutually exclusive, but, in fact, each one has a certain appropriateness in Eph. 5: 21–33.

Apart from the occurrences of παρίστημι in Rom. 6 (13, 13, 16, 19) where it must be taken in a sense of yielding or submitting to something or someone, the closest passage of the use of παρίστημι in Eph. 5: 27a is 2 Cor. 11: 2 – a verse already noted as having several features paralleling 5: 21–33.[1] In 2 Cor. 11: 2, as in Eph. 5: 27, the presenting of the Christians or the church to Christ is a formal matter having to do with the procedures involved in marriage. The purity demanded and required of the bride according to Jewish customs is recognized in both verses. In 2 Cor. 11: 2 this purity is indicated by the words παρθένον ἁγνήν whereas in Eph. 5: 27 it is expressed in a series of positive and negative declarations concerning the purity expected in the church.

The other passage that may shed light on the use of παρίστημι in Eph. 5: 27a is Col. 1: 21–2: 'And you, who once were estranged and hostile in mind, doing evil deeds, he has now reconciled in his body of flesh by his death, in order to present you holy and blameless and irreproachable before him'; καὶ ὑμᾶς ποτε ὄντας ἀπηλλοτριωμένους καὶ ἐχθροὺς τῇ διανοίᾳ ἐν τοῖς ἔργοις τοῖς πονηροῖς, νυνὶ δὲ ἀποκατήλλαξεν ἐν τῷ σώματι τῆς σαρκὸς αὐτοῦ διὰ τοῦ θανάτου, παραστῆσαι ὑμᾶς ἁγίους καὶ ἀμώμους καὶ ἀνεγκλήτους κατενώπιον αὐτοῦ, κτλ. This passage comes early in the epistle to the Colossians and follows on the christological hymn of 1: 15 ff. In contrast to Ephesians, Colossians gives no hint of marriage between Christ and the Christians or the church. The context consists instead of a reference to reconciliation resulting from Christ's death. Immediately following the mention of Christ's death in Col. 1: 22a is the occurrence of παρίστημι as an infinitive of result. Whereas in 2 Cor. 11: 2 and in Eph. 5: 27 the Christians or the church were represented τῷ χριστῷ (2 Cor. 11: 2) and ἑαυτῷ (Eph. 5: 27a), in Col. 1: 22 the presentation is formalized by κατενώπιον. Providing one more point of contact between

---

[1] Above, pp. 83–4.

Col. 1: 22 and Eph. 5: 27 is the customary description of the purity expected of the Christians or the church at the time of the presentation. This description is accomplished in Col. 1: 22 by three coordinated adjectives ἅγιος, ἄμωμος and ἀνεγκλήτος. Ἀνεγκλήτος is missing from both 2 Cor. 11: 2 and Eph. 5: 27 possibly because of its inappropriateness in a context of discussion of marriage. The presence of ἅγιος and ἄμωμος in Col. 1: 22 is clearly parallel with Eph. 5: 25 ff. where ἁγία and ἄμωμος occur in v. 27c and ἁγιάζω appears in v. 26a.

Colossians, 2 Corinthians, and Ephesians manifest a configuration of terminology associated with the verb παρίστημι that portrays an eschatological presentation of Christians to Christ. Consistently the terminology associated with παρίστημι describes these Christians as pure and holy. The possibility arises that the early church had a widespread convention in which the verb παρίστημι functioned in a hieros gamos of Christ and the church. The similarities in each of the three letters are clear enough to indicate that the common tradition is shared by all three and that the differences in these traditions may be accounted for by the divergent purposes made clear in the context of each letter.

The author of Ephesians, in his appropriation of the traditional formula of the presentation of the bride to her husband, uses a single word in the immediate context to carry the weight of the description of the qualities that should pertain to the church. That word is ἔνδοξος: 'in order that he himself might present to himself the church' ἔνδοξος. To be sure, the remainder of v. 27 specifies the content of ἔνδοξος for the author of Ephesians: μὴ ἔχουσαν σπίλον ἢ ῥυτίδα ἤ τι τῶν τοιούτων, ἀλλ' ἵνα ᾖ ἁγία καὶ ἄμωμος. Ἔνδοξος and its related words in v. 27b–c are further confirmation of indebtedness to traditional formulations previously associated with the marriage of YHWH and Israel but now taken over to speak of the marriage of a pure church to Christ, her husband.

Verse 27b–c is an explication of what is entailed in describing the church as ἔνδοξος (v. 27a). Beginning in v. 27b with μὴ ἔχουσαν, the church is the subject both of the participle ἔχουσαν and of the aorist subjunctive ᾖ. Grammatically, this shift of subjects from Christ to the church is made rather easy since the church appears as the object of the finite verb in the second ἵνα clause and stands in last position in that clause. The author of Ephesians then attaches v. 27b–c: μὴ ἔχουσαν σπίλον ἢ ῥυτίδα ἤ τι τῶν τοιούτων, ἀλλ' ἵνα ᾖ ἁγία καὶ ἄμωμος. Ἔχουσαν in v. 27b is an idiomatic or pleonastic participle, and with the negative μή may be translated 'not with' σπίλον ἢ ῥυτίδα ἤ τι τῶν τοιούτων.[1] Thus ἔνδοξος (v. 27a) and the participial phrase beginning with μὴ ἔχουσαν (v. 27b) stand in a similar relationship to τὴν ἐκκλησίαν, the one specifying the quality that the church must have, the other stating a general class of defects that the church must not have. Verse 27b, therefore, extends the limits of the demands included in the word ἔνδοξος simply by disallowing all defects.

Verse 27c ἀλλ' ἵνα ἁγία καὶ ἄμωμος begins with the generally adversative conjunction ἀλλά. The introduction of this clause with the adversative, ἀλλά, does not contrast this third ἵνα clause with the two immediately preceding ἵνα clauses (v. 26a, v. 27a) but distinguishes v. 27c from what has just preceded it, namely v. 27b. Verse 27b has stated that the church is to be devoid of certain blemishes or marks that would characterize it as less than perfect. Therefore v. 27c is set in contrast to v. 27b in that the author makes another claim concerning what should be the characteristics of the church. Blass–Debrunner–Funk point out that ἀλλ' ἵνα may function elliptically to mean: 'on the contrary (but) this happened (or a similar verb), in order that' or 'rather they were to be...'.[2] Either of the latter two translations makes very good sense of ἀλλ' ἵνα in Eph. 5: 27c. The subjunctive of εἶναι as the finite verb associated with ἀλλ' ἵνα produces the following translation: 'rather she is to be ἁγία καὶ ἄμωμος'. Thus, the author, with the introduction of the last ἵνα clause (v. 27c), takes one further step to specify this concern for the purity of the church as the bride of Christ.

The meaning of vv. 25b ff. would be entirely clear without v. 27c but this clause concludes the development of the Christ–church hieros gamos by analogy from the marriage of YHWH and Israel as portrayed in Ezekiel and Song of Songs. For his summation, the author chooses two key words, ἁγία and ἄμωμος (v. 27c). The latter occurs for the first time in 5: 21–33, but the root of the former appeared already in v. 26a. The repetition in

---

[1] *A Grammar*, par. 419.   [2] *Ibid.* par. 448.

v. 27c of the same root word found in v. 26 provides a climactic conclusion of the initial expansion of the Haustafel admonition to the husbands.[1] The occurrence of ἁγία in v. 27c is intended to recall to the reader that Christ's action in loving the church and giving himself up for her had as its purpose a purification of her that was achieved by means of a cleansing by washing with water. She is to be holy or sanctified and ἄμωμος. The significance of ἄμωμος in this connection has been examined extensively.[2] It partakes strongly of the sacrificial qualifications expected of animals due for sacrifice and, as noted by citation of materials above, was extended as a requirement for all priests in the service of YHWH. There is no distinction in Jewish literature between the purity required of the priest and that required of the bride; in v. 27b–c the author of Ephesians specifies that the ἔνδοξος, the glory of splendor that the church is to have, is not to be qualified in any manner but is to encompass that vast understanding of purity called for in the OT of priests, wives and sacrificial animals. Ἄμωμος might have been chosen by the author of Ephesians not only as an appropriate word for the conclusion of his statement concerning the purity expected of the bride, but also as a word whose range of usage includes the meaning 'blameless' in contexts of human behavior. This ambivalence makes easier the transition back to a statement concerning husbands and wives.

4. Eph. 5: 28–30

The appearance of οὕτως at the opening of v. 28 signals a change or movement in the thought of the author from a prime consideration with the relationship between Christ and the church to an extended statement concerning the relationship between the husband and his wife.

There is an opinion among certain scholars that 5: 28 makes a rather abrupt shift from the concern of the preceding verses. In terms of the interpretation thus far established, the question can be put as follows: on what basis does the author shift from a discussion of Christ and the church to a passage related to human marriage and formed on Lev. 19: 18? The answer can be stated in several parts: (1) the previous alternations

---

[1] *Ibid.* par. 493.   [2] Above, pp. 40–9, 68–75.

between Christ–church and man–wife have prepared the reader for the continuation of this pattern; and (2) the purity expected of the church in her betrothal to Christ is easily applied by analogy to the condition of the wife. Parallel evidence of a correlation of purity expected of brides or wives with a reference to Lev. 19: 18 further facilitates the understanding of the movement from a statement about Christ and the church (vv. 25 b–7) to a concern with the relationship of husbands and wives (vv. 28–9). Such a connection may be seen in BT Niddah 17 a: 'R. Ḥisda ruled: A man is forbidden to perform his marital duty in the day-time, for it is said, But thou shalt love thy neighbour as thyself (Lev. 19: 18). But what is the proof? – Abaye replied: He might observe something repulsive in her and she would thereby become loathsome to him.' Here, the 'something repulsive' may be understood in terms of the blemish (מום, μῶμος) of Eph. 5: 27 and is directly related to the quotation of Lev. 19: 18, just as 5: 28 follows immediately upon 5: 27.

Throughout vv. 28–9 b the author applies what he has said about Christ and the church to the Haustafel admonition to the husbands: οὕτως ὀφείλουσιν [καὶ] οἱ ἄνδρες ἀγαπᾶν τὰς ἑαυτῶν γυναῖκας ὡς τὰ ἑαυτῶν σώματα. ὁ ἀγαπῶν τὴν ἑαυτοῦ γυναῖκα ἑαυτὸν ἀγαπᾷ. οὐδεὶς γάρ ποτε τὴν ἑαυτοῦ σάρκα ἐμίσησεν, ἀλλὰ ἐκτρέφει καὶ θάλπει αὐτήν, καθὼς καὶ ὁ χριστὸς τὴν ἐκκλησίαν, ὅτι μέλη ἐσμὲν τοῦ σώματος αὐτοῦ. In v. 28 a the author is once again concerned primarily with the husbands and their action towards their wives.

In v. 28 a, he uses the plural since v. 28 a is, in fact, almost identical to the Haustafel admonition directed to the husbands in v. 25 a: οἱ ἄνδρες ἀγαπᾶτε τὰς γυναῖκας...[1] The major differences between vv. 25 a and 28 a are two. First, there is the introduction of the verb ὀφείλουσιν which changes the occurrence of the verb ἀγαπάω from the imperative as it was in v. 25 a, to the infinitive, as required by common Greek usage with a verb such as ὀφείλουσιν.[2] Second, it is changed by the addition of the comparative phrase ὡς τὰ ἑαυτῶν σώματα. In v. 28

[1] In view of this and other considerations it is difficult to see how Schlier can say 'V. 28 a beginnt einen neuen Gedanken'. Der Brief, p. 260.

[2] Blass–Debrunner–Funk, A Grammar, par. 392.

the author of Ephesians resumes his admonition to the husbands and can now restate it in terms of something that husbands ought to do.

The plural of vv. 28 f. may also be retained as a means of distinguishing between Christ and the husband once again, as was the case with v. 23 b in the section addressed primarily to the wives. In v. 28 a the use of the plural precludes a focus on an individual man as he related to an individual wife. The result is a qualification of the husband–Christ, wife–church correlation.

Οὕτως at the beginning of v. 28 a can denote degree and, when it occurs before a verb, οὕτως may mean 'so intensely'.[1] The simple translation 'thus', used by the RSV, can also convey the meaning of intensity. Even so, it probably refers to what has preceded, and ties vv. 28 f. into the totality of the statement in vv. 25 ff. of the relationship of Christ and the church.

The comparative phrase that concludes v. 28 a – ὡς τὰ ἑαυτῶν σώματα – is significant of the author's purpose. As noted earlier,[2] vv. 28–9 a are deeply indebted to Lev. 19: 18: 'you shall love your neighbor as yourself'. The comparative phrase ὡς τὰ ἑαυτῶν σώματα is this author's way of relating the last part of Gen. 2: 24 – 'and the two shall become one flesh' – to the Haustafel admonition to the husbands that they love their wives. Since a man and his wife become one flesh (Gen. 2: 24; Eph. 5: 31), the author of Ephesians can speak of the wives as the bodies of the husbands. A man's wife is the same as himself or as his body. Therefore the statement that husbands ought to love their wives as their own bodies is the author's combination of his basic OT text, Gen. 2: 24, with Lev. 19: 18 and the Haustafel. This development of the Haustafel admonition by means of reference to Gen. 2: 24 and Lev. 19: 18 is even further informed by the analogy of the marriage of Christ and the church which the author sees as the paradigm for the relation between husbands and wives.

Verse 28 b – ὁ ἀγαπῶν τὴν ἑαυτοῦ γυναῖκα ἑαυτὸν ἀγαπᾷ – shifts from the plural that was to be found in v. 28 a to a singular construction in which the substantivized participle with the article, ὁ ἀγαπῶν, serves as the subject of ἀγαπᾷ. Why does v. 28 b shift from the plural of v. 28 a to the singular.? It is

---

[1] Bauer–Arndt–Gingrich, *A Greek–English Lexicon*, p. 602.
[2] Above, pp. 31–4.

convenient and not at all awkward that the author's statements about the relationship between the husband and the wife in v. 29 *b* – ἀλλὰ ἐκτρέφει καὶ θάλπει αὐτήν – are in the singular, since with v. 29 *c* the author moves from a statement about a man and his wife to a statement about Christ and the church. It is difficult, however, to assess whether in v. 28 *a* the author shifts to the singular in view of this expected movement. Possibly the plural of v. 28 *a* had served the purpose of qualifying the Christ–husband and church–wife correlation, so that in v. 28 *b* the singular may be resumed without confusion.

The use of the participle ὁ ἀγαπῶν in v. 28 *b* as the subject of the sentence introduces the root of ἀγαπάω twice, once as the subject and once as the verb. There results a stress on the idea of love that continues the theme that he has developed from the Haustafel injunction to the husbands (v. 25 *a*) through the Christ–church hieros gamos (vv. 25 *b* ff.).

Verse 28 *b*, apart from the shift from the plural to the singular, actually parallels v. 28 *a* closely. Verse 28 *b* is a declarative statement that the person who does what all men should – namely love their wives – in fact loves himself. The τὰς ἑαυτῶν γυναῖκας of v. 28 *a*, the object of ἀγαπᾶν, is equated with the ἑαυτόν of v. 28 *b* which is, in turn, the object of the finite verb ἀγαπᾷ in v. 28 *b*. In v. 28 *a–b* the object of the husband's love is specified first as his wife, second as his own body and third as himself. The significance of Lev. 19: 18 – 'you shall love your neighbor as yourself' – is readily apparent in v. 28 *a–b* as noted earlier in this study.[1] Both v. 28 *a* and v. 28 *b* unite the Haustafel admonition with the injunction from Lev. 19: 18 – 'you shall love your neighbor as yourself'. Verse 28 *a* gives Lev. 19: 18 as a ground for saying that men ought to love their wives. Verse 28 *b* states that the person who loves his own wife – that is the man who performs what the Haustafel enjoins – is the one who fulfills the OT injunction to love his neighbor as himself.

Verse 29 *a* opens with οὐδείς, the indefinite pronoun used to signify 'nobody' or 'no one'.[2] It functions in v. 29 *a* as the substantive for the verb ἐμίσησεν. Following οὐδείς is the post-positive conjunction γάρ. There are two possible ways of understanding the function of this conjunction in its context in

---

[1] Above, p. 32.
[2] Blass–Debrunner–Funk, *A Grammar*, par. 302.

Eph. 5: 29 a. It may serve to give a ground or a reason for a previous statement, or it may function as an emphatic particle and be best translated by 'indeed' or 'in fact' or 'to be sure'.[1] As a means of making even more emphatic his statement, the author then adds the enclitic particle, ποτε. Associated as it is in Eph. 5: 29 a with a negative particle, ποτε means 'ever'. The first three words of v. 29 a can be translated: 'to be sure (γάρ) no one ever...'.

Since the introduction of the Haustafel admonition to the husbands (v. 25 a), the author of Ephesians has been concerned with love. In 5: 29 a, the author of Ephesians seeks further to substantiate the demand for a husband's love by speaking of the opposite of ἀγαπάω, namely μισέω, which can mean hate, detest, or abhor.[2] He states 'of course no one ever hates his own flesh'.

But the author's purpose is not simply to continue the insistence that the husband love the wife; he extends the argument. On the basis of his general statement that no one ever hates his own flesh he can move to his statement in v. 29 b: ἀλλὰ ἐκτρέφει καὶ θάλπει αὐτήν.

Before analyzing v. 29 b, it must be noted that the occurrence of σάρξ in v. 29 a is clear internal evidence that Gen. 2: 24 (Eph. 5: 31) is informing the author's expansion of the Haustafel address to the husbands. What was a reference in v. 28 a to men's wives as their 'bodies' becomes in v. 28 b 'himself' (ἑαυτόν) and is changed finally in v. 29 a to σάρξ. The author of Ephesians, therefore, makes no distinction between talking of wives as one's own body, as one's self, or as one's flesh. The parallel relationship between the different parts of v. 28 and the first part of v. 29 points up the author's own identification of these three terms – body, self, and flesh – and therefore ties the entire development of vv. 28 f. into the occurrence of the OT quotation in Eph. 5: 31: 'and the two shall become one flesh'.[3]

Verse 29 b – ἀλλὰ ἐκτρέφει καὶ θάλπει αὐτήν – is closely related to v. 29 a by means of the disjunctive preposition ἀλλά. In v. 29 a the author declares what approximates a truism:

[1] Dana and Mantey, *A Manual Grammar*, par. 213.

[2] Bauer–Arndt–Gingrich. *A Greek–English Lexicon*, p. 524.

[3] John A. Allan's comment that in v. 29 'the word FLESH is not quite suitable' misses the mark entirely. *The Epistle to the Ephesians*, p. 130.

'nobody ever hates his own flesh'. With the reader's assent thus secured, the author has prepared for the movement to v. 29*b* 'but nourishes and cherishes it'.

The two finite verbs ἐκτρέφει and θάλπει are placed in paratactic relationship to one another (ἐκτρέφει καὶ θάλπει) and assume as their subject that of ἐμίσησεν in v. 29*a*. The epexegetical relation of these two verbs gives reason to assume that the author of Ephesians does not intend further specification by the listing of both verbs. On the contrary, a generalization results, so that ἐκτρέφει and θάλπει in v. 29*b* must be understood in context to say 'no one ever hates his own flesh but does everything possible to take care of it'. The author of Ephesians has been careful in his discussion of love and its requirements to avoid the notion that love is a vapid emotion. The portrayal of Christ's death as a measure of his love for the church throughout the epistle of Ephesians and especially in 5: 25*b* f. has been established as the paradigm for the love the Christian owes his wife. In v. 29*b* the requirements of love in the marital relationship are spelled out in terms of one's nourishing and cherishing his wife. Such a claim about the husband's obligation towards his wife elicits for the author an obvious connection with Christ's continuing commitment to the church. By this movement to an analogous statement about Christ and the church the author specifies even more fully the commitment the husband should have towards his wife.

Two further observations must be made about v. 29*b*. First, ἐκτρέφει and θάλπει are both in the present tense whereas in vv. 25*b* ff. the main verbs were consistently in the aorist. The nourishing and cherishing of one's own flesh is no punctiliar, completed action, but is a continuing action. Second, αὐτήν in v. 29*b* is important because the author of Ephesians assumes in v. 29*b*, as the object of both ἐκτρέφει and θάλπει, the object of ἐμίσησεν (v. 29*a*): τὴν ἑαυτοῦ σάρκα. The αὐτήν of v. 29*b* is singular feminine accusative in agreement with τὴν ἑαυτοῦ σάρκα. Σάρξ is introduced in v. 29 in view of the quotation of Gen. 2: 24, as most interpreters assert, but that is only a part of the picture. Equally important to the author is the parallelism that the author maintains between statements that fall on opposite sides of the tabulation of 5: 21–33 set forth above.[1] The

[1] Above, p. 104.

situation on one side of the table consistently is shaped so that movement to the other side will be accomplished with the greatest ease. Verse 29 b – ἀλλὰ ἐκτρέφει καὶ θάλπει αὐτήν (σάρξ) – is the last comment in column A before moving to column B, where v. 29 c reads: καθὼς καὶ ὁ χριστὸς τὴν ἐκκλησία. At every change of columns in which verbs are shared on both sides, the author has constructed a noticeable parallelism. The shift from v. 29 b (column A) to v. 29 c (column B) is no exception. In v. 29 b the subject of ἐκτρέφει and θάλπει – viz., he – is paralleled in v. 29 c by ὁ χριστός.[1] Had the author retained either the σῶμα of v. 28 a or the ἑαυτόν of v. 28 b the parallelism between v. 29 b and v. 29 c would have been destroyed. The feminine noun ἐκκλησία of v. 29 c required a feminine noun or pronoun in v. 29 b. This the author provided when he drew σάρξ from the quotation of Gen. 2: 24 and inserted it in v. 29 a.

Once the shift to column B (v. 29 c) has taken place and the author speaks of Christ and the church he may then revert to his use of σῶμα as indeed he does in v. 30: ὅτι μέλη ἐσμὲν τοῦ σώματος αὐτοῦ. In v. 29 c – καθὼς καὶ ὁ χριστὸς τὴν ἐκκλησίαν – καθὼς καὶ is no different from its occurrence in v. 25 b discussed earlier.[2]

Verse 30 is rather short – ὅτι μέλη ἐσμὲν τοῦ σώματος αὐτοῦ – and is related to the close of v. 29 with the causal conjunction ὅτι. Previously in 5: 21–33 the terms κεφαλή, σῶμα, and σάρξ have been encountered. To this list is now added a related word μέλος, 'member' or 'part'. The body referred to in v. 30 is Christ's: the church. Therefore, in v. 30 the author declares that he and his readers, viz. those persons who have been baptized (v. 26 b), are members or parts of that body, the church. Verse 30 must be taken as the conclusion of the entire comparison between Christ and the church and husband and wife; it is the author's way of concluding his statement. He makes

---

[1] The problems related to the alternative readings χριστός/κύριος are similar to those already treated in the identical variants found for v. 21. Cf. the treatment of that problem on p. 117, n. 2. Here occurs the same basic division of witnesses, with the Koine text supporting κύριος while the Hesychian group again favors χριστός. With the evidence provided by vv. 22–9 b, in which the author has consistently chosen to relate χριστός and ἐκκλησία, there is no reason to assume a shift in terminology when parallelism figures so prominently in the structuring of these verses.

[2] Above, p. 127.

clear, just prior to the introduction of the quotation from Gen. 2: 24, that what he has said in and through the Haustafel form (vv. 22–9) applies to himself and to all of his readers since they too are a part (μέλος) of Christ's body, namely the church. Thus, everything said in the preceding lines concerning the church has also a relevance for the readers of this epistle since it pertains directly to them because of their involvement in and being part of the church.

Verse 30 – 'because we are members of his body' – serves an important function in 5: 21–33. It concludes the expanded treatment of the hieros gamos of Christ and the church and gives the reader one further insight into his place in the total picture of Christ's relationship to the church. All that has been said prior to v. 30 is, by that verse, applied to the reader since the readers themselves belong to or are part of the church. Verse 30 shows that what has been said relates to them because they are, in fact, members of Christ's body, the church.

It is important to note that, with v. 30, the author of Ephesians has completed his developmental section within the Haustafel. What occurs after this point is simply a citation of the OT verse that has been prominent in the author's mind from the beginning and a recapitulation or summary of the position taken in vv. 22–30.

5. *Eph. 5: 31–2*

Verse 31 is the quotation from Gen. 2: 24: 'for this reason a man shall leave his father and his mother and shall cleave to his wife and the two shall become one flesh'. As noted,[1] v. 31 is part of a traditional pattern that involves associating an OT text – particularly one relating to Adam and Eve or at least to the Torah – to a question of submission of wives. The extent of the author's indebtedness to the OT in 5: 21 ff. gives assurance that the author is not in the habit of giving a standard introduction to a citation of the OT at every point of his reference to it.

Following the citation of the OT verse in Eph. 5: 31 is the author's terse comment: τὸ μυστήριον τοῦτο μέγα ἐστίν. The significance of this phrase and of the occurrence of μυστήριον in it has been discussed above.[2] The exposition of Eph. 5: 21 ff.

[1] Above, pp. 97–100.   [2] Above, pp. 86–96.

has made clear that the author of Ephesians interprets Gen. 2: 24 to refer not only to the human marriage but also to the marriage of Christ and the church: ἐγὼ δὲ λέγω εἰς χριστὸν καὶ [εἰς] τὴν ἐκκλησίαν (v. 32 b).

6. Eph. 5: 33

Πλὴν καὶ ὑμεῖς οἱ καθ' ἕνα ἕκαστος τὴν ἑαυτοῦ γυναῖκα οὕτως ἀγαπάτω ὡς ἑαυτόν, ἡ δὲ γυνὴ ἵνα φοβῆται τὸν ἄνδρα.

Since the construction of 5: 33 has been adequately treated, there remains only the assessment of its function in the larger context of 5: 21–33.

Eph. 5: 33 is a very integral part of the development that constitutes all of 5: 21–33. It is in v. 33 that Lev. 19: 18 was first observed; it then became apparent that it was the foundation for 5: 28 ff. With v. 33 the author's literary pattern is completed: the Haustafel injunction to the husbands that was first stated in 5: 25 a is repeated. Furthermore, it is in 5: 33 that the admonition to the wives, first set forth in 5: 22, is freely restated – only to be combined with the φόβος of the Haustafel superscription (v. 21). Verse 33 provided the first clear evidence that 5: 21–33 must be considered as a literary unit whose interpretation must reflect that unity. Verse 33 completes the literary form of the unit 5: 21–33 by a chiasmus incorporating the entire passage: wives (vv. 22–4), husbands (vv. 25–30) and husbands (v. 33 a), wives (v. 33 b).

Faithful to the Haustafel form that he has taken over and adapted for his own purposes, the author of Ephesians, in this verse, concludes the first section of the Haustafel by a slightly expanded recapitulation of the admonitions to both classes that constituted the opening set of relationships. Having finished with the treatment of husbands and wives by his modified restatement of the fundamental injunctions to wives and husbands, the author has prepared for an easy transition to the next set of relationships – those of children and fathers (6: 1 ff.) – provided by the Haustafel.

CHAPTER VIII

CONCLUDING OBSERVATIONS

The stage is now set for the consideration of further questions relating to 5: 21–33 and the importance of this passage in the epistle to the Ephesians. There are certain isolable concerns to which the study now turns.

A. IMPLICATIONS OF 5: 21–33 FOR THE REMAINDER OF THE HAUSTAFEL

This investigation has thus far focused on the first set of relationships in the Haustafel (5: 21–33) and has reserved comment upon 6: 1–9, the remainder of the form. Whereas thirteen verses are devoted to wives and husbands (5: 21–33), a total of nine verses is allotted to the remaining classes in the Ephesian Haustafel (6: 1–9).

It has been determined above that 5: 21 not only bears a special relationship to 5: 22 ff. but is, in fact, an introduction to the entire Haustafel.[1] 'Be subject to one another out of reverence for Christ.' Though the Ephesian Haustafel insists that the wives, children and slaves be obedient or submissive to their counterparts, the subjection is placed in somewhat different perspective by the superscription to the Haustafel. The phrase, 'Be subject to one another', is directed to all members of the household, even though the author's inherited Haustafel form does not suggest any such mutuality. 5: 21 states very succinctly the interdependence of the believers. The remainder of v. 21, 'out of reverence for Christ', points to the governing factor for all Christians; all believers are incorporated into Christ and are governed by this commitment. The author of Ephesians, then, urges his readers to govern themselves with reference to Christ, in submission to one another. This mutual submission of one Christian to another pertains not only to wives and husbands, but also to children, fathers, slaves and masters as well.

The Haustafel is almost ideally suited to the purposes and

---

[1] Above, pp. 114–17.

perspective of the author of Ephesians. The Ephesian Haustafel, as indeed would be the case with any Haustafel, portrays an idealized understanding of the household and the relationships that compose the family. For the author of Ephesians the entire household functions as a reflection of the larger Christian community. It is in the family that unity, order, mutual respect and subordination may be realized with Christian devotion. Within earlier passages in Ephesians, the author occasionally pictures the Christian community as a larger family with God as Father (2: 19; 3: 15; 4: 12; 5: 1, 8).

Within the Haustafel, the section dealing with wives and husbands (5: 21–33) is expanded disproportionately since, for the author of Ephesians, the marriage relationship is transparent to God's purposes on a larger scale. It is this transparency that permits the analogy between wife and husband and the church and Christ that is developed so intricately in 5: 21–33.

A further implication of the study of 5: 21–33 for the remainder of the Haustafel (6: 1–9) is that the interpreter ought to expect traditions of the early church, of Judaism, and of the world about him to be interwoven into a fabric similar to that encountered in 5: 21–33. It is hardly conceivable that the author should limit his incorporation of extensive traditional materials to 5: 21–33. In fact, the realization of the extent of the author's dependence on the OT in 5: 21–33 lends added importance to the quotation from the decalog in 6: 2: '"Honor your father and mother" (this is the first commandment with a promise), "that it may be well with you and that you may live long on the earth"' (6: 2–3).

Once the author committed himself to the inherited form of the Haustafel, he carried it through, placing a clear emphasis on the opening set addressed to wives and husbands. The treatment of wives and husbands, expanded as it is, stands at the head of the list because of the natural priority of the husband and wife in the household itself and because no other relationship within the family so fully mirrors God's purposes in the universe. For that reason 5: 21–33, though it shares many characteristics with the remainder of the Haustafel, is the most elaborate and extended portion of that inherited form.

B. INTERRELATION OF 5: 21–33 WITH THE REMAINDER OF EPHESIANS

Already within this investigation certain lines of contact between 5: 21–33 and the remainder of the letter have been noted. It is now appropriate to highlight some of these relationships and to elaborate upon them.

The structure and movement of thought of 5: 21–33 manifests the same alternation apparent throughout the epistle: the situation of the believers is set forth, followed by comment about Christ or God, and return is made to the situation of the believers.[1]

The epistle to the Ephesians throughout focuses attention upon the church and its relationship to God through Christ. The author as a master of received tradition has a variety of ways of talking about and portraying the church. He speaks of the believers as children (5: 1) or a family (3: 15). He refers to them as a household (2: 19), as a house or a building (2: 20–1), or even a temple (2: 21). At other times he refers to them as a body, using the widespread organic terminology already noted.[2] Occasionally the metaphors are mixed and intertwined with one another.

Twice the readers are referred to as children (5: 1, 8).[3] The emphasis on God as Father is clearly set forward at the very opening of the epistle to the Ephesians where God is praised as Father (1: 3) and the readers are said to be sons (1: 5). Already in 1: 2 God is characterized as 'our Father'. The opening words of the epistle, therefore, establish one of the themes that is

---

[1] Above, pp. 103–8.   [2] Above, pp. 61–6.

[3] Missing in these references to the believers as children is the ironic note of sarcasm found in 1 Cor. 3: 1 and Heb. 5: 12 ff. The mention of children in 5: 1, 8 holds more in common with the reference to children in 1 Cor. 4: 14 and 1 Pet. 2: 2. Ephesians manifests one occurrence of the term 'children' that runs counter to those instances just cited. In an appeal to the readers to live a life worthy of their calling (4: 1), the author calls for a unity of the believers in the hope that the readers will go on to what he calls a 'mature manhood' (4: 13), 'so that you may no longer be children, tossed to and fro and carried about with every wind of doctrine' (4: 14). In chapter 4 the argument for unity is advanced by the author's admonition that the believers cease to be like children. The context provides an occasion for the author to speak of children in a way that really bears no relationship to his more prevalent picture of God as Father and the believers as faithful children.

to pervade the letter – the portrayal of God as Father and the believers as sons, children or family – and provide the *raison d'être* of the occurrence of the Haustafel in the later stage of the epistle.

The pervasive Ephesian emphasis on the Christian community as God's family provides the proper context for understanding the comments about inheritance in 1: 14 and 18. The same theme occurs as chapter 3 builds in crescendo towards the doxological formulation of 3: 20 f. 'For this reason I bow my knees before the Father, from whom every family in heaven and on earth is named' (3: 14). Once more God is described as Father and the prominence of the family as a cosmic reality in God's overall purposes is clearly set forward. The believers are properly children as they, in the household of God, relate to Christ.

The unity of the believers in Christ is asserted in various ways throughout Ephesians. Apart from 5: 21–33, the solidarity of the believers in Christ is stated by a variety of metaphors including house, building, body and temple. Only in 5: 21–33, in the context of human marriage, is the relationship of the believer to Christ discussed in terms of an hieros gamos. At no other point would the bridal imagery be appropriate.

Consistently in Ephesians, the church is the recipient of God's beneficent action in Christ. At no point does the church merit God's action on her behalf. Implicit throughout Ephesians, this statement is explicit in 2: 8 f.: 'For by grace you have been saved through faith; and this is not your own doing, it is the gift of God – not because of works, least any man should boast.' Apart from God's actions, the readers of the epistle were without hope (2: 12).[1] The church comes into existence by God's own election: 'He [God] chose us in him [Christ] before the foundation of the world, that we should be holy and blameless before him' (1: 4). This provides one of the closest connections of 5: 21–33 with the remainder of the epistle. Whereas in 1: 4 terminology of election is used, the same thrust is accomplished in 5: 26 by speaking of Christ's sanctifying the church or setting her apart for himself. Furthermore, the

[1] This emphasis is reminiscent of the helplessness of Jerusalem in Ezekiel's portrayal of her as a lonely waif nurtured by YHWH (Ezek. 16: 4 ff.).

purpose of the election (1 : 4) and the sanctification or setting apart (5 : 26) is identical: the believers, the church, should be holy and blameless. Striking confirmation of the connection between 1 : 4 and 5 : 26 ff. is the appearance in both places of the important terms 'holy' and 'blameless'.[1]

God's election or sanctification of the church places an eschatological claim upon her that she be holy and blameless for all time. As a body set apart for God the church must be holy to God.

Little is known about the specific purposes that occasioned the writing of Ephesians. A persistent theme and call for unity pervades the entire epistle and gives rise to the suspicion that the author has some knowledge, or at least fear, that disunity among believers was a problem. The call to unity comes most clearly in 4 : 1 ff.:

I therefore, a prisoner for the Lord, beg you to lead a life worthy of the calling to which you have been called, with all lowliness and meekness, with patience, forbearing one another in love, eager to maintain the unity of the Spirit and the bond of peace. There is one body and one Spirit, just as you were called to the one hope that belongs to your call, one Lord, one faith, one baptism, one God and Father of us all, who is above all and through all and in all.

With a view towards establishing the unity that should exist among believers, the author urges upon the readers a humility (4 : 2) closely related to the mutual submission of Christians demanded in 5 : 21. The Haustafel provides the author an opportunity to develop an idealized picture of the unity that must pertain in the smallest units of the Christian community, the family. The unity that husband and wife are to manifest has as its paradigm the close relationship that exists between Christ and his church. In 5 : 31, the oneness of husband and wife is grounded in the OT ordination for marriage (Gen. 2 : 24) where man and wife are said to be 'one flesh'.

There is one other major connection between 5 : 21–33 and the remainder of the epistle. In 2 : 11 ff. the author develops the theme that the Gentiles who are now incorporated into the church have not always been so blessed. The previous situation

---

[1] Cf. 4 : 24 – 'and put on the new nature, created after the likeness of God in true righteousness and holiness' – where the holiness of the believers is again stressed.

of the Gentile believers is described in two ways. First, their prior condition is defined in terms of their separation from Israel: 'alienated from the commonwealth of Israel, and strangers to the covenants of promise' (2: 12). Second, without reference to Israel, their former condition was described as one of 'no hope and without God in the world' (v. 12). The second is of no consequence for an investigation of 5: 21–33, but the former is of considerable importance.[1]

When, in 5: 21–33, the author of Ephesians adopted the hieros gamos of YHWH and Israel as a means of depicting the relationship of Christ and the church, he made certain implicit connections between YHWH's promises in the past and Christ's commitment in the present. For the author of Ephesians the church stands in continuity with Israel just as Christ's actions on her behalf continue YHWH's loving kindness to Israel. Gentiles are now fellow heirs with the Jews, members of the same body, i.e. the church, and are partakers of the promise in Christ Jesus through the gospel (3: 6). An important theological assumption provides the foundation for the assertion of the continuity of the church with Israel and of Christ with YHWH. YHWH's purposes and promises to Israel in the past have not been declared void or of no effect. The church is the new recipient of these past commitments and is now charged with a mission in the world.

C. PORTRAIT OF THE CHURCH IN 5: 21–33

The dominant characteristic of the church in 5: 21–33 is her submission to her Lord, Christ. She is consistently portrayed as being subject to him and the recipient of his actions on her behalf. The author understands the origin of the church to be grounded in Christ's giving himself up for her, i.e. in his death and in his setting her apart for himself (vv. 25 b and 26 a). To emphasize the historicity of the death of Christ, the author employs the aorist tense, thus stressing the punctiliar kind of

---

[1] Cf. also 2: 19, where the believers are told 'so then you are no longer strangers and sojourners'. The terminology of 'strangers' and 'sojourners' is deeply rooted in Israel's own traditions, and describes those persons who, though they may happen into the midst of Israel, are not direct sharers of God's promises and covenant.

action appropriate to Christ's death as the founding moment in the church. Thus, the historical point of departure for understanding the life of the church is the loving death of Christ. The punctiliar character of the aorist in v. 25 b is a means of expressing the ingressive effect of Christ's death for the church.[1]

In 5: 21–33 the present tense occurs several times and expresses a durative kind of action. The relationship thus suggested by the use of the present tense is reserved in 5: 21–33 for statements describing relationships that the author expects to continue into the future. Such statements are v. 23 b, 'Christ is the head of the church', and v. 29 b, 'Christ does [nourishes and cherishes] the church'. The same durative relationship is manifested in v. 24 a: 'The church is subject to Christ.'

Throughout 5: 21–33 there is an eschatological tension between what has already been done for the church, and what is to be expected in the future of the church. Clearly the submission of the church to Christ that has characterized her to the present is to continue and the church is to pursue her single-minded devotion to Christ as her head. Also the cleansing of the church in the past (*Urzeit*) is to be an eschatological characteristic of the church (*Endzeit*). As the author stated in 1: 4, God's election of the believers had as one of its purposes that they might be holy and blameless before him. So also the cleansing in 5: 26 b of the bride by Christ is designed to prepare her for a continuing relationship with Christ. The cleansing, having the dual overtone of nuptial bath and baptism, is designed to institute a purity that will be characteristic of the church until the end of time. The correlation between the *Urzeit* and *Endzeit* of the church provides the context for understanding the purity presupposed in the phrase ἵνα παραστήσῃ αὐτὸς ἑαυτῷ ἔνδοξον τὴν ἐκκλησίαν.[2] Verse 27 a may be literally translated: 'in order that he himself might present the church to himself glorious'. Verse 27 a portrays Christ as presenting the church to himself so that he is at the same time the subject and the

---

[1] Blass–Debrunner–Funk, *A Greek Grammar*, par. 318.

[2] The RSV, in its translation 'that the church might be presented before him in splendor', offers a simplistic resolution of an admittedly difficult and curious passage. The RSV loses some of the impact of this verse by failing to make clear that Christ remains the subject, as is made quite clear by the intensive αὐτός.

indirect object of the presentation. This action by Christ is grounded in Christ's loving and giving of himself for the church (v. 25b). He loved her and gave himself for her so that she might be ἔνδοξος, glorious in her origin and to the end of time. If the eschatological concern with purity is overlooked in 5: 21–33, then v. 27a is indeed a curiosity. When that eschatological note is understood, however, the phrase 'present her to himself' suggests that Christ is understood not only as the bridegroom but also as the eschatological judge who will finally render a verdict concerning the splendor and purity of the church. Therefore the phrase 'present her to himself' serves the double function of relating to the initial marriage of Christ and the church and the eschatological judgment in which Christ will stand over against the church. Ephesians is careful throughout not to make a simple identification of Christ and the church. Unlike the human husband and wife who are one flesh, Christ is always the head of the church. The church is always his body. Therefore Christ's relation to the church is not in 5: 21–33 simply to be relegated to his past act of establishing her or to his nourishing and cherishing her, but also includes his eschatological judgment of her purity.

Verse 30 – 'because we are members of his body' – is short but very essential to the development of 5: 21–33. The author presupposes that he is not converting his readers but rather that they are already believing, baptized Christians. Verse 30 is his way of reminding the readers that, as Christians, they are individually members of that body, the church, that has been spoken of in such detail in vv. 22–9.[1] Also, v. 30 makes clear that the ambivalence of v. 26b – 'having cleansed her by the washing of water with the word' – must be retained. Verse 26b no doubt refers not only to the nuptial bath prior to the church's marriage to Christ, but also to baptism as a means of entry, or as the mark of the believer. By this cleansing the individuals are incorporated into the body of Christ, the church.

According to 5: 21–33 the church looks not to itself but to Christ for its sustenance. He is its creator and he cares for it (v. 29b). He qualifies as the church's savior (v. 23c) by his death (v. 25b). In part, the church retains her purity and her

[1] Cf. 4: 7–11. Though there are many different gifts distributed among the believers, all believers are equally members of the body of Christ.

splendor insofar as she depends faithfully upon Christ to lead her as head and to sustain her as husband.

Clearly, 5: 21–33 presents an exalted view of the church. The interpreter does not meet here the 'church in your home' of Philem. 2. Also, though there are many similarities between the portrayal of the church in 5: 21–33 and Jerusalem in Ezek. 16, there is no Ephesian parallel to the harlotry expected of Israel (Ezek. 16 and 23). Only the most idealized picture of the church is presented in 5: 21–33. Clearly, a definite hortatory function is involved in this portrayal of the church. By depicting it as holy and without blemish the author, in effect, has issued a challenge, or a call, that the church live up to its portrait. Or as it is stated in 4: 1, the church ought to 'lead a life worthy of the calling to which you have been called'. The indicative statement is explicit: the church is the object of Christ's love. He has sanctified her, cleansed her, and caused her to be pure. An imperative is implicit in this description: 'be what Christ created you to be'.

At the same time that the church is described as having its prime concern in a pure obedience to Christ, it also has a cosmic task and significance. The church fits into God's total plan described by the author as 'the mystery hidden for ages in God who created all things; that through the church the manifold wisdom of God might now be made known to the principalities and powers in the heavenly places' (3: 9–10). The church now has a cosmic function in manifesting God's plan and purpose. It is precisely in this context that the interpreter must understand 6: 10–20, the armament passage immediately following upon the Haustafel. The believers are in a cosmic contention with principalities, powers, world rulers, and spiritual hosts of wickedness in the heavenly places (6: 12). In this warfare the Christians, as members of the church, manifest God's purposes throughout the cosmos. Consistent with the portrait of the church in 5: 21–33, the Christian does not carry on this battle for himself; he is empowered by the armament of God to withstand the evil day (v. 13). Through prayer and supplication, the believer is given the panoply of God and enabled to stand against evil (v. 18). The Christians, as members of the church, Christ's body, will be empowered to stand firm in face of resistance to God's purpose. Only as he stands fast in the battle does the believer continue to manifest what God in Christ has done for the church of which he is a member; only by standing firm does he remain spotless and holy before God.

D. UNDERSTANDING OF MARRIAGE IN 5: 21–33

Such an exalted view of the church and its relation to Christ, intertwined as it is with the author's assertions about the relationship that should subsist between husband and wife, leads without fail to an exalted portrait of marriage. Eph. 5: 21–33 is one of the contributing factors in Christian tradition's high regard for marriage. According to the author of Ephesians marriage is a reflection of the paradigm relationship that subsists between Christ and his church.[1]

Since the human family is the microcosm of God's larger purposes in the cosmos and since in the family the marriage relationship is of central importance, it is necessary that the mutuality and solidarity of the marital partnership be clarified. Frequently the basic Haustafel injunction of submission upon the wives (vv. 22 a and 24 b) is taken out of context and understood as the remnant of outdated cultural and sociological patterns. To be sure, there is some accuracy in this. In part, the author of the Ephesians does reflect the thinking and sociological structures of his own times. The Haustafel is a codification of widespread practice contemporary to the author of Ephesians and it must be recognized that the author did not modify the basic injunction of submission to the wives itself, but brought it over intact.[2]

In large measure, the subjection urged upon the wife is ideal for what the author wants to say about the church. In the church's relation to Christ there is no qualification of submission. To be sure, for the purposes of his statement about the submission of the church, the author found a ready format in the unmodified Haustafel admonition to the wives.

It has already been observed, however, that 5: 21 – 'be

---

[1] The Vulgate's translation of μυστήριον by *sacramentum* functioned, in the traditional interpretation of the Roman Catholic Church, to formalize the high regard for marriage set forth in the opening section of the Ephesian Haustafel.

[2] Above, pp. 28–30.

subject to one another out of reverence for Christ' – stands as a superscription to the entire Haustafel and qualifies the submission urged upon the wives, children and slaves, as well as the authority of the husbands, fathers and masters. All familial relations are governed by mutual submission in the fear of Christ. Furthermore, by his exposition of Gen. 2:24, the author of Ephesians argues that the marriage relationship must be understood as a union of husband and wife as one flesh. For this reason the wife is spoken of as the husband's body and his self (vv. 28–9). The author's development of the line of thought of Gen. 2:24 by means of Lev. 19:18 provides a further qualification of the submission incumbent upon the woman in 5:22 a.

E. ASSESSMENT OF TRADITIONS INCORPORATED IN 5:21–33 AS A CLUE TO THE PURPOSE OF EPHESIANS

Käsemann's statement that Ephesians is a mosaic of traditional formulations has been taken as a working hypothesis of this investigation.[1] 5:21–33 has been seen to contain no single verse that lacks such a conventional formulation.

The question then arises as to why there are so many traditions incorporated in Ephesians. Clearly the author of Ephesians does not know the recipients of the letter and therefore has no set of teachings that he himself has imparted to them. Paul, when writing to congregations that he had founded, could refer to instruction that he had passed on to them (1 Cor. 15:3 and 11:23), but the author of Ephesians has no such background that he has personally communicated to the readers. He is therefore left with no alternative except to presuppose that his readers, by their catechetical training and liturgical practices, have a certain fund of traditions culled from Judaism and the early church, upon which he may draw to communicate his message to them.[2]

A second question arises: why are these traditions and not others inserted? Two rather basic parts of the answer suggest

[1] Above, pp. 1, 3.

[2] If Ephesians is not authentically Pauline, then the heavy use of traditional formulations may have represented a sounder approach to the author since the traditions themselves had a certain authority among the early Christians.

themselves. First, the traditions chosen by the author are germane to his purposes and concerns. Second, the traditions chosen may reflect a problem or problems known or suspected to be current among the recipients. Käsemann's second statement cited at the opening of this investigation may here be reconsidered.[1] Was Ephesians directed to Gentile Christians who were in danger of divorcing themselves from their Jewish–Christian heritage?

The use of the OT in 5: 21–3 is pervasive and perhaps significant of the author's purpose. The author's chief indebtedness to the OT consists of his use of (1) Gen. 2: 24, 'and a man shall leave his father and mother and cleave to his wife and the two shall become one flesh'; (2) Lev. 19: 18, 'You shall love your neighbor as yourself'; and (3) the hieros gamos of YHWH and Israel.

By fulfilling the early Christian convention of a word of submission to women and a reference to Torah by means of Gen. 2: 24, the author of Ephesians has found a passage ideally suited for insertion in a statement about marriage.[2] For the author of Ephesians, marriage between Christians, reflecting the larger purposes of God, is to be understood as grounded firmly in the OT ordination of marriage, Gen. 2: 24. The daily comportment of marriage partners in the Christian family is therefore founded upon a statement from Torah. If the recipients of the epistle to the Ephesians were Christians converted from Judaism the use of Gen. 2: 24 would be less striking. In Ephesians, however, Gentile Christians are addressed.

The author's deep indebtedness to Lev. 19: 18 – 'You shall love your neighbor as yourself' – is in part a reflection of that OT verse's wide circulation among the Christians and Jews in and around the turn of the eras. All of Torah is fulfilled in the loving of one's neighbor. When Lev. 19: 18 is applied to marriage the word 'neighbor' is exchanged for the word 'wife', or πλησίον is understood as a term of endearment for the wife.[3] The combination of Lev. 19: 18 and Gen. 2: 24 indicates that Torah continues as an effective guideline for the marriage partners' relation to one another.

The term 'love' was probably introduced to the author's

---

[1] Above, p. 3.   [2] Above, pp. 97–100.

[3] Above, pp. 30–3.

159

attention in the context of marriage by the received form of the Haustafel injunction to the husbands: 'husbands, love your wives'. The content of what love requires as stated in the Haustafel injunction to the husbands and the author's use of Lev. 19: 18, therefore, is placed within the framework of a christological reference to the love of Christ as shown in his death for the believers.

For his statement of Christ's relationship to the church, the author of Ephesians draws upon a third fundamental OT image: the hieros gamos of YHWH and Israel. The use of this complex set of images, grounded finally in Ezek. 16, Song of Songs and Ps. 45, provides a clue to understanding the purpose of Ephesians. The author of Ephesians distinguishes between the former situation of the believers and their present situation.[1] And most illuminating is the observation that the believers' present and past are defined *vis-à-vis* Israel and the covenant. In 5: 21–33 the present situation of the believers as the body of Christ, the church, is described as a continuation of YHWH's commitment to Israel of old, by baptism into the church the Gentile believers take their part alongside Jewish believers and old Israel. So also, the situation of the recipients before their baptism is defined as an alienation from Israel and from the covenant (2: 12).

It becomes apparent that Ephesians is directed to a congregation or to congregations exposed to, or partaking in schismatic talk. The danger expressed by Paul in Rom. 11 has in fact come true: Gentile Christians have begun to take pride in their new position as believers accepted by God and have divorced themselves from the Jews.[2]

This investigation thus confirms Käsemann's judgment that Ephesians is directed to Gentile believers who reject, or at least question, the necessity of recognizing the continuity of Gentile Christianity with Jewish Christianity and old Israel.[3]

5: 21–33 provides a relatively small but intense part of the total picture of the author's response to the error that he fears among his readers. Basically he asserts that God's promises as

[1] Above, pp. 7–8.
[2] Some tendencies later epitomized in Marcion are incipient in Ephesians. The author rejects the very ground on which those tendencies are founded.
[3] Above, p. 3.

revealed in Christ may not be understood apart from Israel and the church's continuity with her. The OT continues as a guide, not only to the life of the married couple, but to the church as a whole, to the understanding of what she is and, in fact, to God's purposes. The theological stance and the ethical perspective of the author of Ephesians are informed by and grounded in the OT.

In view of the author of Ephesians' commitment to traditions of Judaism it is especially difficult to understand Käsemann's third assertion:[1] the author of Ephesians shows no interest in Jewish Christianity as a context for understanding the present life of the church. Though this study has confirmed the first two statements isolated from Käsemann, it gives clear evidence that this third assertion cannot stand without modification. In fact, it is precisely through OT traditions that the author calls his readers back to a realization of their place in God's overall purposes extending from creation to the end of all times.

Several striking similarities between 5: 21–33 and 2: 11–22 confirm the argument here set forward. In the context of the discussion of the former situation of the readers as separated from Israel and the covenant, the author of Ephesians expresses in various ways the unification of Jew and Gentile in the death of Christ.[2] Within 2: 14–18 the author refers three times to τὰ ἀμφότερα ἕν (vv. 14, 16, 18). Verses 14 ff. develop the thought that Christ banishes the enmity that formerly stood between those near and those far away and makes peace between them so that the two (τὰ ἀμφότερα) become one (ἕν).[3] The phrase, 'making peace' (ποιῶν εἰρήνην), reoccurs immediately in v. 15, and there is grounded in Christ's death. Though the phrase τὰ ἀμφότερα does not occur in v. 15, a similar construction does: 'that he might create in himself one new man in place of the two (τοὺς δύο)'. The terminology is not identical, but the same idea is clearly in view. Verse 16 states that through the crucifixion of Christ 'the both' (τοὺς ἀμφοτέρους) were

---

[1] Above, pp. 3–4.

[2] This passage in Ephesians is itself heavily indebted to terminology and imagery drawn from the OT. Isaiah is especially prominent.

[3] In Isa. 57: 19 the terms 'near' and 'far' probably refer to the diaspora. Their occurrence in Eph. 2: 13 has become the occasion to speak of Israel and the Gentiles.

reconciled to God in one body (ἐν ἑνὶ σώματι). Verse 17 brings to the surface a quotation of Isa. 57: 19 that has been in view since v. 13.[1] Verse 18 contains the last occurrence of ἀμφότερα: 'for through him we both (οἱ ἀμφότεροι) have access in one spirit to the Father'.[2] Jew and Gentile equally have access to the Father through the one Spirit. The emphasis in 2: 11 ff. on the unity of Jew and Gentile in the church is mirrored in 5: 21–33 no less clearly in the unity of husband and wife. 2: 11 ff. speaks of God's all-inclusive plan, whereas 5: 21–33 carefully shows the implications of God's cosmic purposes as they bear on human marriage.

The recipients of Ephesians are urged to recognize that they, together with Jews, share in God's cosmic purposes. Gentiles have no basis upon which to understand their new situation before God apart from Israel. They are bound inseparably with the Jews in God's plan.

Whereas the language about the incorporation of Gentile and Jew into the body of Christ remains more universal and therefore more general, 5: 21–33 is the author's specific application of the theme of unity to the smallest unit into which the church may be divided. In his talk about marriage the author remains consistent to his commitment that Gentiles cannot understand their new place before God apart from Israel. In 5: 21–33 the marital relationship is shown to be grounded in Torah and patterned on YHWH's marriage to Israel as reflected in Christ's relation to the church.

A detailed examination of Eph. 5: 21–33 has contributed further insight into the liturgical and catechetical traditions extant in the early church and has shed light on the author's creative mastery of diverse traditions. The study of this passage has also yielded evidence of early Christian exegesis, its methodology and its sources.

Eph. 5: 21–33, since it reflects in microcosmic fashion several of the concerns of the entire epistle, has provided

[1] Notice should be taken here of the exegetical pattern of the author of Ephesians, since 2: 13 ff. presents an exegetical method similar to that noted in 5: 21–33 where, from v. 22, the author has in view the quotation from Gen. 2: 24 that appears finally in v. 31. Cf. above, pp. 89–90.
[2] Note the use of the title 'father' for God. Cf. above, pp. 150–1.

illumination for some of the theological and christological concerns and purposes of the author. The task of determining the purpose or purposes of Ephesians is not hereby solved, but hopefully some initial steps have been taken.

Eph. 5: 21–33 is indeed an elaborate passage, but not labored. The author pursues very carefully and judiciously an intricate train of thought, with careful literary balance and structure from beginning to end. In 5: 21–33, the author of Ephesians has extolled human marriage and glorified God 'in the church and in Christ Jesus to all generations' (3: 21).

BIBLIOGRAPHY

1. PRIMARY SOURCES

The Babylonian Talmud. Translated under the auspices of I. Epstein. London: The Soncino Press, 1935–48.

Biblia Hebraica. Edited by Rud. Kittel. Stuttgart: Privileg. Württ. Bibelanstalt, 1937.

The Book of Tobit. An English translation with introduction and commentary by Frank Zimmermann. New York: Harper & Brothers, 1958.

Charles, R. H. *The Apocrypha and Pseudepigrapha of the Old Testament*. Oxford: The Clarendon Press, 1913.

The Dead Sea Scriptures in English Translation. Translated with an introduction and notes by T. H. Gaster. 2nd ed. revised. New York: Doubleday & Company, Inc., Anchor Books, 1964.

The Holy Bible. Revised Standard Version. New York: Thomas Nelson & Sons, 1952.

The Mishnah. Translated by Herbert Danby. Oxford: Oxford University Press, 1933.

Philo. With an English translation by F. H. Colson and the Rev. G. H. Whitaker. London: William Heinemann Ltd, 1958.

Seneca. *De Clementia*. Translation by John W. Basere (The Loeb Classical Library). London: William Heinemann Ltd, 1958.

  Epistulae Morales. Translation by R. M. Gummere (The Loeb Classical Library). London: William Heinemann Ltd, 1958.

Septuaginta. 2 Vols. Edited by Alfred Rahlfs. Stuttgart: Privileg. Württ. Bibelanstalt, 1935.

Die Texte aus Qumran: Hebräisch und deutsch. Edited and translated by Eduard Lohse. München: Kösel-Verlag, 1964.

2. REFERENCE WORKS

Bauer, Walter, Arndt, William F. and Gingrich, F. Wilbur. *A Greek–English Lexicon of the New Testament and Other Early Christian Literature*. Chicago: The University of Chicago Press, 1957.

Blass, Friedrich, Debrunner, Albert and Funk, Robert. *A Greek Grammar of the New Testament and Other Early Christian Literature*. Translated by Robert Funk. Chicago: The University of Chicago Press, 1961.

Brown, Francis, Driver, S. R. and Briggs, Charles A. *A Hebrew and English Lexicon of the Old Testament*. Oxford: Clarendon Press, 1952.

Dana, H. E. and Mantey, Julius R. *A Manual Grammar of the Greek New Testament.* New York: The Macmillan Company, 1927.

Hatch, Edwin and Redpath, Henry A. *A Concordance to the Septuagint and other Greek Versions of the Old Testament.* Oxford: The Clarendon Press, 1897.

Jastrow, Marcus. *A Dictionary of the Targumim, the Talmud Babli and Yerushalmi, and the Midrashic Literature.* New York: Pardes Publishing House, Inc., 1950.

Moffatt, James. *The First Epistle of Paul to the Corinthians (The Moffatt New Testament Commentary).* New York and London: Harper and Brothers Publishers, 1938.

Moulton, J. H. *A Grammar of New Testament Greek.* 3rd ed. Edinburgh: T. and T. Clark, 1908.

Robertson, A. T. *A Grammar of the Greek New Testament in the Light of Historical Research.* Nashville: Broadman Press, 1934.

Strack, H. L. and Billerbeck, P. *Kommentar zum Neuen Testament aus Talmud und Midrasch,* 1922–6.

Trench, R. C. *Synonyms of the New Testament.* 9th ed. Grand Rapids, Michigan: Wm. B. Eerdman's Publishing Company, 1963.

3. BOOKS

Abbott, T. K. *A Critical and Exegetical Commentary on the Epistles to the Ephesians and to the Colossians.* Edinburgh: T. and T. Clark, 1897.

Allan, John A. *The Epistle to the Ephesians.* London: SCM Press Ltd, 1959.

Barrett, C. K. *A Commentary on the Epistle to the Romans.* New York: Harper & Row, 1957.

From First Adam to Last: A Study in Pauline Theology. New York: Charles Scribner's Sons, 1962.

The Pastoral Epistles. Oxford: The Clarendon Press, 1963.

Barth, Markus. *The Broken Wall: A Study of the Epistle to the Ephesians.* Chicago: The Judson Press, 1959.

Beare, Francis W. 'The Epistle to the Ephesians', vol. x of *The Interpreter's Bible.* Edited by G. A. Buttrick. New York: Abingdon Press, 1953.

The First Epistle of Peter. 2nd ed. revised. Oxford: Basil Blackwell, 1958.

Bultmann, Rudolf. *Theology of the New Testament.* Translated by Kendrick Grobel. New York: Charles Scribner's Sons, 1951.

Carrington, Philip. *The Primitive Christian Catechism.* Cambridge: Cambridge University Press, 1940.

Chavasse, Claude. *The Bride of Christ: an Enquiry into the Nuptial*

Element in Early Christianity. London: The Religious Book Club, 1939.

Dahl, Nils A. *Das Volk Gottes: Eine Untersuchung zum Kirchenbewußtsein des Urchristentums*. Darmstadt: Wissenschaftliche Buchgesellschaft, 1963.

Dibelius, Martin. *An die Kolosser Epheser an Philemon*. 3. Auflage. Tübingen: J. C. B. Mohr (John Siebeck), 1953.

Dodd, C. H. *According to the Scriptures: the Sub-structure of New Testament Theology*. London: James Nisbet and Company Ltd, 1952.

Eichrodt, Walther. *Theology of the Old Testament*, vol. 1. Translated by J. A. Baker. Philadelphia: The Westminster Press, 1961.

Feine, Paul, Behm, Johannes and Kümmel, W. G. *Introduction to the New Testament*. Translated by A. J. Mattill, Jr. 14th ed. revised. Nashville: Abingdon Press, 1965.

Goodspeed, Edgar J. *The Key to Ephesians*. Chicago: University of Chicago Press, 1956.

The Meaning of Ephesians. Chicago: University of Chicago Press, 1933.

Heschel, Abraham J. *The Prophets*. New York: Harper & Row, 1962.

Holtzmann, H. J. *Kritik der Epheser- und Kolosserbriefe*. Leipzig: Wilhelm Engelmann, 1872.

Kamlah, Ehrhard. *Die Form der katalogischen Paränese im Neuen Testament*. Tübingen: J. C. B. Mohr (Paul Siebeck), 1964.

Käsemann, Ernst. *Leib und Leib Christi*. Tübingen: J. C. B. Mohr (Paul Siebeck), 1933.

Kirby, John C. *Ephesians: Baptism and Pentecost*. Montreal: McGill University Press, 1968.

Knox, John. *Philemon Among the Letters of Paul*. 2nd ed. revised. New York: Abingdon Press, 1959.

Knox, W. L. *St Paul and the Church of the Gentiles*. Cambridge: Cambridge University Press, 1939.

Lindars, Barnabas. *New Testament Apologetic*. London: SCM Press Ltd, 1961.

Lindblom, Johannes. *Prophecy in Ancient Israel*. Philadelphia: Fortress Press, 1962.

Lohse, Eduard. *Die Briefe an die Kolosser und an Philemon*. Göttingen: Vandenhoeck and Ruprecht, 1968.

Masson, Charles. *L'Épître de Saint Paul aux Éphésiens*. Paris: Delachaux et Niestle, 1953.

Minear, Paul S. *Images of the Church in the New Testament*. Philadelphia: Westminster Press, 1960.

Mitton, C. Leslie. *The Epistle to the Ephesians: Its Authorship, Origin and Purpose*. Oxford: The Clarendon Press, 1951.

Moore, George Foot. *Judaism in the First Centuries of the Christian Era:*

The Age of the Tannaim. Cambridge, Mass.: Harvard University Press, 1958.

Ochel, Werner. *Die Anname einer Bearbeitung des Kolosser-Briefes im Epheser-Brief.* Marburg: Konrad Triltsch, Würzburg, 1934.

Percy, Ernst. *Die Probleme der Kolosser- und Epheserbriefe.* Lund: C. W. K. Gleerup, 1946.

Robert, A. and Tournay, R. *Le Cantique des Cantiques: Traduction et Commentaire.* Paris: J. Gabalda et Cie, 1963.

Robinson, John A. T. *The Body: a Study in Pauline Theology.* London: SCM Press Ltd, 1952.

Schille, Gottfried. *Frühchristliche Hymnen.* Berlin: Evangelische Verlagsanstalt, 1965.

Schlier, Heinrich. *Der Brief an die Epheser.* Düsseldorf: Patmos-Verlag, 1962.
Christus und die Kirche im Epheserbrief. Tübingen: J. C. B. Mohr (Paul Siebeck), 1930.

Scott, E. F. *The Epistles of Paul to the Colossians, to Philemon and to the Ephesians.* New York: Harper and Brothers Publishers, 1930.

Smith, Morton. *Tannaitic Parallels to the Gospels (The Journal of Biblical Literature Monograph Series,* vol. VI). Philadelphia: The Society of Biblical Literature, 1951.

Synge, F. C. *St Paul's Epistle to the Ephesians: A Theological Commentary.* London: SPCK, 1941.

Weidinger, Karl. *Das Problem der urchristlichen Haustafeln.* Leipzig, 1928.
Die Haustafeln: ein Stück urchristlicher Paränese. Leipzig, 1928.

Zimmerli, Walther. *Ezechiel (Biblischer Kommentar Altes Testament,* Herausg. von Martin Noth). Neukirchen Kreis Moers: Neukirchener Verlag, 1958.

4. ARTICLES

Bornkamm, Günther. 'μυστήριον', vol. IV of *Theologisches Worterbuch zum Neuen Testament.* Herausgegeben von Gerhard Kittel. Stuttgart: W. Kohlhammer Verlag. IV, 809–34.

Brown, Raymond E. 'The Semitic Background of the New Testament Mysterion (II)', *Biblica,* **40,** 74–84.

Colpe, Carsten. 'Zur Leib-Christi-Vorstellung im Epheserbrief', *Zeitschrift für die Neutestamentliche Wissenschaft und die Kunde der Alteren Kirche.* **26,** 170 ff.

Dahl, Nils A. 'Addresse und Prooemium des Epheserbrief', *Theologische Literaturzeitung,* **7,** 24 ff.
'Bibelstudie über den Epheserbrief', *Kurze Auslegung des Epheserbriefes.* Göttingen: Vandenhoeck & Ruprecht, 1965. 7–83.
'Dopet i Efesierbrevet', *Svensk Teologisk Kvartalskrift.* **21,** 85–103.

Daube, David. 'Participle and Imperative in I Peter', in E. G. Selwyn's *The First Epistle of St Peter*. 2nd ed. London: Macmillan and Co. Ltd, 1961. 467–88.

Hauck, Friedrich. 'ἀγνός', *Theological Dictionary of the New Testament*. Translated by G. W. Bromiley. Grand Rapids: Wm. B. Eerdman's Publishing Company, 1964. I, 122–4.

Käsemann, Ernst. 'Das Interpretationsproblem des Epheserbriefes', *Exegetische Versuche und Besinnungen* (Göttingen: Vandenhoeck & Ruprecht, 1964), II, 253–61.

'Epheserbrief', *Die Religion in Geschichte und Gegenwart*. 3. Auflage. Tübingen: J. C. B. Mohr (Paul Siebeck), 1957–62. II, 517–20.

'Ephesians and Acts', *Studies in Luke–Acts*, ed. L. E. Keck and J. L. Martyn. Nashville: The Abingdon Press, 1966, p. 297, n. 1.

Kittel, Gerhard. '῎Ενδοξος', *Theological Dictionary of the New Testament*. II, 254–5.

Kuhn, K. G. 'Der Epheserbrief im Lichte der Qumrantexte', *New Testament Studies*, **7**, 334 ff.

'The Concept of Holiness in Rabbinic Judaism', *Theological Dictionary of the New Testament*. I, 97–100.

Lehmann, Manfred R. 'Gen. 2: 24 as the Basis for Divorce in Halakhah and New Testament', *Zeitschrift für die Alttestamentliche Wissenschaft*, **31**, 263–7.

Nauck, W. 'Eph. 2: 19–22 ein Tauflied?', *Evangelische Theologie*, **13**, 362 f.

Procksch, Otto. 'ἅγιος' and 'ἁγιάζω', *Theological Dictionary of the New Testament*. I, 100–12.

Robinson, James M. 'Die Hodajot-Formel in Gebet und Hymnus des Frühchristentums', *Apophoreta; Festschrift für Ernst Haenchen*. Berlin: Alfred Töpelmann, 1964, pp. 194–235.

Soden, Hans von. 'ΜΥΣΤΗΡΙΟΝ und sacramentum in den ersten zwei Jahrhunderten der Kirche', *Zeitschrift für die neutestamentliche Wissenschaft und die Kunde der alteren Kirche*. **12**, 188–227.

Wendland, Hein Dietrich. 'Zur sozialethischen Bedeutung der neutestamentlichen Haustafeln', *Die Leibhaftigkeit des Wortes*. Theologische und Seelsorgerliche Studien und Beiträge als Festgabe für Adolf Koberle zum 60. Geburtstag, Hrsg. Otto Michel und Ulrich Mann. Hamburg: 1958.

5. UNPUBLISHED MATERIAL

Schroeder, David. 'Die Haustafeln des Neuen Testament: Ihre Herkunft und ihr theologischer Sinn.' Unpublished Ph.D. dissertation, Hamburg, 1959.

INDEX OF PASSAGES CITED

C. WRITINGS OF THE EARLY CHURCH

D. QUMRAN

E. APOCRYPHA AND PSEUDEPIGRAPHA

F. HELLENISTIC WRITINGS

G. MIDRASH, MISHNA, TALMUD

INDEX OF AUTHORS

INDEX OF SUBJECTS

INDEX OF SELECTED GREEK WORDS